MEN OF PROPERTY

MEN OF PROPERTY

THE VERY WEALTHY IN BRITAIN
SINCE THE INDUSTRIAL REVOLUTION

W.D. RUBINSTEIN

CROOM HELM LONDON

©1981 W.D. Rubinstein
Croom Helm Ltd, 2-10 St John's Road, London SW11

British Library Cataloguing in Publication Data

Rubinstein, W. D.
    Men of property.
    1. Upper classes - Great Britain - History
    I. Title
    305.5'2   HT653.G7

    ISBN 0-85664-674-1

Typeset by Leaper & Gard Ltd, Bristol
Printed and bound in Great Britain by
Biddles Ltd, Guildford and King's Lynn

CONTENTS

MEN OF PROPERTY

ACKNOWLEDGEMENTS

I have accumulated many debts in writing this book. The first is to my thesis supervisor, Professor David Spring, whose shrewd and sensible comments on my work, and confidence on the success of this venture, were all-important. (I must also mention Professor Vernon Lidtke of Johns Hopkins, the second reader of my thesis.) Professor Harold Perkin of the University of Lancaster, for whom I acted as Research Associate in 1974-5 in undertaking the SSRC-sponsored research project 'Wealth and Social Origins of British Elites, 1880-1970', allowed me to augment my knowledge of British elites far beyond the elite of money; at all times I was stimulated by his ingenious and important ideas on the development of British society. I also owe a special debt to Professor F.M.L. Thompson (formerly of Bedford College and now Director of the Institute of Historical Research), as well as to other academic figures in Britain, especially Professors Colin Harbury and Eric Hobsbawm. Much of this research was undertaken at the Institute of Historical Research (the best club in England) and the Public Record Office, and, without them, the work could not have been attempted. The staff, always helpful if sometimes puzzled, of the probate archives at Somerset House (and elsewhere) were also all-important.

I should also say something of my colleagues in Australia, since arriving in 1976, especially Professor F.L. Jones, Oliver MacDonagh, and Dr F.B. Smith of the Australian National University, and Professor Francis West of Deakin University. Rosemary Boston, Frances Baensch, Sue Leach and Tricia Wynd of Deakin University typed the manuscript.

I owe a special debt to the major public and county libraries of Great Britain. Perhaps every single local library of any importance was approached at some stage for biographical information about local wealth-holders. Those public libraries to whom the author is especially indebted include: Liverpool, Glasgow, Bradford, Leeds, Birmingham, Newcastle-upon-Tyne and Edinburgh. Most of the work in tracking down individual careers and genealogies, however, was done at the Institute of Historical Research, which contains the best open-shelved reference library for historians I have seen.

I am also indebted to the Borthwick Institute of Historical Research, St Anthony's Hall, York; and to Dr Murray of the Historical Department of the Scottish Record Office in Edinburgh, who brought to my attention that the Scottish Inventories of Goods and Gear were available to the researcher, and that Scottish probate indexes for the period 1824-75 existed. Among other individuals who must be thanked are: Mr Ian Lloyd, MP, whose intervention allowed me to see the Scottish series I.R.9; the late Richard Gatty JP, of Pepper Arden, Northallerton, holder of the Morrison Papers; Dr Daniel Duman, formerly my fellow graduate student at Johns Hopkins University and now of the Ben-Gurion University, Israel, who told me of the existence of the pre-1858 probate records at the Public Record Office; and my wife Hilary, specifically for her help and assistance in abstracting the names of the nineteenth-century wealth-holders from the probate calendars, and generally for so much more. I dedicate this work to her.

1 STUDYING THE WEALTHY IN BRITAIN

The rich are always with us. What is commonly regarded as the subject-matter of history has always consisted of surprisingly little apart from their affairs, punctuated from time to time by eruptions from below. In the dark spots, as Lawrence Stone has put it, 'Here be the rich' has always been the unstated assumption of most historians and a safe guide to the course of events.[1] Yet as a historical or social category in themselves the rich have received relatively little attention. On the face of it the reasons for this are powerful and compelling. Wealth has nearly invariably been a trapping, a corollary, of power or status, and with comparatively few exceptions, not a goal to be sought in itself. Those peoples, like the Jews or English dissenters, who successfully sought out wealth as an end in itself, were much of the time excluded from power and status, while in the new world of America the possession of wealth took on the importance it did only because America lacked a formal status structure. Furthermore, while the possession of wealth may be an important defining characteristic of classes or groups in society, it would be naive to assert that the mere fact of wealth is a meaningful clue to predicting the behaviour of individuals or groups at similar wealth levels. The rich may be different from the rest of us, but it is not always easy to point to where this is so. Wealth in itself is not synonymous with social class, nor is it even the prime determinant of class, and clearly it has often been the case that those individuals and groups at similar wealth levels were antagonistic and hostile. Two historical distinctions more important than the degree of wealth have been those of 'How and when was it made?' and 'Who made it?'

In Britain — not only the first industrial nation but one whose livelihood had historically derived from trade and commerce — wealth, whatever its origins, quickly masked itself in the ordered trappings of the traditional social structure. The time-honoured pattern whereby the merchant or business family soon merged with the landed gentry, often acquiring a title while intermarrying freely with the older elite within a few generations, has a history stretching back to before the De la Poers in the fourteenth century. The coming of the Industrial Revolution, with its new modes of entrepreneurship and wealth, did little to alter this: indeed the point has recently been made that the acquisition of social status was an important motivating force behind the efforts of the early industrialists.[2] Despite the great social and political differences between the industrialists of the nineteenth century and their landed contemporaries it is quite plausible to view the last 150 years as a long period of gradual co-option of the business classes by the older aristocracy — a fusion symbolised by the flood of business peerages after 1886.[3] Throughout British history, men have been classified and marked by characteristics other than sheer wealth: title, land ownership, religion, politics, education. The extent of wealth has not commonly been a part of the evidence employed to comprehend the British social structure, except in the sense that the leaders of society were normally expected to be richer than those whom they led. With the exception of the work of historians concerned with the great landowners, very little work has been undertaken on the rich as a social group in Britain; indeed the non-landed wealthy might be termed a class of invisible men. To be sure, there have been studies of individual businessmen, business dynasties and firms which have flourished in the past two centuries, but our knowledge of the wealth structure of Britain, has necessarily been limited by the vagaries of authorship. To cite one example, the Marshalls, the flax spinners of Leeds, are only part of our perspective of British economic development during the nineteenth century because they were the subject of a well-known study.[4] There are certainly many other families just as successful at entrepreneurship, and many times wealthier, who have never been studied and who hence remain largely unknown. The choice of subject matter in business history is itself dictated by the prevalent perceptions of economic structure and of economic change in Britain during the past two centuries. The overriding importance attached to industrialism and industrialisation has often led to the neglect of commerce, finance and landowning. That this prevalent view is belied by the statistics of wealth and entrepreneurship will form one of the clearest arguments in this book. There are famous businessmen, and then there are wealthy and successful ones, and these two classes may not be identical.

This work is a study of the very wealthy in Britain since the Industrial Revolution. It is based on probate valuations to be found in London at Somerset House and at the Public Record Office, at the Scottish Record Office in Edinburgh, in the Borthwick Institute in York and elsewhere. My research has consisted in abstracting from these sources the names and wealth of all persons leaving £500,000 or more from 1809 (when these records begin in a usable form) to 1939; in addition I have conducted some further research on wealth-holders at this level deceased from 1940 to the 1970s. Besides this group of millionaires and half-millionaires, two groups of early wealth-holders at a somewhat lower level of affluence were also included. These two groups of 'lesser wealthy' consisted of those leaving between £160,000 and £500,000 in 1809-29, and those leaving between £250,000 and £500,000 during the period 1850-69. These two groups were included because until the 1870s the number of millionaires and half-millionaires was too small to justify far-reaching statistical inferences. Most of this book will examine the primary social and economic characteristics of Britain's wealth elite as identified by the probate records, among them occupations and range of wealth, geographical venues, social origins and mobility, religions and political connections and inheritance patterns.[5]

A keen if hidden interest in the wealthy has always been manifested by Englishmen, both in order to help fit a man into his proper slot in society and in order to acquire an insight into a field in which reticence has been the rule. When in 1872 the *Spectator* published a list of the largest fortunes left during the previous ten years their readers' response astounded the editors:

> People who rarely read anything spelled over that long, closely-packed column of names and figures as if they somehow expected to find a notice within it of some legacy coming to themselves, and quoted the amount with a sort of smacking of the intellectual lips, and in many cases took great pains to recall hazy memories of the will-maker's career. We would venture to say the list obtained more readers than the best essay on politics we ever published, and that if we would or could publish a similar one of the living rich, beginning with the fifteen or sixteen peers who receive £100,000 a year, our publishers would be unable to meet the day's demand.[6]

It was perhaps the same hidden interest which caused one London club's copies of the *Return of Owners of Land* to be 'reduced to rags and tatters within a fortnight of its arrival',[7] and this same attitude may help explain the continuing popularity of gossip columns and society journals in Britain since the nineteenth century.

British scholars working in this area are fortunate to possess a number of sources of information about the very rich which are probably as comprehensive in scope and as reliable as any available in the other industrialised countries where research of this kind has, or usefully might, be undertaken. In this introductory chapter, these various sources, their histories, scope and utility, accuracy, comprehensiveness, and the *caveats* which must be made to their use, will be discussed.

Probate Calendars

The *probate calendars* at record offices in London and elsewhere are
the main source of information for this study. Since they record the
names and probate valuations of everyone leaving property in Britain,
the calendars provide a comprehensive guide not only to the wealth-
holders who were household names, but also those who are virtually
unknown, but who were often far wealthier than the famous.

The probate returns are obviously not perfect, and no one would
claim that they provide us with knowledge of the peak wealth of all
very wealthy men. Yet any conclusions about the structure of wealth
in Britain which employ the probate returns — and most do — are
based upon the presumption that the cohort of wealthy men deceased
during a relatively brief period are an accurate sample of all wealthy
men alive at that time. It is my firm belief that this assumption is
largely true, but the critical historian must examine the available data
and the possible sources of bias or inaccuracy with considerable care.
It is therefore appropriate at this stage to set out the most salient
features of the data in the probate calendars.

(1) Everyone leaving property at death in Britain must have the value
of his holdings totalled by the executors or administrators of his
estate for the various purposes entailed in the probate process. This
applies equally to persons leaving a will or dying intestate.
(2) Since January 1858 an inventory of the assets and liabilities of the
deceased has been lodged at the Principal Probate Registry, which
since 1874 has been situated at Somerset House in central London. Its
role is to deal with all testamentary aspects of the probate process,
and is the great central storehouse of all wills and letters of administration
left in England and Wales.
(3) Prior to the formation of the Principal Probate Registry the process
of probate in England and Wales was exclusively the business of the
Church of England, and probate was transacted under one of more
than 50 Ecclesiastical Courts.[8] If any testator left property worth £5 or
more within two or more dioceses, his estate was required to be proved
in one of the two Prerogative Courts, those of Canterbury and York,
whose dominion extended respectively to the southern two-thirds of
England (and to all of Wales) and to the northern third of England —
including Lancashire and Yorkshire.[9]

Because, however, of two important aspects of the ecclesiastical
system, the bulk of wealthy testators had their estates proved in London.

First any estate containing Bank of England funds ('consols') had to be proved in the Canterbury Court regardless of the place of residence of the testator;[10] and second, the offices of the Canterbury Prerogative Court were located not in Canterbury but at Doctor's Commons, Great Knightrider Street, in the City of London.[11] For these reasons, and probably for others related to professional expertise and despatch, the estates of most wealthy persons were proved in the Canterbury Court: about 90 per cent of all estates worth £100,000 or more probated between 1809 and 1858, and 63 of 66 estates worth £500,000 or more in this period. There is, however, some evidence of a rise in the importance of the provincial courts in these years.[12]

(4) Although the disposition of property at death dates back to medieval times valuations, in cash terms, of the global worth of an estate became universal only in the eighteenth century. But prior to the year 1809, estates of £100,000 or more (£10,000 or more before 1803) were termed 'Upper Value' in the Canterbury Courts Probate Act Books, rather than sworn to a specific sum. This study therefore begins at 1809 for comprehensive probate valuations at a very high level of wealth do not exist prior to that date.

Up to 1881, both in the Ecclesiastical Courts and in the Principal Probate Registry, the value of an estate was given in the style, e.g., 'Effects Under £300,000', and only after that date was an estate in England and Wales valued to a precise figure. Thus up to 1881 any such estate was worth slightly less than the figure stated: among very large estates, up to £50,000 or £100,000 less.

The Scottish and Irish probate records have a different history. The Scottish probate calendars appear in a published alphabetical form only from 1875. Until 1825 Scottish probate records were kept only at the level of individual shire courts rather than nationally in a central repository; for the years 1825-75 there exists a manuscript calendar held at the Scottish Record Office. I have, after much difficulty, been able to consult this manuscript index as well as the post-1875 records for this research.[13]

From their origin these Scottish probate sources recorded the precise valuation of an estate rather than an approximate figure, as in England until 1881. The Scottish probate records also differ from those in England (and Ireland) in one key and singular respect, for there the historian is permitted to see the inventory of property (known as the 'Inventory of Goods and Gear') of any estate proved in Scotland. Included in these inventories are not only an item-by-item account of all of the deceased's stocks and shares, but also all holdings in those categories of property (such as settled land prior to 1926) not included in the English calendar valuations. I have made use of this important source at several places in this work.[14]

The printed Irish probate calendars originate in 1858; most pre-1858 Irish probate documents were destroyed in the Four Courts fire of 1922. These Irish calendars were compiled until 1917; Northern Irish calendars since 1922. I have included all Irish wealth-holders deceased in the period 1858-1917 and Northern Irish wealth-holders since 1922.[15]

(5) The estates of foreigners leaving property in Britain are included in the probate calendars in the same manner as British subjects. A number of such persons left very substantial estates in Britain, including among them 20 millionaires.[16] None of these has been included in the discussions in this work, since the focus is British wealth, although both foreigners whose careers were largely passed in Britain and lived in Britain, and Englishmen whose fortunes were earned abroad, are included. Had these foreign wealth-holders been included in the data below, the financial and commercial (and, probably, self-made) proportion of the wealth class would have risen still further.

(6) More important than these distinctions and, indeed, crucial to the accuracy of this venture, are the types of property which are included in the valuation figures and the types which are excluded. The probate valuations are not all-encompassing, and have varied in their coverage from one period to another. There are several basic distinctions to be noted here, most importantly the distinction between settled and unsettled personalty and that between realty and personalty.

The valuation figures in the English calendars have always included *unsettled personalty* — any property other than land which the testator had in his absolute possession.[17] *Settled personalty* was not included in the valuation figure unless this property ceased being in settlement at the death of that testator. (It should be stressed that settled personalty is property *settled upon* the testator, and not property settled under a provision of the testator's will). In general, the property left to the chief male heir of the deceased was seldom tied up in this way; most settled personalty was left to women and more distant relatives, and would not much affect the statistics of the wealthy.[18]

Real property (apart from leaseholds) was not included in the calendar valuations prior to 1898 when, in accordance with a provision of the Land Transfer Act of 1897, *unsettled realty* was included in the global valuation figure. Between 1898 and 1926 — the date of the next major change in this category of valuation — there were several examples of wealth-holders whose realty must to a large extent have been included in the calendar valuations (for example, Hubert, second Marquess of Clanricarde (d. 1916) who left £2.5 million). Unfortunately, for this period of 27 years it is not possible to differentiate in the global valuation figure between personalty and realty, and one cannot — as before — add the personal wealth of a landowner to a multiple of his annual rental to arrive at his total wealth.

Under a provision of the Settled Land Act of 1925, *settled land* came to be included in the calendar figures from 1 January 1926.[19] The valuation figure for settled land is customarily entered separately from his other property in the calendars, which enables the researcher to gauge the value of agricultural land in the more recent period, although substantial estate duty avoidance probably began soon after this change was made. In any case, and most fortuitously, the historian has at his disposal the official statistics of the *Return of Owners of Land* of 1871-4 and the distilled figures in Bateman's *Great Landowners*. Despite their omission of London land and other confusions and lapses, they offer a near-total compensation for the omission of land valuations from the probate valuations prior to this century. Thus this area of omission, seemingly of the greatest seriousness, is in reality of minor significance.[20]

(7) Although the legal and administrative details of the process of valuation are not of paramount importance or can be compensated for from other sources, there is still the problem of voluntary estate duty avoidance. Certainly the rich have always indulged in some avoidance of duty. However, one must presume that the degree of avoidance was far lower before the era of very high duties on top levels of wealth. Although death duties existed from 1694 onwards they had only reached a level of 11 per cent on millionaire estates by 1907, and only attained what might be termed a confiscatory rate (of 40 per cent) in 1919.[21] Before the present era, it seems improbable that many men voluntarily gave away their fortune to avoid losing 11 per cent or even 20 per cent of it after their death. It seems more likely that it would require some psychological threshold in the level of duty — perhaps 40 per cent or 50 per cent or more — before most wealthy persons would seriously consider this.[22]

Furthermore, and perhaps more importantly, even if substantial numbers of wealth-holders do give away most of their property before death, this will not necessarily affect a study like this in a critical way. Since every very wealthy man has an identical motive for avoiding death duties, omissions caused by *inter vivos* gifts will be *random*, and will not much affect the statistics of the basic divisions — occupational, geographic, old *vs* new wealth — we are trying to trace here, provided that the remaining sample is of sufficient size. In fact, certain groups, particularly landowners and the London financial elite, have probably engaged in estate avoidance practices more frequently in the post-1945 period than the less sophisticated or those situated at a distance from the tax accountants and lawyers of London. But no objective motive accounts for any such distinctions.[23]

(8) Aside from the valuation figures contained in the calendars at Somerset House and elsewhere, there exists (from 1894 onwards) another set of valuation figures somewhat more extensive than the calendar figures. These are the figures of the *Estate Duty Office of the Inland Revenue* and they — rather than the figures given in the probate calendars — form the basis of virtually all current statistics of wealth-holding in Britain, and for most of the contemporary debate among economists and social commentators on the distribution of British wealth.[24] The Inland Revenue statistics are superior to the probate calendar figures in that they include settled property, property situated abroad, and property 'caught' by the seven year time limit on *inter vivos* gifts prior to death, which are not included in the probate calendars. But they are closed to all researchers for 125 years — no exception to this rule has ever been made, so far as I am aware — and the published statistical tables which derive from them are invariably anonymous. It should also be noted that the Inland Revenue figures are again inevitably for the *net* rather than the gross value of estates.[25]

Other Sources

(1) Apart from the two series of probate records, a number of other sources of major importance exist and have been used in this work, as necessary. By far the most important of these is the *Income Tax*, which was levied in Britain between 1799 and 1815, and again from 1842 onwards. The Income Tax, however, presents a number of very serious problems to the researcher. In keeping with all of the records maintained by the Inland Revenue, its statistics are presented in the form of anonymous tables. No individual Income Tax records may be consulted, and it is exceedingly unlikely that any individual returns are kept when no longer current. The researcher has only the extensive array of annual tables about the distribution of taxable incomes in Britain in the *Annual Reports of the Inland Revenue*, and the manuscript statistical records (often more extensive and useful — but still

anonymous) deposited at the Public Record Office among the Inland Revenue ('I.R.') classes of documents. But he has little or nothing more.[26]

This basic difficulty would not be so important if it were possible, from published statistical sources, to establish the distribution of incomes, especially at the highest levels, throughout the nineteenth century. Unfortunately this is impossible as well, for between 1803 and 1911 the Income Tax was divided into, and levied according to, a system of five schedules, rather than upon the total income of an individual.[27] Thus, except for one early table of income distribution in 1801,[28] it is impossible to ascertain how many individual *persons* were in possession of annual incomes of a particular range until 1911 (when Lloyd George's 'Super-Tax' provide us with such statistics for the highest ranges of incomes for the first time), for these five schedules were assessed upon *types* of income, and a single individual might find himself assessed under several schedules at once. Furthermore, *companies* were included with *persons* in enumerating the number of 'taxpayers' and their taxable incomes: there are many other anomalies as well.[29]

Although the nineteenth-century Income Tax thus raises seemingly insuperable difficulties for the researcher, in reality – and these difficulties notwithstanding – the statistics are nearly as useful as the probate records. First they provide a check on the main trends evidenced by the probate records against a different statistical measure, assessing a similar but, strictly speaking unrelated measure of affluence compiled by different government agencies for different purposes. Should the main conclusions about the British wealth structure emerging from the probate records be paralleled by the Income Tax data, the researcher has greater confidence in both. Second, whatever the limitations of the Income Tax statistics, they can address some key problems, especially the important matter of the geographical distribution of the middle class and of the elites. They can also be used in determining income distribution since 1911. Such possibilities present considerable scope for the historian of the subject.[30]

(2) Britain possesses a number of other statistical sources of information on the wealthy of very considerable interest and importance. Perhaps the most promising of these is the *Inhabited House Duty*, which was one of the so-called Assessed Taxes[31] levied from the eighteenth century onwards upon a bizarre collection of items likely to be owned or employed by the well-to-do, including carriages, coats-of-arms, men servants and hair powder (for wigs). As its name implies, the House Duty was levied on all inhabited dwellings in Britain. Its special potential

stems from two facts: the impressively long span — 1778 till 1834, and again from 1851 to 1926 — when it was levied, and the highly income-elastic nature of its assessments, which were levied according to the rental (or in the case of freeholds, imputed rental) of a house. Given the close ratio (except perhaps at the very top) between rentals and incomes, the distribution of incomes ought to be discernible from these statistics in at least a rough way. Unfortunately, major difficulties exist in the data: in particular, there were very considerable regional variations in the rates of house rentals with London rentals, especially after about 1870, anomalously high.[32]

(3) There is a range of hidden treasures to be found in the *Parliamentary Papers*, but they need careful sifting. In particular during each round of Parliamentary reform or mooted reform during the nineteenth century, and especially during the years 1825-33 and 1857-67, there appeared in the Parliamentary Papers a spate of official tables on all matters relating to the distribution of income, wealth and property, and particularly the relative amount of property in each geographical locality or parliamentary constituency in Britain. This material has never been systematically explored, and can be traced only in the (often misleadingly classified) indexes to the Parliamentary Papers. One table — to give an idea of the important material of this type — presents for each parliamentary borough in England and Wales in 1859-60 the number of male taxpayers liable to schedules B and D of the Income Tax or to any of the Assessed Taxes, and is thus, so far as I am aware, the solitary exception between 1803 and 1911 to the rule that the historian can never determine the number of individual persons assessed to Income Tax.[33] Any keen student of this field ought certainly to acquaint himself with these sources; there are doubtless many gems still undiscovered.

(4) The last of these other sources has also been mentioned before. It is the *Return of Owners of Land*, compiled by Parliament in 1871-4, and it is a listing of all persons (and corporate bodies and business firms) owning land in Britain apart from London — together with the acreage and gross annual rental of each.[34] For reasons which remain obscure, John Bateman, an Essex squire, undertook the thankless but invaluable task of collating and revising the original returns, and published several editions of his *Great Landowners of Great Britain and Ireland* between 1876 and 1883. In his work is listed every substantial landowner in Britain (except London landowners), with county and national totals for their acreages and incomes, and biographical information on each. This is the single most important source on the territorial and financial

aspects of nineteenth-century British landowning, and forms the basis for most of the discussions in Chapter 7 below.

Previous Research

Research into the fields of wealth-holding and wealth distribution which relies wholly or partly upon the statistical sources described here, has interested scholars in economics, economic and social history and sociology. Something can here be said only of the first two of these.[35] Particularly significant is the widespread and lively debate into the distribution of wealth and income in contemporary Britain, which has itself grown out of a previous debate on this subject. Such works as Dudley Baxter's *National Income* (1868), Leone Levi's *Wages and Earnings of the Working Classes* (1867) and Leo Chiozza Money's *Riches and Poverty (1910)* (1911) opened a debate which then remained closed for nearly half a century.[36] In recent years[37] such economists as J.R.S. Revell, A.B. Atkinson, and C.T. Sandford have addressed themselves to the question of contemporary wealth distribution, employing the Inland Revenue's probate figures as their major source of evidence. Perhaps the economist whose work most closely bears on the topic under discussion here is Professor Colin Harbury of the City University, London, who, with his research associates, has investigated intergenerational social mobility in an admirably precise and painstaking way among top wealth-leavers of the 1900s, 1950s, 1960s and 1970s. Harbury's work was in part inspired by Josiah Wedgwood's investigation of the inheritances of top wealth-leavers deceased in the period 1924-5, *The Economics of Inheritance* (London, 1929). A very great deal — indeed, one might argue, too much — has appeared in recent years on the distribution of wealth and income in Britain, to which the statistical sources on wealth and income distribution are of central importance; the appointment of the Royal Commission on this subject headed by Lord Diamond and its several major *Reports* are evidence of this.

The disciplines of economic and social history have contributed much less to this topic in recent years. Since 1945 economic historians have been more concerned with economic growth and development where aggregate and national statistics of the national economy have been more important than the wealth-gathering efforts of individual men. Social historians have tended to concentrate on the working-class and poverty, particularly factory and urban poverty: as a result the study of the rich, as a social group, has fallen between stools. The only exception to this are the many fine studies of landowners and landed society which have appeared over the past 15 years and the Namieresque analyses of nineteenth- and twentieth-century political leaders. There is some considerable evidence that this is now changing, with such works as John Foster's important *Class Struggle and the Industrial Revolution* (London, 1974) incorporating accurate and illuminating data on the wealth of the new industrial bourgeoisie of northern England. The utility and comprehensive nature of the probate records are now more widely known among historians than ever before — as witness the listing of the probate valuations of nearly all the working-class leaders in John Saville and Joyce Bellamy's *Dictionary of Labour Biography* — commonly pathetic in their smallness, occasionally more surprising still for their grandeur.[38]

But, needless to say, public interest in the rich is no new thing. It is at least as old as the eighteenth-century guide naming the unmarried women in England with the largest dowries (and the sums their lucky suitors could expect to receive). Although interest in the rich must have risen as the amount of wealth, especially business wealth, increased during the nineteenth century, the public's hunger for works which would name names and tell how it was done, was aroused permanently by popular Victorian writers like Samuel Smiles and his many imitators. This pattern was essentially set by the 1880s, which saw the publication of two of the more typical of such efforts, both produced anonymously, *Fortunes Made in Business* (London, 1883) and *Millionaires and How They Became So*, reprinted in 1884 from a series of articles which first appeared in *Tit-Bits*. *Millionaires* opens with an incomplete list of all British probate fortunes of £250,000 left in the previous decade — an unusually precise touch in a subject whose general hallmark is vagueness as to size of fortune. Although the title page promises to show 'How twenty-seven of the wealthiest men in the world made their money', this work (rather in the manner of Falstaff's 'eleven buckram men grown out of two') discusses the careers of 15 alleged millionaires, beginning, for some reason, with the American robber-baron Jay Gould, and proceeding to such genuine British millionaires as the Rothschilds, Thomas Brassey and Sir William Armstrong. It then surveys a number of celebrated business figures of the day whose fortunes were, in actual fact, considerably less, such as the Budgetts, a family of Bristol retailers, Sir John Brown the shipbuilder and the engineer Sir William Fairbairn. A miscellany of erstwhile millionaires, like Warren Hastings and Sir Richard Arkwright, and foreign ones like Stephen Girard and Peter Cooper, round out the work. Several of the characteristics which mark all such studies appear in this work, as it were, in full colour. There is, first, the extremely slapdash manner in which subjects are chosen for inclusion: there is no serious effort to assess the relative wealth of the wealthiest men of 1884 and include only the richest; fields like banking, brewing and landowning, though highly lucrative, are virtually unrepresented.[39] This era being the zenith of influence of Samuel Smiles, most of the essays are in the classical rags-to-riches vein and, indeed, virtually the only common denominator linking the subjects together is that most appear to be 'self-made men'.

Similar qualities are the hallmark of another, perhaps better-known work of collective biography published at the same time, *Fortunes Made in Business* (London, 1883). This time there are 14 family fortunes, all of them British. The 'fortunes' here vary from bona-fide millionaires and half-millionaires like the Fieldens, Fosters, Kitsons, Peases and Platts, to those far less wealthy (though probably more celebrated) like the Brights. There is again the same panegyrical emphasis on the 'self-made' aspects of the dynasties' rise, the same overemphasis on manufacturing and heavy industry to the exclusion of finance and commerce (only two of the 14 families here were not in manufacturing, and none at all in finance), with the consequent overestimation of the numerical importance of northerners and dissenters among successful nineteenth-century British entrepreneurs. Remarkably, and no doubt in the absence of anything better, this farrago has been used as a source for a discussion of entrepreneurship by a major economic historian of our day.[40]

In this century, though this type of book has had a good many imitators, very little has ever been added to the form of such collections. Indeed, a work like T.C. Bridges and H. Hessel Tiltman's *Kings of Commerce* (London, 1928) is even more eulogistic than *Millionaires and How they Became So*, omitting any hint of questionable practice by the businessmen described. A certain veil of obscurity had passed over the making of great fortunes in Britain. This affected even the opposition for there are few if any British equivalents to the American muckraking tradition of millionaire-bashing from the Gilded Age's *America's Sixty Families* by Gustavus Myer to Felix Lundberg's *The Rich and the Super-Rich* (New York, 1968).[41] Indeed, perhaps the only meaningful attempt to raise the veil, for purely tactical reasons, occurred during the Lloyd George Honours scandals, led by the extreme right in the House of Lords. While in recent years much of the old caginess has surely gone — no one has ever accused *Private Eye* of failing to wash a millionaire's dirty laundry in public — little has been added to the old tradition, except perhaps a new emphasis on the psychology of money-making, much of it far-fetched.[42] Perhaps the most useful and interesting of recent serious writings on the rich in Britain has been at the level intermediate between serious scholarship and journalism, such as Roy Perrott's *The Artistocrats* (London, 1968) or Oliver Marriott's remarkable and justly-celebrated *The Property Boom* (London, 1969). Yet the overall conclusion must be that serious social analysis of the wealthy in Britain, both historically and in the contemporary world, has been neither particularly searching nor profound.

Yet, once again, it goes almost without saying that the British public's interest in the subject of great wealth is as keen as is its interest in any subject can possibly be. This is evident on many levels: by the lengthy and continuing popularity of gossip columns and journals of the *Tatler* variety (it is, of course, difficult to separate the interest in the monied from the equally pronounced fascination with royalty and the aristocracy); by the unique excellence of genealogical guides, above all of *Burke's Peerage* and *Burke's Landed Gentry* (which dates back to the 1830s and had many predecessors even then) and of biographical reference works like *Who's Who* and the *Directory of Directors*, both products of the nineteenth century; by the attention paid to the rich and to all the subtle ramifications of social differentiation at a high level by British writers from Jane Austen, Thackeray and Dickens to C.P. Snow and Anthony Powell or, in a vulgarised form, by the ten thousand and one writers of popular fiction and detective stories.

There is, in other words, a yawning gap to be explained. Cold, hard facts about great wealth simply do not match the public's undoubted interest in them: it is T.S. Eliot's 'objective correlative' in reverse. Although there are many reasons for this, perhaps the most basic one is the sheer lack of knowledge about who is rich and who is not, how the rich came to be that way, and what this implies about the nature of British society in the past century and a half. The remainder of this book is an attempt to fill the gap.[43]

Notes

1. Lawrence Stone, *The Crisis of the Aristocracy* (Oxford, 1965), p. 1.

2. Harold Perkin, *The Origins of Modern English Society, 1780-1880* (London, 1969), Chapter III, esp. pp. 63, 85.

3. Ralph E. Pumphrey 'The Introduction of Industrialists Into the British Peerage. A Study in the Adaption of a Social Institution', *Amer. Hist. Rev.* LXV (1959), pp. 1-16 *passim*. I should state that I myself do not wholly agree

with this view.

4. W.G. Rimmer, *Marshalls of Leeds. Flax Spinners. 1788-1886* (Cambridge, 1960).

5. The term 'wealth-holder' will be used throughout this work to denote those men included in this study. At the present time this is the common academic term to denote *either* the very rich *or* any individual possessor of wealth or property (when the general distribution of wealth in society is discussed) and was, I believe, first introduced into scholarly parlance by the American economist R.J. Lampman in 'Changes in the Share of Top Wealth-holders, 1922-56', *Review of Economics and Statistics*, 41 (1959). More accurately the term for those *leaving* large fortunes is 'wealth-leaver' (which is preferred by e.g., Professor Harbury), which I have rejected as unwieldy. Indeed, many of the neutral circumlocutions employed in this work, for instance 'half-millionaire', are inelegant in the extreme, but are none the less necessary for all that. It is a commentary on both the vagueness and excitability engendered by talk of great wealth that even the basic terminology is unsatisfactory.

6. 'The Fascination of Money', *Spectator*, 23 November 1873, pp. 1486-7.

7. John Bateman, *The Great Landowners of Great Britain and Ireland*, (4th edn, London, 1883), pp. v-vi.

8. The authoritative guide to the probate process and its ramifications is Anthony J. Camp, *Wills and Their Whereabouts* (London, 1974). See also L.D. Powles and T.W.H. Oakley, *The Law Relating to Probate and Administration* (London, 1892), Sir Roland L. Vaughan Williams, *A Treatise on the Law of Executors and Administrators* (9th edn, London, 1893) and Thomas Gwynne, *The Law Relating to the Duties on Probate and Letters of Administration* (3rd edn, London, 1841).

9. Should a deceased person have left property within both areas, his effects in each were proven separately within either court; neither court held jurisdiction within the area of the other.

10. [George] Walter Thornbury, *Old and New London* (London, n.d. [1873]), vol. I, p. 289.

11. This remained the seat of the later principal Probate Registry until 1874.

12. In the course of my research, I have systematically examined the indexes of the Canterbury and York Prerogative Courts (currently held, respectively at the Public Record Office, London, and the Borthwick Institute, York), of the two local Lancashire courts whose records are now housed at the Lancashire Record Office (those of the Episcopal Consistory Court of Chester and the Consistory Court of the Archdeaconry of Richmond), and (from 1825) of the Scottish probate records for the period 1809-58, and abstracted the names and other pertinent data of all persons leaving £100,000 or more. I did not, however, examine the indexes (classified at PROB. 6, 7 and 9, rather than PROB. 8) of intestacies and limited probates in the Canterbury Court.

On this subject, see Gerald Hamilton-Edwards, *In Search of Ancestry* (London, 1966), esp. p. 56.

13. The 1825-75 indexes remain technically in the possession of the Inland Revenue (and hence are indexed as 'I.R. 9'), and are subject to that body's restrictions on access by researchers to many of its documents for a period of 125 (formerly 150) years. My own attempt to consult them was successful only after the intervention of a local MP on my behalf.

14. Copies of these Scottish inventories may be found at Somerset House in cases where the testator also left property in England.

15. On the complicated matter of Irish probate, see Camp, *Wills*, pp. 207-25.

16. There is a list of these men in W.D. Rubinstein, 'British Millionaires, 1809-1949', *Bulletin of the Institute of Historical Research* (1974).

17. Gwynne, *Duties on Probate*, p. 20. Such unsettled personalty included the value of leaseholds let for a period of years.

18. Were a wealth-holder to settle his personal fortune for several generations and no more, it would – if kept intact – eventually be 'caught' in the calendar valuations several generations later. This has in fact happened among several wealthy families.

19. Except in Scotland, where settled land remained excluded from the valuation figure until 1964.

20. Two other important points about the type of property valued in the probate calendars should be noted. First, real property situated abroad, as well as foreign shares for which no deed or title may exist except in the books of that foreign state, are excluded from the valuation figures. However, a detailed examination of a large number of Scottish inventories makes clear that most foreign shares, for instance American railway shares, were certainly included in these calculations. Second, all probate calendar valuations consist of the *gross* rather than the net value of an estate: the difference between these two figures consists of personal debts and funeral expenses. Accordingly, the *gross* values of estates have been used throughout this work. In more than 90 per cent of the cases where I have seen both figures, the difference between the two amounted to between 5 per cent and 15 per cent of the gross value. The net value may be obtained for estates proved after 1881 (on payment of a further fee), but is unavailable before that date.

21. On the history of the early death duties see Sidney Buxton and George Stapleton Barnes, *A Handbook to the Death Duties* (London, 1890); a modern survey of this field may be found in C.T. Sandford, *Taxing Personal Wealth* (London, 1971), pp. 43 ff.

22. Taxes on 'death bed gifts' and *inter vivos* gifts made before a time limit (for instance, three years) prior to death were levied from 1881 on. It is interesting to note that the amount raised by this tax, known in the nineteenth century as 'Account Duty' was always very small, although it was levied at the same rate as Probate Duty on ordinary probates. It reached even £100,000 in this period only once, in 1891-2.

23. Such omissions would affect much more materially those conclusions about wealth-holding which depend crucially upon having a complete series of all estates of deceased persons – for instance, the changing distribution of wealth within the entire nation.

24. See, e.g., Sandford, *Taxing Personal Wealth*, A.B. Atkinson, *Unequal Shares* (London, 1972), *The Economics of Inequality* (Oxford, 1975) and (with A.J. Harrison), *The Distribution of Wealth in Britain* (Cambridge, 1978). The last of these is the most comprehensive study of this source, particularly for the very recent period. For a devastating critique, from a right-wing perspective, of these statistics and the conclusions commonly drawn from them, see G. Polanyi and J.B. Wood, *How Much Inequality?* (London, Institute of Economic Affairs, 1974).

25. Colin Harbury and D.M.W. Hitchens, in their *Inheritance and Wealth Inequality* (London, 1980), explore the differences between the two series in considerable detail. See also C. Harbury's 'Inheritance and the Distribution of Personal Wealth in Britain', *The Economic Journal*, 72 (1962).

26. The most useful of these documents are I.R. 16, 'Tax Abstracts and Statistics', which detail the annual assessments and payments of each schedule of the Income Tax, by county and local registration district, between 1845/6 and 1911/12 and I.R. 2, which presents similar statistics by *parish* at intervals between 1857 and 1904. Also of great interest are the surviving records of the first Income Tax (1799-1815), explored by

Arthur Hope-Jones in his *Income Tax in The Napoleonic Wars* (Cambridge, 1939). These are held by the P.R.O. but classified at E (for 'Exchequer') 181 and 182, and similarly detail the tax statistics by geographical areas. A full list of the individual classes of Inland Revenue material held at the P.R.O. was published in the *Social History Newsletter*, vol. 2, number 2 (Autumn, 1977).

27. The authoritative work on the subject, which all researchers in the field must consult, is Josiah Stamp's *British Incomes and Property* (London, 1916), which I personally regard as the most astonishing work ever written on nineteenth-century British economic history. It is quite impossible that this work will ever be superseded as the authoritative book in its field. On the history of the Income Tax see also Hope-Jones, *Income Tax in The Napoleonic Wars*; Stephen Dowell, *History of Taxation and Taxes in England* (London, 1884; reprinted 1965), B.E.V. Sabine, *A History of the Income Tax* (London, 1966); and D.J. O'Brien, 'British Incomes and Property in the Early Nineteenth Century', *Econ. Hist. Rev.*, 2nd ser., XII (1959-60).

28. Reprinted in Stamp, *British Incomes*, p. 501.

29. On the details of the system of schedules, see Stamp, *British Incomes*, *passim*; and W.D. Rubinstein, 'Victorian Middle Classes', *Econ. Hist. Rev.*, 2nd ser., XXX (1977), esp. pp. 615-19. The lower limit of *individual* income liable to Income Tax ranged from £100 to £160 at different times during the nineteenth century.

30. Much exists in the Parliamentary Papers of very considerable interest. In particular, there are a number of very important tables detailing the assessment of taxable income by geographical area. See especially P.P. 1882, LII, *Parliamentary Constituencies (Population)*, listing the assessment of four schedules of the Income Tax by Parliamentary constituency, and P.P. 1860, XXXIX, pt. II, *Property and Income Tax*, an even more detailed breakdown by *parish*. There are at least a dozen other tables of similar significance, especially in the years 1803-15, 1827-33 and 1857-66.

31. On these taxes see Dowell, *Taxation and Taxes*, vol. three, esp. pp. 178-92; Stamp, *British Incomes*, pp. 107-41, 444ff; and L.D. Schwartz, 'Income Distribution and Social Structure in London in the late Eighteenth Century', *Econ. Hist. Rev.*, 2nd ser., XXXII (1979).

32. There are a number of very interesting and unusual returns in the Parliamentary Papers which make use of House Duties. At various times in the 1820s and 1830s (e.g., P.P. 1833, 503, 'House Duties') there appeared named lists of the most expensive houses in Britain! In the April 1833 return, the five most expensive private houses in London were owned by – in descending order – the Dukes of Sutherland and Devonshire, the Earl of Chesterfield, the Duke of Wellington and the Marquess of Lansdowne.

33. P.P. 1861, L, 785, 'Parliamentary Boroughs (Assessed Taxes, etc)'.

34. It originally appeared in the Parliamentary Papers in instalments: P.P. 1874, LXXII, Pts. I and II; P.P. 1874, LXXII, Pt III; P.P. 1876, LXXX.

35. For other references to previous research in this area and to the use of wealth data by social scientists in Britain, see the chapter 'Modern Britain' in W.D. Rubinstein (ed.), *Wealth and the Wealthy in the Modern World* (London, 1980).

36. Money's work is particularly interesting and historically important in that it made use of probate records to ascertain the distribution of wealth, the first time these were used for this now-familiar purpose. Money – whose real name was Chiozza and who changed it to Money on inheriting a legacy, strange as this may seem – was an unusually intelligent radical Liberal MP of the Edwardian period whose career ended in a notorious sexual scandal in the 1920s.

37. For some reason the debate on the distribution of wealth in Britain virtually disappeared between the First World War and the 1960s. Some exceptions in the interim are: A.L. Bowley's important *The Change in the Distribution of the National Income, 1880-1913* (Oxford, 1920); Josiah Wedgwood, *The Economics of Inheritance* (London, 1929) and D. Seers, *The Levelling of Incomes since 1938* (Oxford, 1951).

38. This increased interest is only indirectly related to the very wide interest in the history of wealth-holding evident among scholars abroad, particularly in France and America. In France, the leading scholar in this field is Professor Adeline Daumard and her monumental *Les Fortunes Françaises au XIX Siècle* (Paris, 1973). The leading American historians of wealth-holding are probably Professors Edward Pessen and Lee Soltow; there is now a very considerable body of able scholars in this area. On foreign research, see the references in Rubinstein, *Wealth and the Wealthy*. There is little evidence that much of this foreign research, except in a general way, has been absorbed by British historians.

39. Although the compilers of this work do estimate (p. 101) that the number of millionaires in the world in 1884 was 700, of whom 200 were in Britain, 100 in America and Germany, 75 in France, 50 in Russia, 50 in India (!) and 125 in other countries. The British figure is an underestimate — though not a wild one — if landed millionaires are counted; an overestimate otherwise.

40. Charles P. Kindleberger, *Economic Growth in France and Britain* (New York, 1969), pp. 126-31. Use of such sources, unfortunately, has resulted in a fair number of warped perceptions about nineteenth-century British entrepreneurship by Professor Kindleberger, e.g., 'Why did not new enterprises elbow their way to the forefront in Britain after 1880? . . . The hungry outsiders — immigrants, Quakers, Jews, and lower-class aspirants to wealth — diminished either in numbers or in the intensity of their drive.' (p. 133.)

41. Simon Haxey, *Tory M.P.* (London, 1938), is one of the very few such works. Probably the main reasons for this were the reticence of Fleet Street reporters to delve into this question and the stringent British libel laws.

42. See, e.g., Thomas Wiseman, *The Money Motive* (London, 1974); cf., Raymond Pinter, *Fortunes to be Made* (London, 1970).

43. A number of other basic conventions adopted in the discussion throughout the book should be made explicit. Women are excluded from the discussion, chiefly because of the haphazard nature of inheritance of large fortunes by women in Britain, and the difficulties of tracing biographical details of their lives. The Appendix deals with women wealth-holders.

It must also be made clear the lower limit of wealth for inclusion in this study was held steady and does not vary with time. The difficulties of, e.g., calculating a plausible inflation index for the wealthy are considerable. Finally we generally employ date-of-death cohorts in the discussion rather than date-of-birth groupings, as rich men continue to earn money up to the time of their deaths.

2 THE NUMBER OF WEALTH-HOLDERS AND THE RANGE OF WEALTH

Perhaps the most basic dimension of the British wealth structure is the number of wealthy persons and the range of their wealth and income. How much did it take to be rich, to be numbered among a country's wealthiest men? How many men at any one time were in fact 'rich'? The answer to these questions will vary with time: 'wealth' has only a relative meaning and denotes considerably different levels of riches at different times. However, this chapter will present a broad picture of the changing numbers of top wealth-holders or high income-earners, together with the levels of their wealth and income, from 1809 when official records became available. In a sense, the sources from which this chapter are derived are somewhat different from subsequent ones in that, for the most part, they are anonymous, revealing less about individual identities or careers among the very wealthy than is the case elsewhere. This is so because so much of the data here is derived from the Inland Revenue data. Mere numbers in the abstract can be the most tedious of all impressions made upon the human senses: it is hoped that here the inherent fascination of the subject will to some degree prove to be a compensation.

Before discussing the relative handful of top wealth-holders in nineteenth-century British society, it would perhaps be helpful to start by detailing the overall place of the wealthy within the whole of society and to discuss, at least in a cursory manner, something of the distribution of wealth throughout society as a whole. Although we have spoken of the definitive answers which the British sources can provide, it is perhaps ironical that, in the matter of the distribution of wealth throughout British society as a whole, there is virtually no consistent evidence for the nineteenth century.

Only in 1895, with the Harcourt death duties, did the Inland Revenue begin to record the numbers of estates probated by level of wealth.[1] Perhaps the most unfortunate consequence of this is that it is impossible to discuss, except in a crude way, the changing distribution of personal wealth during the period of industrialisation, and the degree of inequality which resulted. No one — and certainly no statistical agency of the government — took it upon himself to collect and publish this material.[2] There are, however, two or three exceptions to this void in our knowledge. A table exists in the Parliamentary Papers detailing the number and size of all estates proved in the Canterbury Prerogative Court in 1824 (and which is, accordingly, biased toward the wealthy).[3] More important is the full statistical discussion of the wills and letters of administration probated in 1858, the first year of the Principal Probate Registry, to be found – inappropriately enough – in the *Twenty-second Annual Report of the Registrar-General of Births, Marriages and Deaths*, which appeared in the Parliamentary Papers in 1861.[4] Among the details given in this remarkable document is a unique breakdown of the *occupations* of all wealth-leavers in England and Wales by sex and size of estate.[5] The uniqueness of this data should be stressed: from that day to this, no other source has ever published the occupations of wealth-leavers.

It is thus that we know that in 1858, of 65 male estates given in this source as worth £100,000 or more,[6] ten belonged to peers, five to bankers, four to merchants, three to clergymen, two to East India Company officers, and one each to a naval officer, to a hotel-keeper, to a corn merchant and to a cotton manufacturer. In 37 cases the testator was described as 'gentleman', 'esquire', 'of independent means' or the like. But we also learn from this source much about the other end of the social scale: that, for instance, of 33 'mechanics' who left any probated estate in 1858 (doubtless there were hundreds of mechanics who did not), 29 left under £1000 (12 under £100), but four left between £1,000 and £4,000, and one thrifty mid-Victorian mechanic took not less than between £6,000 and £8,000 to his cold and lonely grave. No 'labourer'[7] deceased in 1858, however, could claim to have left more than between £1,000 and £2,000 (five did so); on the other hand, somehow four blacksmiths did this, the richest of whom was possessed of between £30,000 and £50,000.

What, indisputably, this *Report* does show, however, is that during the nineteenth century the average man, and still more the average woman, left nothing: at least nothing which the probate statistics chose to call property. Only 14.7 per cent of all persons aged 21 or more dying in 1858 left any property recorded by the probate statistics: 21.0 per cent of adult men, 8.6 per cent of all adult women.[8] Because of the singular nature of this source, it is worth recording its main findings in Table 2.1.

As Table 2.1 makes clear at once, the distribution of personal wealth in Britain in 1858 was exceedingly unequal, probably far more unequal than in any generation since. One man alone – the sole millionaire whose estate was proved in 1858[9] – left 1.6 per cent of all the traceable

Table 2.1: Number of Wills and Administrations Probated in 1858 in England and Wales, by Size and Aggregate Amounts of Estates

Amounts £	Persons	Numbers of Estates		Aggregate amount of Estates (£'000)
		Men	Women	
Under 20	1,935	1,316	619	29
20-100	6,368	4,146	2,222	382
100-200	4,670	3,195	1,475	701
200-300	2,512	1,758	754	628
300-450	2,426	1,670	756	910
450-600	1,877	1,326	551	985
600-800	1,622	1,161	461	1,135
800-1,000	1,103	775	328	993
1,000-2,000	2,671	1,909	762	4,007
2,000-4,000	2,058	1,484	574	6,174
4,000-6,000	806	599	207	4,030
6,000-8,000	439	341	98	3,073
8,000-10,000	303	221	82	2,727
10,000-20,000	602	468	134	9,030
20,000-30,000	231	189	42	5,775
30,000-40,000	126	107	19	4,410
40,000-50,000	61	48	13	2,745
50,000-75,000	73	64	9	4,563
75,000-100,000	29	24	5	2,537
100,000-200,000	43	42	1	5,860
200,000-400,000	19	19	–	4,700
400,000-500,000	3	3	–	1,500
500,000-1m	1	1	–	800
1m +	1	1	–	1,000
Totals	29,979	20,867	9,112	69,893

Source: *Twenty-second Annual Report of the Registrar-General of Births, Marriages and Deaths*, p. 181.

Note: The divisions in the ranges of wealth are as in the Parliamentary Papers, except that those above £100,000 have been somewhat condensed.

wealth passing by probate that year, a degree of inequality more reminiscent of the erstwhile Indian maharajah who received his weight in diamonds each year than of a modern industrial society. The wealthiest *67 persons* deceased in 1858 among them left nearly £14 million, *22 per cent* of all the wealth passing by probate in that year. Conversely, the poorest 1,935 wealth-leavers collectively left a pathetic £29,000. Even this by no means is the whole story, for it must not be forgotten that the vast majority of adults dying in England and Wales in 1858 — 189,000 of 211,000 — left *nothing*.[10] Obviously most of these people were not tramps sleeping on the benches of such parks as existed in 1858. Persons owning only chattels or property not requiring a deed or title to be transferred would not be caught in the probate net, and it may well be imagined that most mid-Victorian working-men were simply *de facto* outside the legal network of probate. On the other hand it must not be forgotten that the value of land was excluded from the nineteenth-century probate figures. This was perhaps the most unequally distributed commodity of all, and its exclusion from the 1858 statistics means that the real degree of inequality is even greater than that recorded here: many of the peers and landed gentry given here as worth hundreds of thousands were in fact worth millions.

Beginning in 1895, the official series maintained by the Inland Revenue are available and it is worth looking at some of their returns, in light of the findings for 1858. The Inland Revenue statistics include real property, some settled personalty not brought into the Principal Probate Registry figures, and are for the net rather than the gross value of the estate. By 1900-1, the distribution of British wealth as evidenced in the probate returns was as per Table 2.2.[11]

Again, the distribution of wealth appears phenomenally unequal, but perhaps less so than in 1858 when it is remembered that landed wealth is now brought into the picture. Nine persons accounted for more than five per cent of the wealth passing by probate; 67 persons left 16 per cent; fewer than 700 estates accounted for 41 per cent of the total value of all estates. At the other end of the scale, it was still true that only a small minority of the population left any property at all caught in the probate: there were some 343,000 adult deaths in England and Wales in 1900, but only 49,799 estates proved there in 1900-1: about 17 per cent of the population, only marginally greater than in 1858, despite four decades of Britain's imperial zenith. Again, it should in fairness be stressed that the remainder of the population could hardly have been utterly destitute, and that the scope of estate duties automatically precluded certain types of property from entering at all into the statistics; this property was more likely to be owned by the poor than the rich. But the figure of 17 per cent of the population

Table 2.2: Number of United Kingdom Estates, 1900-1, by Size and Aggregate Amounts

Amount	Number	Total Value (£'000)
Small estates, not exceeding £300 gross value	18,237	3,557
Small estates, exceeding £300 but not exceeding £500 gross value	8,707	3,499
* £ Net		
100-500	6,460	3,568
500-1,000	9,434	8,463
1,000-10,000	15,814	60,641
10,000-25,000	2,290	40,768
25,000-50,000	887	33,597
50,000-75,000	263	18,167
75,000-100,000	133	13,000
100,000-150,000	140	18,141
150,000-250,000	81	17,755
250,000-500,000	51	16,667
500,000-1m	17	13,088
1m +	9	13,603
Totals	62,523	264,514

*Net value, as are all subsequent amounts in this table. The dimensions in this column are from the Parliamentary Papers.

is suspiciously like that generally given as the percentage of the middle-class in the total population, and the probate figures, recording as they do primarily the rich and the thrifty, may reveal the precise limitations of Victorian and Edwardian opportunity with startling clarity.

In more recent times (the post-1945 situation will be surveyed in another chapter), the period between 1900 and 1938-9, the next period surveyed here, reveals itself to be a time of continuing gain in the spread of wealth, without touching the main features of inequality, as Table 2.3 reveals.

Again, the glaring inequality of the top end is still evident: four millionaires by themselves accounted for nearly two per cent of all wealth passing by probate, 30 half-millionaires for nearly four per cent, while 35,383 of the smallest estates recorded here between them

Table 2.3: Number of Estates in Great Britain, 1938-9, by Size and Aggregate Amounts

Amount	Number	Aggregate Amount (£'000)
Small estates, not exceeding £300 gross value	35,383	7,272
Small estates, exceeding £300 but not exceeding £500 gross value	23,195	9,305
£ Net		
100-1,000	38,470	27,318
1,000-10,000	46,127	155,457
10,000-25,000	6,066	96,126
25,000-50,000	2,031	72,527
50,000-100,000	943	65,779
100,000-150,000	224	27,580
150,000-250,000	141	26,481
250,000-500,000	98	34,744
500,000-1m	30	19,908
1m +	4	10,774
Totals	152,712	553,271

Source: P.P. 1938-9, 12, 16-17.

Note: Divisions given here have been grouped as in Table 2.2 wherever possible.

made up only 1.3 per cent of the total wealth. But one feature of these statistics had markedly changed: the percentage of all deceased adults leaving some property had greatly increased. A total of 136,794 out of about 420,000 adults dying in England and Wales left property caught by the probate net, just under 33 per cent. This still meant that two-thirds of the adult population left nothing, while most of the increase came in the lowest wealth brackets rather than among substantial estates. It is likely, too, that inflation accounted for much of the increase. Yet on the face of it the ownership of wealth was substantially greater than in Victorian times.

Number of Wealth-holders

Just as in the case of the distribution of personal wealth among the whole population there are apparently irremoveable limitations on the available statistical evidence, so with the probate records and the light they shed on the identity and magnitude of great fortunes there is the blunt fact that the sources begin in a usable form in 1809, and it is not possible to extend this research back in a comprehensive way before that date. But this does not mean that we know nothing about the rich prior to that time or that it is impossible to make important general-isations, based upon more selective evidence. As in the later period, this evidence emerges from the probate records.[12] During the late eighteenth and very early nineteenth centuries, it appears that a personal fortune of £500,000-£1 million would have been sufficient to place its holder among the very richest of Englishmen whose money was derived from non-landed sources − from trade or government patronage. This figure was seldom if ever exceeded by any personal fortune of the period. At this level of wealth were such men as John Moore, Archbishop of Canterbury (d. 1805), who left £1 million; Samuel Fludyer (d. 1786), 'probably the richest clothier in England', whose estate totalled £900,000; the miser John Elewes, worth about £800,000 in 1789; the financier Abraham Franco (d. 1777), the banker John Denison (d. 1806) and the great pottery magnate Josiah Wedgwood (d. 1795), each worth between £500,000 and £600,000 at their deaths.[13] This list cannot be regarded as comprehensive: yet it would be surprising if any vastly greater British personal fortunes existed prior to the nineteenth century. (The capital value of the land owned by the great aristocrats is, of course, another matter). Indeed, it is not unlikely that the level of wealth of the richest Restoration and even Jacobean merchants had already reached this level on occasion; during the eighteenth century such fortunes were seldom if ever exceeded: they only occurred more often.[14]

From 1809, fairly precise figures can be given for the number of large personal fortunes. Until the Inland Revenue statistics first become available in 1894, however, in order to construct such a continuous series, it is necessary to abstract a list of the largest estates from these sources by hand. A close examination of these figures reveals that there are very wide yearly variations in the total number of such estates: for example, there were 21 estates of £100,000 or more in 1821 and 1823, but 36 in 1822; similarly there were 21 estates in 1846, but 36 in 1847. To some extent this must have been the result of wide annual economic variations, but such variations are probably to be expected in any case considering the tiny number of such estates: of all the thousands of adults dying in Britain, only on average one per month left a fortune of £100,000 or more in 1811, only two per month in 1839, only three per month in 1856. In 1840 there were 182,000 male deaths in England and Wales, perhaps 135,000 of whom were adults.[15]

Table 2.4: Estates of £100,000 or More, Five-year Annual Averages, 1809-58

	Numbers
1809-14	16.5
1815-19	18.2
1820-4	25.6
1825-9	29.0
1830-4	29.4
1835-9	30.4
1840-4	30.2
1845-9	29.2
1850-4	31.6
1855-8	37.0

Much of these wide yearly variations disappear if five-yearly averages are taken instead of yearly figures, as Table 2.4 makes clear for the probate figures prior to the establishment of the Principal Probate Registry in 1858. It would thus appear that the trend in the wealth picture between 1809 and 1858 may be divided into three parts. First, the period of the Napoleonic War and the fifteen post-war years witnessed a sharp rise in the number of wealthy deaths, from 16.5 per annum in 1809-14 to 29.0 in the period 1825-9. There then ensued a span of 25 years when the number of wealthy deaths hardly varied: no more than 31.6 per annum (in the period 1850-4), no fewer than 29.0 in 1825-9. Finally there occurred a rise in the last period of the Ecclesiastical Court Records, the annual number rising from 31.6 to 37.0 during the 1850s.

In view of the sharp rise in the cost of living during the Napoleonic War — the Rousseaux Price Index reached a peak of 206 in 1809, a level not surpassed until the First World War[16] — and of the wide distortions of supply and demand caused by the war, a rise in the number of large estates was to be expected. Many merchants made themselves rich overnight:

A Bristol merchant, worth at the beginning of the [Napoleonic] war under £1000, possessed half a million when Farington met him at its conclusion. A shopkeeper of the Exeter Exchange in the Strand amassed £100,000 merely by selling shilling packets of powder to sharpen razors.[17]

The number of deceased wealth-holders continued to rise until the period 1825-9, and although the cost of living fell dramatically — the Rousseaux Index declined from 202 in 1814 to 122 in 1824 — and war-caused economic distortions were no longer present, it is not surprising that the number of wealth-holders should continue to rise. The merchants of the Napoleonic War period were by definition active in trade prior to 1815, and began to die in substantial numbers only several years later. Furthermore, with the reopening of normal trade routes and markets abroad, home production was stimulated.[18]

However much the increase of the Napoleonic War and post-war period might be expected, the failure of the number of wealth-holders to rise at all until the mid-1850s is clearly surprising. During this period the number of male deaths increased from 175,000 in 1838 to 222,000 in 1854,[19] while national income expanded from £291 million in 1821 to £523 million in 1851.[20] Furthermore, the best evidence on this much-vexed issue supports the view that there is little if any evidence of a shift of income away from the middle classes — let alone the wealthy — to the working classes during this period. There was probably a distinct long-term rise in the working-class standard of living during the first half of the nineteenth century, with the exception of a few years around 1845, but there was also an increase in the income and wealth of the middle and upper classes.[21] Without further evidence, one can only speculate on the reasons for this puzzling set of figures. It might be the result merely of the sources, and most especially of a rise in the number of large fortunes proved in provincial courts which may have occurred in this period. In fact the percentage of very large estates proved in the Canterbury Court did decline somewhat during the span 1809-58 among those courts whose records were examined.

Alternatively, this trend may have been the result of a shift of a substantial portion of the property of the wealthy into sources not included in the probate valuations. There may have been a rush by wealthy businessmen to purchase land in this period: if indeed this was the case, the failure of the large estates to expand in number could be satisfactorily explained, for businessmen would not have to purchase land on the scale of a grandee like Lord Overstone or James Morrison to distort the figures. At the peak of the land price rise after 1837, to purchase a small estate of 3,000-4,000 acres would require a capital expenditure of around £100,000 and any businessman who wished to transmute his wealth into high status in this manner would certainly have to part with a very sizable portion of his personal wealth. So far as I am aware, however, there is no real evidence to support such a contention, but F.M.L. Thompson does note that during this period when small farmers were forced to sell out 'their land was sometimes bought by local tradesmen, but more often in this period the small holding was bought by a neighbouring large landowner, or one of the rising new gentry . . .',[22] presumably former businessmen in large measure. Another factor doubtless at work was the profitability of land: land prices were generally higher, in the period under discussion, after 1837 than before.[23] Yet, as Table 2.4 makes clear, there is no break around 1837 in the number of personal estates over £100,000. If the price of land was a factor in convincing businessmen to purchase realty — which would seem plausible — one must question why there was in fact no break at this date.

It might be supposed that a factor at work may have been an increase in foreign investment. In 1850 the 'grand total of Britain's foreign holdings' was £255 million.[24] National wealth is always difficult, and perhaps impossible to assess precisely, including as it does freehold houses and buildings of all kinds, as well as works of art, which yield no income, but Giffen estimated the British national capital at £4,000 million in 1845 and £6,115 million in 1868.[25] Assuming that the national capital was about £4,500 million in 1850, it is clear that foreign holdings could not have accounted for more than about 5 per cent of the total, and although such holdings were owned by the wealthier classes to a disproportionate extent, it must not be forgotten that most foreign holdings were included for probate purposes as British personalty and would hence have been included in the probate valuations. It is more than likely that this factor is of only minor importance.

Still another consideration may lie in a changing style of life among the very wealthy: if they earned more money in 1850 than in 1810 they also spent more, and hence left less. Necessarily this is a thesis about which insufficient evidence exists for quantification, and against this view must be put the consensus opinion of contemporaries and later historians alike, that saving was preeminently a Victorian virtue. It can hardly be suggested that the years between 1825 and 1853 witnessed more display among the very wealthy than the 30 preceding years, and in particular the wealthy businessmen of the early Victorian period are universally supposed to have been as sober as they were acquisitive. In sum this is a suggestion which can probably be discounted.

It is not impossible that the decades in this period constituted, as it were, a trough between two stages of the Industrial Revolution which might be termed the 'cotton' and 'railway' phases. While the first generation of industrialists left their fortunes in substantial numbers just after the Napoleonic Wars, the second did not do so until after 1853. The Brasseys, Bairds and second generation of Crawshays, entrepreneurs in metals and railways, begin to appear in the probate records only after about 1860. But such an argument is not without its flaws, for, as will be shown, the bulk of the early leavers of fortunes above £100,000 were not first-generation industrialists but, disproportionately, entrepreneurs in London commerce and finance. Certainly the fact that the provincial ecclesiastical registries − where industrial wealth would be found − became of importance only just before 1858 does not add weight to this suggestion.

It may not, however, have been until the mid-century that industrialists and manufacturers possessed equipment and plant stock of sufficient capital value to gain their place among the very rich: the early industrialists, as is well-known, operated on a comparatively small scale, with the rare exception of an Arkwright, Peel or Strutt. Thus it is possible that the near-constant number of persons in the £100,000 class between 1825 and 1855 was an accurate reflection of the scale of industry in Britain at the time, always allowing for the time lag between the date in which a man is active in business and his death. Professor Chapman has indeed noted that the early factory masters were very largely just such relatively small-scale operators.[26] This explanation may be the most satisfactory of any. If the failure of the number of large personal fortunes to keep pace with the ever-expanding national product during the first half of the nineteenth century is indeed an accurate reflection of the position of the wealthy at the time, rather than a statistical or historical illusion, it raises very large questions about the distribution of wealth at the time and even, at least by inference, about the time-honoured matter of the working-class standard of living. If wealthy businessmen did not increase in number as fast as the national income as a whole, this necessarily implies that these income gains must have gone elsewhere and, again necessarily, this must have been to those comparatively poorer. In any case this is a phenomenon which calls for a more detailed and searching examination.

Table 2.5: Estates of £100,000 or More, 1858-94, by Five-year Annual Averages

Period	Annual Number	Percent Increase over Previous Period
1858-9	49.5	
1860-4	53.4	+ 11.9
1865-9	76.2	+ 37.5
1870-4	114.8	+ 50.7
1875-9	115.0	+ 0.2
1880-4	141.6	+ 29.1
1885-9	149.6	+ 2.1
1890-3	185.5	+ 30.0

In Table 2.5 the annual numbers of top wealth-holders deceased in the period 1858-93 are set out. Thus there was a sharp rise in the number of large personal fortunes during the latter part of the nineteenth century, with the exception of the two plateaus during the late 1870s and late 1880s. The rise in top fortunes at this time was unparalleled in previous British experience, their number doubling between 1858-9 and 1870-4, and nearly doubling again before the end of the period. This could hardly have failed to have influenced the ways in which British writers and social critics viewed the role and place of wealth in society, and indeed the period centring around the 1870s was something of a watershed in this respect. Most of Trollope's great novels of business life and society were written at that time, including *The Way We Live Now* (1875), on the rise and fall of the charlatan financier Auguste Melmotte — perhaps the great English novel with wealth as its theme between Thackeray and Galsworthy. This was also the decade in which *The Return of Owners of Land* (1871-4) was compiled, the *Spectator's* millionaire lists (1873 and 1883) were published, and works like *Millionaires and How They Became So* (1874) appeared. Samuel Smiles produced the majority of his most characteristic works in this decade, including the aptly-titled *Character* (1871), *Thrift* (1875) and *Duty* (1880) (*Self-Help* had appeared in 1859). A sensation was made in Britain by the appearance of the American Henry George's *Progress and Poverty* (1879), with its central idea of a single tax on land. The problems created by the unequal distribution of wealth in British society were of prime importance to the socialist thinkers who, a few years later in 1884, founded the Fabian Society.

The maximum expansion in the number of deceased wealth-holders occurred in the first half of the 1870s: thereafter the rise was less dramatic, and in two of the four remaining half-decadal periods there was no increase at all. This levelling-off occurred during the agricultural depression after 1879, and since land was excluded from these figures, this may suggest that businessmen were still purchasing land, despite, or perhaps because of, its relative cheapness. Yet ironically it was apparently during this period that ownership of land ceased to be the automatic prerequisite of new peerage creations.[27]

A phenomenon of the period was the apparent shift, within the wealth structure, toward the very wealthiest estates. The tip of the wealthy group, those estates whose minimum value was £300,000 to £500,000 or more, increased during this period at a rapid rate. Only four millionaire estates, for example, had been proved in the five years 1858-61 inclusive, but five were proved in 1890 alone and six in the following year. Another noteworthy feature of the period was the increased importance of Scotland as a centre of wealth-production. In 1855-7 only six Scottish estates of £100,000 or more had been probated, but in 1859 and 1861 this figure rose to seven in each year, and in the 1870s to about 12 per annum. This period coincided with the emergence of Clydeside as a national centre of commerce, engineering and ship-building.[28]

The third series of probate data begins with the establishment of the Estate Duty Office of the Inland Revenue in 1894, and the data available in the *Annual Reports of the Inland Revenue* is used to the close of this section of the study in 1939, and, indeed, can be used up to the present day. The Estate Duty Office figures, which form the basis of the post-1894 statistics here, differ from both of the previous series in two important respects. First, they record the net, rather than the gross value of the estate. The effect of this is to decrease the number of very large estates by about ten per cent, if the difference between the net and gross values in those cases in which both were known to me is indicative of all estates over £100,000. On the other hand, and conversely, these figures include most of those categories of property excluded from the calendar valuations, including realty, both settled and unsettled, settled personalty and the value of gifts *inter vivos* 'caught' by the time-limit in force at the time and added to the total value of the testator's estate. Therefore these official statistics are a complete listing of all estates passing in a particular year, and no further additions to their number are required for accuracy, beyond a possible addition for the number of gross estates.[29]

Table 2.6: Estates of £100,000 or More, 1895-1939, by Five-year Annual Averages

Period	Number	Change over Previous Period %
1895-9	264.6	
1900 4	292.8	+ 10.7
1905-10	303.8	+ 3.8
1910-14	299.8	− 1.4
1915-19	351.8	+ 17.3
1920-4	372.0	+ 5.7
1925-9	495.0	+ 33.0
1930 4	466.2	− 5.8
1935 9	540.0	+ 15.8

Table 2.6 details the five-year averages between 1895 and 1939, as has been done for the two previous series of data.[30] As with the yearly totals abstracted from the Act Books and probate calendars, the official statistics often produced wide yearly variations, which are to a considerable extent smoothed out by taking five-year averages. Yet overall, the totals of wealth-holding follow the broader trends in Britain's economic performance to a marked degree, reaching a peak in the late 1920s, and declining during the worst years of the Depression — though it is noteworthy that even then the rich hardly disappear. These figures, moreover, follow the trends in economic performance to a greater extent than was the case during the nineteenth century, and especially for the period 1815-50.

It is interesting to note that the annual averages for all wealth-holders do not alter by very much until the First World War and, indeed, the ten-year figures between 1905 and 1914 are virtually stationary. Although there is little doubt that economically, as in many other spheres, the Edwardian period was a troubled one,[31] the general impression in literature and other sources, both contemporaneous and subsequent, is that the rich had never previously been better off. To a certain extent this impression may have been the result of external causes, of the rise of new fortunes in the United States or South Africa, rather than an accurate representation of the British picture.[32] Yet it is important to note (and this is not brought out by any of the figures here) that the number of really large fortunes, those in excess of £2 million, totalled 30 in the period 1895-1914, including those of women and foreigners (22 among British men) compared with only six during the previous 22 years 1873-94. Four of the estates proved during this period reached the hitherto unknown level of wealth of £5 million or more – those of Charles Morrison (1817-1909), Henry O. Wills (1828-1911), Alfred Beit (1853-1906) and Sir Julius Wehrner (1850-1912); additionally, several fortunes among the greatest ground-rent landlords, like those of the 1st Duke of Westminster (1825-99) and the 16th Earl of Derby (1841-1908) were probably also in this class. Before the mid-1890s it is doubtful if any non-landed wealth-holder in British history had ever amassed a fortune of more than about £5 million.

There are thus two apparently contradictory trends at work in the period 1895-1914 – a great expansion in the size and number of the very largest fortunes, occurring at the same time as a plateau was reached among all fortunes above £100,000. Some of this levelling trend may have been the result of early instances of estate duty avoidance in the wake of the Harcourt duties and several subsequent increases in the top rates of duty under the Liberal government after 1906 – although it must be emphasised that the 'worst' three-year period by far for large estates during this era were the Tory government years 1902-5 (in 1904-5 only one net millionaire estate was probated). The rapid decline in land values, hitting the gentry and lesser aristocracy particularly hard – rather than the great landowners with their substantial mineral deposits and ground-rents – may have been a prime cause of the plateau among all fortunes over £100,000. The merely very rich (as opposed to the very, very rich) were by no means a booming class during the Edwardian period.

The immediate effect of the First World War was to produce a significant increase in the number of top fortunes – except at the millionaire level – of 17.3 per cent for the five-year period 1915-19 as opposed to the previous half-decade. It is of course true that prices rose at a rapid pace, but the feeling was then widespread, and as universal among Conservatives as among radicals, that the war had spawned a great crop of profiteers among munitions contractors, shipowners, merchants and even retail shopkeepers who grew wealthy not through any entrepreneurial effort, but merely by exploiting the government's contracts and temporary dislocations in other spheres caused by the war.[33] The fact remains, however, that the increase which undoubtedly did occur in the number of top fortunes failed to keep pace with inflation, and that this expansion took place not among the very wealthiest contractors and armaments manufacturers, but at a lower level of wealth.[34]

During the 1920s the number of large estates, fanned by the post-war boom in the south of England and by the price spiral, reached levels very much higher than before the war, at a figure about 54 per cent above that prior to 1914. Yet, once again, by far the greatest part of this expansion came at the lower end of the wealth scale, while estates above £500,000 (and, most especially, millionaire estates) did not increase in number to the same extent. The average annual number of net millionaire estates rose from 9.8 in 1910-14 to 13.1 in 1925-9, a sizable increase, but not as great as the increase lower down the scale. Once again, it is difficult to pinpoint the reasons for this. It is more than likely that there was a growing amount of estate duty avoidance among the very rich, which would presumably have become more common still among millionaires than at a level of wealth only one-tenth as great. Moreover, it is probable that some estates which were 'really' worth in excess of £1 million (or at least a very large amount) appear in the figures not at this level but at a considerably lower one, the testator having successfully avoided duty on much, but not all, of his estate. Such estates would swell the figures at the lower end of the scale recorded here. It should be noted, however, that there was certainly no dearth of very large estates. In the period 1920-30 there were in fact 12 estates valued at £4 million or more, with three worth in excess of £10 million. The figures for the 1920s may genuinely reflect the economic possibilities for entrepreneurship during the period: for example, it may have been significantly easier for a new man to acquire a fortune of £100,000 or so than one at the millionaire level. As during the 1870s, there was a good deal of public awareness of wealth and the wealthy during this decade. The novels of Arnold Bennett, or the scenarios of detective fiction which focused — for the first time — on the 'body in the library' in the country house,[35] the fiction of Michael Arlen or the popularity of gossip columns in the popular press are evidence of this. Moreover, the scandals at the beginning of the decade, concerning the sale of honours to wealthy men of otherwise unknown merit, was evidence that sheer wealth had acquired a new importance as an element in the British status system.[36]

The last decade discussed in this chapter is that of the Great Depression. It will be seen in Table 2.6 that the average number of large estates did not fall by anything like the extent which might have been supposed, in view of the decline in the economy as a whole. The drop from an average of 495.0 estates above the £100,000 level proved annually in 1925-29 to 466.2 in the early 1930s is rather nugatory. This was, however, only slightly less than the decline in the net national income at current prices.[37] When it is recalled that the rich, unlike the poor, are free to switch their portfolios to take advantage of current areas of profitability in economy, and that much of their assets was held in secure government or war bonds, or in art works, rare stamps or the like, it is perhaps not surprising that their decline in net worth was as little as it was. Even at the very worst stage of the Depression the average annual number of estates of £100,000 or more exceeded the number proved in 1920-4, and in 1933 Sir John Ellerman left his £37 million.

The latter half of the 1930s witnessed a remarkable improvement in Britain's economic circumstances, though this was heavily masked by its sectional and regional nature.[38] The net national income at current prices rose to an average of £4,564 million, much above the average for even the late 1920s,[39] and the average annual number of estates of £100,000 or more rose to 540.0, an increase of about 16 per cent over the figures for the earlier part of the decade and again, significantly higher than the average figure for the late 1920s. This was apparently somewhat below the increase of 21 per cent in the net British income at current prices,[40] but it remains true that, prior to the Second World War, the two years with the largest number of estates proved in excess of £100,000 were 1937-8 with 618 and 1936-7 (597), not 1929-30 (581), 1928-9 (535) nor 1913-14 (318). For the rich at least, the late 1930s were the Indian summer of British capitalism.

Top Fortune-holders

Along with the change in number of wealth-holders went a rise in the amount of wealth owned by Britain's richest men. We noted above that no personal fortune of the eighteenth century was known to have exceeded about £1 million. How this changed, and how the size of individual fortunes grew, can best be grasped from Table 2.7, which divides the span 1809-1939 into successive 30-year intervals.[41]

Since these figures exclude realty for nearly all of the nineteenth century, they probably exaggerate the upward rise in the peaks of British wealth-holding. Although the wealth of those landowners continued

Table 2.7: Top Wealth-leavers, 1809-1939

		£m
1809-1839:		
1. Nathan M. Rothschild (d. 1836), merchant banker	*c.*	5[a]
2. George, first Duke of Sutherland (d. 1833), landowner	*c.*	2
3. Sir Robert Peel, 1st Bt. (d. 1830), cotton manufacturer	*c.*	1.5
1840-79:		
1. James Morrison (d. 1857), warehouseman and merchant banker	*c.*	4
2. Thomas Brassey (d. 1870), railway contractor		3.2
3. Giles Loder (d. 1871), Russia merchant		2.9
1880-1909:[b]		
1. Charles Morrison (d. 1909), warehouseman and merchant banker		10.9
2. Herman, Baron de Stern (d. 1887), merchant banker		3.5
3. Wentworth Beaumont, first Baron Allendale (d. 1907), landowner		3.2
1910-39:		
1. Sir John R. Ellerman, 1st Bt. (d. 1933), shipowner and financier		36.7
2. Edward A. Guinness, first Earl of Iveagh (d. 1927), brewer		13.5
3. James Williamson, first Baron Ashton (d. 1930), linoleum manufacturer		10.5

a. Most of the millionaire estates proved before about 1860 were sworn in the probate calendars at 'Upper Value' (i.e., above £1 million) or 'Above £1 million'. The figures given here are based on contemporary estimates.

b. Sir Julius Werhner (d. 1912) and Alfred Beit (d. 1906) the South African gold and diamond magnates left, respectively, £10.0m and £8.0m in Britain. Samuel J. Loyd, first Baron Overstone (d. 1883), the banker, left £2.1m in personalty plus land which had cost about £3.1m to purchase.

to rise with the increasing value of their urban property and mineral deposits, it is probably the case that the personalty of an early nineteenth-century landowner like the first Duke of Sutherland (recorded in Table 2.7) would, if added to his purely landed wealth (which it is not), exceed even the fortune of a Rothschild: 'I believe he was the richest individual who ever died', was Greville's comment at his death.[42] By the end of the nineteenth century, the Duke of Westminster was said to be worth £14m on his London holdings alone,[43] with the very greatest landed magnates like the Dukes of Devonshire, Bedford or

Portland, or the Earl of Derby, not far behind. Westminster, according to C. Northcote Parkinson, may have been wealthier than W.H. Vanderbilt, the richest American millionaire, as late as 1885.[44]

None the less, these figures serve to indicate the progressive rise in the size of the greatest personal fortunes in the 130 years surveyed here, and the extent to which the growth of the British economy allowed a handful of the keenest or luckiest businessmen to enrich themselves. To be sure, each of these men was anomalous in some sense, each deserving of several paragraphs in his own right. James Morrison, for instance, was the son of a Hampshire innkeeper, found a job at the Fore Street Textile Warehouse in London, married the boss's daughter, and never looked back: he was probably the greatest textile wholesaler in England and a merchant banker on a great scale in America.[45] His eldest son Charles, who lived from the reign of George III until the year of the first cross-Channel flight, tripled or quadrupled the millions left him by his father. A bachelor, living quietly outside the public gaze, he 'habitually kept a large sum in gold as a reserve against serious financial loss'.[46] He was probably the second wealthiest man in Britain at his death. The case of Sir John Ellerman, who deserves not merely a paragraph but a searching biography,[47] was more striking yet, and indeed, was probably the most astonishing and extraordinary business career in British history. A self-made man whose father died leaving £600 when the son was nine, Ellerman began as an accountant, forming his own London accountancy firm at 24 and at 29 acquired the old-established Liverpool shipping company of Frederic Leyland & Co. His empire eventually extended into shipping, finance, brewing, property development and newspapers; he was a long-time backstairs power in the Conservative party. The full story will probably never be known.[48] What little is known of his private life suggests that he was as vulgar and ignorant a *nouveau-riche* as has ever lived.[49] His fortune of £37 million, left at the bottom of the Depression, virtually defies belief. His only son, who died in 1973, left £53 million, the largest estate ever proved in Britain. He was the world's greatest expert on African rodents.[50]

It is evident from Table 2.7 that the top ranges of personal wealth were continuously growing, although the estimated fortune of the first Rothschild was not exceeded until this century. The peaks drew the bulk of the wealth pyramid with them. In the 30 years 1809-39, only two male British personal fortunes of £2 million or more were left. During the next 30 years (1840-79) there were nine; in 1880-1909, 22; and no fewer than 61 in 1910-39.[51] By 1927, to take one admittedly prosperous but not altogether unusual year, there were three fortunes of £4 million or more – those of Edward A. Guinness, first Earl of Iveagh, the great brewer and art collector (who left £13.5 million), Marcus Samuel, first Viscount Bearsted, founder of Shell Transport & Trading and instrumental in the origins of M. Samuel, the merchant bank; and Weetman Pearson, first Viscount Cowdray, the 'Mex' in 'Shell-Mex' and a great engineering contractor – three of the most notable British businessmen of the past century.

Yet, wealthy as these men were, and as much as the topmost levels of the largest British fortunes had grown, they were not, on an international scale, all that vast. Even before the First World War, a Rockefeller, a Ford, a J.P. Morgan, could have devoured Cowdray, Bearsted, or even Iveagh and scarcely noticed it. Britain's wealthiest men never did attain that level of wealth, measured not in tens of millions but in hundreds of millions of pounds. This comparative measure is a key to understanding the possibilities and limitations which constrained the rich in Britain.

High Incomes

Inconsistent and unsatisfactory as are the probate figures of the very wealthy, they are at least a continuous series, extending back to the early nineteenth century. The statistics of high income earners, in contrast, simply do not exist in any shape or form between 1803 and 1911, that is, between the time the schedule system of the Income Tax was established, and the date of the first statistics of the 'Super-Tax' on very high incomes put through by Lloyd George. The nineteenth century then, is a complete blank.

Even so, only one table appears to exist from the few years of the first Income Tax prior to the origin of the system of taxation schedules, which presents the number of incomes by size of incomes. It is for the year 1801, and was reprinted in an Appendix to Stamp's *British Incomes and Property*.[52] It seems likely that the total income figures given here are underestimates.[53] This table is reproduced here in Table 2.8 (in a compressed form) because of its unique historical importance and the contrast with the income figures available for the twentieth century. No incomes lower than £60 per annum were liable for Income Tax. Thus, in 1801 – if these figures can be believed – only 1,020 Britons possessed an income of £5,000 or more, only 538,904 (about 5 per cent of the population), an income of £60 or more.

Table 2.8: Number of Income-earners of £60 or More, 1801

£	Number of Persons	Amount of Income (£'000)
60-100	147,764	10,246
100-150	70,381	7,859
150-200	34,354	5,420
2-500	42,694	12,239
500-1,000	14,762	9,498
1,000-2,000	6,927	9,041
2,000-5,000	3,657	10,403
5,000 +	1,020	9,970
Total	321,559	74,677

Nothing else of a reliable nature exists for the nineteenth century, although numerous attempts were made at the time to estimate the number of high income-earners by reworking the information provided by the Income Tax through its system of schedules.[54] Dudley Baxter, for example, estimated that in 1865-6 there were 1,262,000 incomes of £100 or more in the United Kingdom, of which 48,800 were in the range of £1,000-5,000, and 8,500 of £5,000 or more — a rise of five-seven times since 1801, more at the highest levels of income than at those just below.[55] Stamp's own estimate, taking both Income Tax and Inhabited House Duty into account, was that the number of incomes of £150 or more stood at between 306,700 and 319,500 in 1860-1, 691,400 and 720,000 in 1881-2, and 1,202,000 − 1,253,000 in 1909-10.[56] Nevertheless, such estimates are at best only approximations, and can only be less reliable still where the very small number at the highest income ranges are concerned.

With the coming of the 'Super-tax' applied by Lloyd George, it is finally possible to provide official figures for the precise number of high income-earners, those with incomes of £5,000 or more. In Table 2.9, the data for the years between 1911/12 and 1939/40 are summarised in five-year annual averages, with incomes at the very top further distinguished.[57]

The variation between the trends in high income-earning evident here, and the twentieth-century probate valuations presented above, requires some comment. Of particular note is the extremely sharp rise during the years of the First World War, lending some credence to the popular notion of 'war-profiteering' at the time — and the

Table 2.9: Incomes of £5,000 or More, Five-year Average Number 1911/12-1939/40, with Percentage Changes over Previous Periods (Current Prices)

Years	£5,000+	Change (%)	£50,000- £100,000	Change (%)	£100,000+	Change (%)
1911/12- 1914/15	13,134	–	182	–	75	–
1915/16- 1919/20	18,047	+ 37.4	307	+ 68.7	115	+ 53.3
1920/1- 1924/5	26,805	+ 48.5	452	+ 47.2	157	+ 36.5
1925/6- 1929/30	28,359	+ 5.8	403	– 10.8	146	– 7.0
1930/1- 1934/5	22,572	– 20.4	255	– 36.7	86	– 41.1
1935/6- 1939/40	25,182	+ 11.2	288	+ 11.3	92	+ 7.0

continuing further marked increase during the early 1920s. However, in contrast to the trend apparent among the top wealth-leavers, there was a slower growth and, at the very top levels, an actual decline during the prosperous late 1920s, and a very marked decline during the Depression. Although an increase in top incomes occurred during the late 1930s, it was not as rapid as was the case among the wealth-holders, and the numbers at this period never reached those attained during the 1920s. The number of incomes of £100,000 or more, for instance, totalled 147 in 1926-7, 135 in 1927-8, and 166 in 1928-9. This figure then declined steadily from 142 in 1929-30 to 111 in 1930-1, 95 in 1931-2, 87 in 1932-3 and touched bottom at 66 in 1933-4. In the upward rise of the latter part of the decade, it never rose above 106 in 1937-8, dropping again to 98 in 1938-9. Although it would be premature to dwell on this, it is perhaps of some interest to note that the number of incomes of £100,000 or more (it is, in fact, rather difficult to believe that there were any at all) totalled 57 in 1945-6, 38 in 1949-50, and reached this century's nadir at only 37 each in 1950-1 and 1952-3, rising again fairly steadily thereafter (though, of course, worth far less in real terms). There were 200, for example, in 1965-6.

Inhabited Houses

The third source of direct statistical information about the size and level of wealth of the rich is the Inhabited House Duty. It is, however, the least useful of these sources, and its utility is much more evident in discussing the middle class as a whole rather than the very wealthy. The main reason for this is that, although expenditure on housing in the form of rentals (or the cost of freehold purchase) is highly income-elastic, and in general varies directly at all levels of the income scale, it is probably true that in modern times there are two major exceptions to this. One was the lower end of the middle class (and, particularly from late Victorian times onward, the London middle class), whose status pretentions both restricted their choice of housing to neighbourhoods not manifestly working-class and who, at least in this century, have prized home-ownership to the extent that they were willing to make virtually any financial sacrifice to achieve it. The rule-of-thumb in nineteenth-century England was that about ten per cent of a family's income was to be spent on housing.[58] (After about 1870, and especially in London, this percentage probably rose to 15 per cent or more.) In the case of the lower end of the middle class, it was likely that this rule-of-thumb was (and is still, in the context of today's prices) considerably exceeded and, that family incomes cannot necessarily be inferred from a knowledge of rentals alone. Ironically, the other exception is the very rich, those whose incomes were so large that no conceivable expenditure on housing, even on the best of the West End or upon the building or upkeep of a country house, was more than a relatively small percentage of it. A shipping clerk, a barrister, a surgeon may have spent ten, 15, or even 20 per cent of his income on housing in Victorian England; but Baron Rothschild or the Duke of Devonshire did not. This being so, the upper end of the rental (or imputed rental) figures of the Inhabited House Duty statistics are conflated (whereas those at low and median ranges more or less accurately reflect actual incomes) in a peculiar mirror-image of the normal pattern: where the annual income of a millionaire was literally a thousand times greater than that of a manual worker, the differential of his annual expenditure on housing was not nearly so great and, when compared to the merely affluent, only a matter of degree. The rentals (or imputed rentals) of the most expensive houses *c*. 1830 are evidence of this: the Duke of Devonshire's Piccadilly residence was assessed at an annual value of £1,200; this could hardly have been more than, at the very most, one-fortieth of the Duke's income at the time and possibly much less. One curious but invaluable Parliamentary return was made in 1831 of the assessment on all houses in Grosvenor, Belgrave and Eaton Squares, with the name of each householder and his annual rental (!)[59] Of the 70 households named here, only two were paying as much as £1,000 in rent (those of Lord Belgrave at No. 15 Grosvenor Square and the Duke of Bedford at No. 6 Belgrave Square). Most were in the range of £300-£600, some lower. The Duke of Beaufort's rental was £500; Earl Cawdor's was £400; Lord Maynard's only £350 − and so on. Clearly these were totally incompatible with the accepted rule-of-thumb as to percentage expenditure on housing.

Nevertheless, the Inhabited House Duty does have some useful features for our study, if its limitations are kept in view. Its statistics (which, as remarked above, exist for an enormously long span) can identify, at least in a general way, growth trends in the affluent class; it can ascertain, too, where the rich lived, bearing the higher prices of south-east England in mind. The second of these points will be explored at a later stage; it is with the first that we are concerned here.

Very little published statistical information survives about the early Inhabited House Duty, that levied between the 1780s and 1834. Most of what has been published dates from the tail end of this period, particularly from just before the 1832 Reform Bill when, as noted above, a good many statistical tables relating wealth to population appeared. One of the most useful of these, which appeared in 1831, detailed the number of houses assessed to Inhabited House Duty by county in the year 1829-30, by range of rental or imputed rental. The lowest rental in this table was £10, the highest range, £400 or more. A total of 378,786 houses in England and Wales were assessed as worth £10 or more in rental; of this number, 116,030 were worth between £10 and £15, 66,394 between £15 and £20, and 74,499 at £20-£30. Under 13,500 houses were assessed at £100 or more, 1,925 at £200-£300, 551 at £300-£400, and just 438 houses in England and Wales at £400 or more. Without anticipating the argument of another chapter, 10,000 of the 13,500 houses worth £100 or more were located in London, Middlesex or Westminster, with the predominance of London steadily increasing with the rise in rentals until no fewer than 419 of the 438 houses assessed at £400 or more were situated in London.[60]

For the late nineteenth century (following the hiatus in the levying of Inhabited House Duty between 1834 and 1851), plentiful statistics at last exist, both in the Parliamentary Papers and in manuscript (classified at I.R. 16) at the Public Record Office.[61] Without dealing at excessive length with the many anomalies of this Duty, the overall

growth in the number of purely residential houses then worth £20 or
more in rental or imputed rental may be outlined as follows:[62]

		Percentage Change over Previous Decade
1870-1	520,795	—
1880-1	734,471	+ 41
1890-1	878,169	+ 20
1900-1	1,187,758	+ 35
1911-12	1,584,456	+ 33

(It will be recalled that in 1829-30 a total of 378,786 houses were
subject to House Duty as it then existed, encompassing both houses
and occupied trading premises.)[63] The number of houses assessed at
very high rates of Duty was, of course, very much smaller. In 1900-1,
for instance, just 5,628 houses (out of 1,187,758 assessed at £20 or
more) were regarded as worth £400 or more — 3,867 in the London
area, 1,761 in the provinces (including Scotland, but not Ireland).
This represented a 13-fold increase in houses at this level in 70 years,
a figure itself an understatement, as the earlier figures included occupied
trading premises. If the larger figure of over 1.1 million houses
represented the middle-class (and, in London, lower-middle class)
housing stock in 1900-1, the total of *5,628* houses assessed at £400
or more is at least indicative of the relative numbers of the very rich —
and not even that, if it is accepted that 15 per cent of income was
spent on rent or its equivalent. It is obvious from these figures (and
from all those presented before) that the very wealthy in nineteenth-
century Britain were a *very* small class indeed.

Notes

1. In the *Annual Report of the Inland Revenue* for 1895 *et. seq.* Professor
Jeffrey Williamson (University of Wisconsin) has published a number of research
papers attempting to measure income inequality in nineteenth-century Britain.
See also, L.D. Schwartz, 'Income Distribution and Social Structure in London
in the Late Eighteenth Century', *Econ. Hist. Rev.*, 2nd ser., XXXII (1979).
2. In theory, it is possible to piece together such a series from the probate
calendars (or from the manuscript Act Books of the Ecclesiastical Courts),
but only with great difficulty and after considerable effort. The most realistic
way of doing this would be to take statistically valid samples of valuations in
several annual calendars at regular intervals. Theoretically, it might be possible to
do the same with the surviving records of the Assessed and Income taxes, but

heroic assumptions must first be made.

3. It is reprinted in A. Aspinall and E. Anthony Smith (eds.), *English Historical Documents, 1783-1832* (London, 1959), p. 574.

4. P.P. 1861, XVIII, 545. I am extremely grateful to Dr Michael King (University of Nottingham) for this valuable reference. Note should also be made of the return in P.P. 1843, XXX, 603, showing the number of estates of £20 or more proved in 1839. ('Total Number of Wills and Extracts (*sic*) of Administration sent to the Legacy Duty Office'.) It is differentiated by size of estate up to £1,000. Approximately 20,000 estates of £20 or more were recorded here, 5,596 above £1,000. (See Chapter 5 for a further discussion.) Anthony J. Camp, *Wills and Their Whereabouts*, (London, 1974), p. xxxviii estimates that in 1796 only 6 per cent of all persons deceased in England and Wales left any estate; by 1873 this figure had increased only to 8 per cent.

5. *Twenty-second Annual Report of the Registrar-General of Births, Marriages and Deaths*, pp. 174ff.

6. In addition, one estate at this level belonged to a woman. My figures later in this chapter for estates proved in 1858 indicate that 55 estates of £100,000 or more were probated in 1858, but I have eliminated those estates which had already appeared in previous calendars, including revised figures, etc.

7. The occupational descriptions here were almost certainly taken from the will or letter of administration, not from, e.g., the death certificate.

8. *Twenty-second Annual Report*, p. xlvi.

9. This man, as it happens, was James Morrison (1798-1857), possibly the richest commoner of the nineteenth century. His total estate was closer to £5 million than to the £1 million declared for probate purposes, and his percentage of the total wealth passing by probate accordingly was much higher than is even indicated here.

10. *Twenty-second Annual Report*, p. xlvi.

11. P.P. 1901, 18, 159.

12. The probate valuation was commonly written on each will or letter of administration after the mid-eighteenth century, but the Act Books or indexes, as noted in Chapter 1, did not record this figure or recorded (if above, say £10,000) only the term 'Upper Value'. The valuation figures quoted here were recorded in newspapers or other contemporary writings which had access to the will or letter of administration. The point is that these exist only on a hit-or-miss basis and are not comprehensive.

13. R.A. Soloway, *Prelates and People: Ecclesiastical Thought in England 1783-1852* (London, 1969), p. 72, n.3; Sir Lewis Namier and John Brooke, *The House of Commons 1754-1790* (London, HM Stationery Office, 1964), p. 103; Thornton Hall, *Romances of the Peerage* (London, 1914), p. 245; *Anglo-Jewish Notabilities, Their Arms and Testamentary Dispositions* (London, n.d., p. 227); *Gentleman's Magazine* (1806), p. 1,181; Sidney Pollard, *The Genesis of Modern Management* (London, 1965), p. 121. Probably a systematic reading of the *Gentleman's Magazine*, the *London Magazine*, and similar journals of the day would provide other names and valuations at this level; *cf*. Namier and Brooke's discussion of the 'richest Commoner'.

14. See Richard Grassby, 'English Merchant Capitalism in the Late Seventeenth Century, the Composition of Business Fortunes', *Past and Present* 46 (1970) and 'The Personal Wealth of the Business Community in Seventeenth Century England', *Econ. Hist. Rev.*, 2nd ser., XXIII (1970). Professor R.S. Neale (University of New England, Australia), who is researching the early eighteenth-century noble placeman and financier, the Duke of Chandos, indicates that, at his peak, his personal fortune may have exceeded £1 million. Cf. also Lawrence Stone, *The Crisis of the Aristocracy* (Oxford, 1965).

15. B.R. Mitchell and Phyllis Deane, *Abstract of British Historical Statistics* (Cambridge, 1962), p. 34.

16. Ibid., p. 471. On this index, the average of 1865 and 1885 = 100.

17. Arthur Bryant, *The Age of Elegance* (London, 1956), p. 310.

18. See S.G. Checkland, *The Rise of Industrial Society in England 1815-1885* (New York, 1964), Chapters I-III.

19. Mitchell and Deane, *British Historical Statistics*, p. 34. This series does not extend prior to 1838, nor is the increase accounted for by a rise in infant or child mortality rates, which remained much the same. (Ibid., p. 38.)

20. Ibid., p. 366. The share of agriculture, forestry and fishing in the national income was £76m in 1821, £106.5m in 1854, and £118.8m in 1861.

21. See, e.g., Harold Perkin, *The Origins of Modern English Society, 1780-1880* (London, 1967), Chapter V, esp. Table 2, p. 137, and pp. 141-3.

22. F.M.L. Thompson, *English Landed Society in the Nineteenth Century* (London, 1963), p. 233.

23. Ibid., p. 122.

24. Checkland, *Rise of Industrial Society*, p. 65, citing A.H. Imlah, 'British Balance of Payments and Export of Capital 1816-1913', *Econ. Hist. Rev.*, 2nd series, vol. 5 (1952), p. 231.

25. Josiah Stamp, *British Incomes and Property* (London, 1920), p. 406.

26. See Stanley D. Chapman, *The Early Factory Masters* (Newton Abbot, 1967), esp. Chapter Seven.

27. Thompson, *English Landed Society*, pp. 295-300.

28. T.J. Byers, *Entrepreneurship in the Scottish Heavy Industries 1870-1900'* in P.L. Payne (ed.), *Studies in Scottish Business History* (London, 1967).

29. And, of course, an addition of unknown but presumably ever-increasing size, to reach the number of 'real' wealth-holders who disappear from the Inland Revenue figures because of estate duty avoidance not caught by the law.

30. It might be useful to look at the gaps between the last years of the first two series and the first years of the next. In the case of the break between the last years of the Ecclesiastical Court Records (1854-8) and the first of the Principal Probate Registry, for the English and Welsh sources alone (i.e. excluding Scotland and Ireland), the number of estates proved in the Canterbury, York and Lancashire Courts at £100,000 or more for the period 1854-9 January 1858 were:

1854	28
1855	38
1856	34
1857-8 (Jan.)	34

The English/Welsh estates proved at this level in the years 1858-62 were:

1858	55
1859	36
1860	47
1861	41

Except for the anomalously high number of large estates proved in 1858, the continuum is not terribly ill-fitting and, indeed, the total of such estates proved in 1855 was higher than the total in 1859. Since neither minor court records nor intestacies at Canterbury were examined, it would seem as if the bulk of the pre-1858 estates were traced.

The gap between the 1890-3 Principal Probate office figures (which of course continue to the present) and the first Inland Revenue figures from 1894 are much more difficult to match, as the very substantial portion of great wealth in landed property is entirely excluded from the Principal Probate Registry figures, as well as the other distinctions between the two noted above. For what it is worth, the number of estates over £100,000 in the years 1890-4 in the older series was 185.5; the number in 1895-9 according to the new statistics was 264.6, an increase of 42.6 per cent.

31. See, e.g., D.H. Aldcroft, (ed.), *The Development of British Industry and Foreign Competition 1875-1914* (London, 1968) and W. Ashworth, *An Economic History of England 1870-1939* (London, 1960) on the economic side of this period; R.E. Dangerfield, *The Strange Death of Liberal England* (London, 1936) on the political and social side.

32. See, among others, Walter J. Macqueen-Pope, *Twenty Shillings in the Pound* (London, 1949).

33. See A.W. Kirkaldy, (ed.), *British Finance During and After the War, 1914-21* (London, 1921) and F. Fairer Smith, *War Finance and Its Consequences* (London, 1936). For the patriotic view, see G.A.B. Dewar, *The Great Munitions Feat 1914-18* (London, 1941).

34. In the course of my detailed biographical research on the very wealthy, which extends to those leaving £500,000 or more in 1969, I never found a clear case of a man who earned his money during the First World War nor, indeed, of more than a handful who added significantly to their wealth during this period. Needless to say, few would admit to being 'war profiteers', but the lack of any evidence at all on this point is striking.

35. See Erik Routley, *The Puritan Pleasures of the Detective Story* (London, 1972), pp. 119-28.

36. See Gerald MacMillan, *Honours For Sale* (London, 1954).

37. David Butler and Anne Freeman, *British Political Facts 1900-75* (London, 1975), pp. 306-7.

38. For the debate among economic historians on the degree of economic recovery during the Depression, see B.W.E. Alford, *Depression and Recovery? British Economic Growth, 1918-1939* (London, 1974).

39. Mitchell and Deane, *British Historical Statistics*, p. 368.

40. Butler and Freeman, *British Political Facts*, pp. 306-7.

41. For a complete list of millionaire estates left between 1809 and 1949, see W.D. Rubinstein, 'British Millionaires, 1809-1949', *Bulletin of the Institute of Historical Research* XLVIII (1974).

42. Eric Richards, *The Leviathan of Wealth* (London, 1973), p. 12.

43. *The Times*, 23 December 1899.

44. C. Northcote Parkinson, *The Rise of Big Business* (London, 1977), p. 109. This was probably incorrect as Vanderbilt was, according to his own admission, worth $194m, or more than twice as much as Westminster.

45. James Morrison, *Dictionary of National Biography*; Morrison Papers in the possession of the late Richard Gatty, JP, of Pepper Arden, Northallerton and in the London Guildhall.

46. *The Times*, 26 May 1909.

47. James Taylor, *Ellermans. A Wealth of Shipping* (London, 1976), the first family-cum-company history, covers the firm to the 1970s.

48. 'Sir John R. Ellerman', *Dictionary of National Biography*.

49. See Robert McAlmon, *Being Geniuses Together* (London, 1933). One is bound to note that McAlmon may well have been jaundiced and prejudiced. The author was briefly married to Ellerman's daughter (the novelist 'Bryher'). He was a bohemian American poet and, it goes without saying, was not on Ellerman's wavelength.

50. Taylor, *Ellermans*.

51. Rubinstein, 'British Millionaires, 1809-1949', p. xx.

52. Stamp, *British Incomes*, p. 501. I have never succeeded in finding the

original of this either in manuscript form or as a printed table in the Parliamentary Papers. No specific reference to the whereabouts of this return is given by the usually meticulous Stamp; it is apparently taken from William Farr's evidence before the Select Committee on the Income Tax in 1852. (Ibid., p. 431.)

53. Ibid.

54. The best account of these efforts remains Stamp, *British Incomes*, Chapter XIII (pp. 430-65).

55. Ibid., p. 432, citing Baxter's *National Income*, Chapter Three.

56. Ibid., p. 448.

57. Statistics taken from the *Annual Report of the Inland Revenue* in the Parliamentary Papers, 1912, *et.seq.* The final revised figures have been used wherever given.

58. See J.A. Banks, *Prosperity and Parenthood* (London, 1954).

59. P.P. 1831, 'House Duty: Grosvenor Square, etc'.

60. In addition, 36,405 Scottish houses were assessed as worth £10 or more, of which just two (both in Edinburgh) were worth £400 or more. P.P. 1831, 'House and Window Duty, Scotland'.

61. See also, e.g., 'Return of Houses Assessed in Each County, 1851-2', P.P. 1852-3, LVII, 433.

62. Taken from I.R.16, 30 (1870/71) *et.seq.* Purely residential houses were taxed at 9 pence per pound, other buildings occupied for trade were subject to Inhabited House Duty at 6 pence per pound. These included shops, pubs, tenant farms and certain lodging houses (when these had living-in residents), as well as certain miscellaneous types of buildings. Again, see Stamp, *British Incomes*, pp. 107-41.

63. The number of occupied trading premises, etc., taxed at 6 pence was: 1870-1, 275,598; 1880-1, 346,512; 1890-1, 379,306; 1900-1, 442,457; 1911-12, 463,637.

3 THE OCCUPATIONAL AND GEOGRAPHICAL DISTRIBUTION OF WEALTH-HOLDERS

In this chapter the occupations or sources of wealth of the very rich will be examined. Unlike the discussion in the previous chapter, which dealt with trends among all estates of £100,000 or more, and with the separate and largely anonymous statistics provided by the Income Tax and Inhabited House Duty, this chapter — and others which follow — will specifically focus on those British males leaving £500,000 or more, with the addition of the two groups of lesser wealthy deceased in 1809-39 and 1850-69. There is little that either the Income Tax or the Inhabited House Duty statistics, as they have come down to us, can add which is of very much relevance here, and no analysis has been undertaken by this author of those who, though wealthy, left less than £500,000, beyond the two nineteenth-century groups mentioned above.

The rationale behind a detailed examination of the occupations or sources of wealth of the very rich needs no lengthy elaboration. It is perhaps the most basic characteristic of all, and the very first dimension which must be traced in order to give flesh to the bare bones of numbers and size of fortune outlined in the previous chapter. In conjunction with the other social dimensions dealt with in the remainder of this book, and especially with the subsequent discussions of the geography of the rich and their social origins, such an analysis permits the researcher to construct an accurate anatomy of wealth in Britain in modern times, to identify the most salient features of the wealthy class, including the divisions within it, and the sources of stability, change and conflict. It is also, as we shall see, to no small extent the key to understanding the evolution of British society during the past two centuries.

The Occupations of the Wealthy

The most common and most fruitful way of classifying occupational distribution in Britain is termed the Standard Industrial Classification (henceforth referred to as 'S.I.C.'), which since 1948 has been officially adopted by the Central Statistical office of the United Kingdom.[1]

Previous to 1948, forerunners of the S.I.C. had been adopted by the Census and the Bureau of Labour Statistics as the basis of occupational classification.[2] There therefore exists a very great deal of comparable material available for the nineteenth and twentieth centuries about the occupational distribution of the total labour-force with which to compare the data concerning wealth-holders, and additionally some analysis of the earlier data has been made by economic historians.[3]

The S.I.C. system is based upon industries, not upon occupations: that is to say, in classifying the category of employment to which an individual belongs, members of the administrative, technical or clerical staff of that industry are counted with other employees in that industry, the 'unit' of an industry consisting of 'an establishment . . . normally the whole of the premises, such as a farm, a factory, or a shop at a particular address', and including 'all the activities carried on at that address (including for example departments engaged in selling, bottling, packaging, or transport . . .)'.[4]

The system of schedules employed by the *Standard Industrial Classification* divides the labour force into 24 Orders.[5] From the point of view of weighing and evaluating the occupational distribution among the top wealth-holders in light of their historical position and role, this system may be improved upon without distorting the basic structure of the S.I.C.[6] The occupational grid finally employed in this section to classify the wealth-holders is as follows:

I.   Agriculture and Landowning
II.   Manufacturing and Industry:
     1. Coal Mining
     2. Other Mining
     3. Iron and Steel Manufacturing
     4. Shipbuilding
     5. Engineering
     6. Chemical Manufacturing
     7. Cotton Manufacturing
     8. Woollen Manufacturing
     9. Other Textile Manufacturing
    10. Construction
    11. Other Manufacturing
III.   Food, Drink and Tobacco:
    12. Brewing and Related
    13. Distilling
    14. Tobacco Manufacturing

15. Foods and Foodstuffs (including non-alcoholic beverages)
IV.   Commerce and Finance:
16. Banking
17. Merchant Banking
18. Other Finance
19. Foreign Merchants (i.e., merchants trading abroad, import-export merchants, etc.)
20. Retailing
21. Other Merchants (including warehousemen, auctioneers, etc.)
22. Insurance
23. Stockbrokers
24. Shipowners
25. Other Commerce
V.   ) Publishing and Miscellaneous:
26. Newspaper Proprietors
27. Publishers
28. Other Miscellaneous
VI.   Professionals and Public Administration:
29. Professionals — Law
30. Other Professionals
31. Public Administration and Defence
VII.   Others

Perhaps the chief value of the system of occupations adopted here, and of the S.I.C. classification on which they are based, is that they carefully divide commerce and finance from manufacturing and industry proper. Additionally, they separate professionals and government employees and functionaries; and they detach landowners and others concerned in the land from businessmen and professionals.

In the following tables each wealth-holder was assigned to one and only one occupational category even if he held multiple interests. Although this may seem questionable, it was the case — and this will be demonstrated with further evidence in another chapter — that the vast majority of Britain's wealth-holders earned their fortunes overwhelmingly in one trade or line of business, and held other interests only as a clear sideline to their main field. It is true, however, that examples of wealth-holders with multiple interests did occur; these tended to cluster in a number of related fields, most importantly shipowning/shipbuilding and colliery/ironmastery. (Those who possessed multiple interests of similar lucrativeness in completely unrelated fields

were much rarer.) Such individuals were assigned to whichever field
seemed to predominate as judged by a wide range of biographical
material and by sources like the *Directory of Directors* and *The Stock
Exchange Yearbook*. A wealth-holder who inherited his money but was
not himself actively engaged in trade was assigned to the field in which
his family earned its fortune, and not to the particular occupation or
profession (for instance, diplomat or barrister) which he may have
adopted as his career.[7] After three generations of non-participation in
the business in which the family fortune was earned, wealthy descendants
were nearly always classified as landowners; it was found that almost
invariably such men (who were few in number) had become part of the
landed gentry, participating in the life of the country and indistinguishable from the older gentry. Although most such men died after
the compilation of Bateman's *Great Landowners* in 1883, it is apparent
from their obituaries that they lived in country estates and apparently
owned or rented some landed property.

Before discussing the statistics relating to non-landed wealth, something should perhaps be said first of the position of landowning in the
occupations structure of British wealth.[8] Since only personal property
was included in the probate valuations until 1898, and only unsettled
realty until 1926, it is evident that any occupational tables drawn
exclusively from the probate calendars must seriously understate the
position of landowning in the wealth structure. Despite this, it will be
seen from the occupational tables below that landowning is a most
important element despite the omission of real property. Until 1898
or 1926, the landowners who appeared in the probate calendars did so
by virtue of the substantial mineral, dock, or urban property interests
which they owned, or their holdings in stocks and shares or other
forms of non-landed wealth. (A later chapter of this work is devoted
to this most important segment of the British wealth structure.)

Wealthy Landowners

There are thus two sets of figures concerning the number of wealthy
landowners, the number to be found in the probate calendars
including personalty only until 1898 or 1926, and the 'real' number,
arrived at by taking into account the capital value of their land. The
number of probate calendar landed wealth-holders, divided by the
dates employed throughout this chapter, is detailed in Table 3.1. Even
without any addition for the capital value of their land, it is evident
that, from the probate calendars alone, landowners were a most
significant part of the wealth structure. They generally accounted for

Table 3.1: Number of Landed Wealth-holders, Probate Calendar Data 1809-1939

	Date of Death						
	1809-19	1820-39	1840-59	1860-79	1880-99	1900-19	1920-39
Millionaires	1	1	0	4	8	19	24
Half-millionaires	2	4	7	13	16	29	37
		1809-29		1850-69			
Lesser Wealthy		31		34			

10 per cent to 20 per cent of each of the nineteenth-century cohorts; among some groups their percentage was higher still. Significant as the percentage of wealthy landowners seems here, this is as nothing compared with their total numbers if the figures are reworked to take into account the capital value of their land in order to identify the number of 'missing' landed wealth-holders. These figures must be derived by multiplying the number of landowners at appropriate gross annual incomes given in Bateman's *Great Landowners* by the years' rental, and subtracting those who have already appeared in the probate calendar data. The figures here are so striking they ought to be given in a separate table (Table 3.2).[9]

Table 3.2: 'Missing' Landed Wealth-holders, 1809-1939

	1809-58	1858-79	1880-99	1900-19	1920-39
Millionaires	179	114	28	14	5
Half-millionaires	338	149	122	78	25
		1809-29		1850-69	
Lesser Wealthy		784		660	

It should be kept carefully in mind that these figures are, and can only be, tentative estimates. They can take no account, for example, of the indebtedness which afflicted so many landowners, nor, on the other hand, do they include any of the realty owned by wealth-holders classified elsewhere than in Order I. Yet the meaning of these figures is plain. Until about 1880 (see Tables 3.2–3.8), more than half of all the really wealthy men in Britain were landowners, and during the first half of the nineteenth century — one or two full generations after the beginnings of the Industrial Revolution — the non-landed wealth-holders were a virtually insignificant percentage of the entire wealthy class. An observer entering a room full of Britain's 200 wealthiest men in 1825 might be forgiven for thinking that the Industrial Revolution had not occurred.

Non-landed Wealth-holders

If the nineteenth century saw the absolute predominance of landed wealth until surprisingly late in the day, it also witnessed the overtaking of landowners by businessmen even at the very peak of the wealth scale. Tables 3.3–3.8 present the occupational figures of the non-landed wealth-holders; as these make clear, the total number of non-landed wealth-holders began to surpass the landed portion from the mid-nineteenth century.

Tables 3.3, 3.4 and 3.5 provide extended statistics for each of the 32 occupational categories employed in this chapter. This somewhat unwieldy and lengthy set of tables is summarised in the three additional tables 3.6, 3.7 and 3.8, which recapitulate the data under the major, very broad occupational categories — industry and manufacturing; food, drink and tobacco; commerce and finance; publishing; professionals and public administration; and miscellaneous.

A number of persistent and highly important occupational patterns are evident from these tables. It is clear that wealth-holding was not randomly distributed among all occupational categories, but clustered disproportionately in a smaller number of trades. Above all, although there were indeed a substantial number of wealthy fortunes in certain manufacturing and industrial trades like cotton manufacturing and engineering, the wealthy in Britain have disproportionately earned their fortunes in commerce and finance — that is, as merchants, bankers, shipowners, merchant bankers and stock and insurance agents and brokers, rather than in manufacturing or industry. *This is probably the most important point to be made in this book*, and is, as this author has argued elsehwere,[10] one of the keys to understanding, not merely the wealthy, but the anatomy of British elites and, through them, the social structure of modern British society since the eighteenth century.[11] To be sure, this does not mean — and this must be made quite clear — that there were no wealthy industrialists or manufacturers. As remarked above, several of the industrial fields were extremely well-represented among the wealth-holders. Among millionaires, for example, engineering,

Table 3.3: Non-landed Millionaires, 1809-1939

	1809-19	1820-39	1840-59	1860-79	1880-99	1900-19	1920-39
1. Coal Mining	0	0	0	1= 3.4%	2= 3.3%	3= 3.0%	4= 2.6%
2. Other Minerals	0	0	0	0	1= 1.7%	1= 1.0%	2= 1.3%
3. Iron & Steel	1=100%	0	0	4=13.8%	2= 3.3%	2= 2.0%	3= 2.0%
4. Shipbuilding	0	0	0	0	2= 3.3%	1= 1.0%	1= 0.7%
5. Engineering	0	0	0	2= 6.9%	5= 8.3%	5= 5.0%	7= 4.6%
6. Chemicals	0	0	0	0	3= 5.0%	5= 5.0%	6= 3.9%
7. Cotton Mfc.*	0	0	1=20.0%	3=10.3%	4= 6.7%	8= 7.9%	7= 4.6%
8. Woollen Mfc.	0	1=25.0%	0	1= 3.4%	1= 1.7%	1= 1.0%	1= 0.7%
9. Other Textiles	0	0	1=20.0%	1= 3.4%	0	1= 1.0%	6= 3.9%
10. Construction	0	0	0	0	0	0	1= 0.7%
11. Other Mfc.	0	0	0	0	3= 5.0%	0	6= 3.9%
12. Brewing	0	0	0	1= 3.4%	10=16.7%	9= 8.9%	13= 8.5%
13. Distilling	0	0	0	0	2= 3.3%	1= 1.0%	4= 2.6%
14. Tobacco	0	0	0	0	0	5= 5.0%	11= 7.2%
15. Foods	0	0	0	0	2= 3.3%	4= 4.0%	12= 7.8%
16. Banking	0	0	1=20.0%	4=13.8%	7=11.7%	5= 5.0%	5= 3.3%
17. Merchant Banking	0	1=25.0%	0	5=17.2%	3= 5.0%	14=13.9%	6= 3.9%
18. Other Finance	0	0	1=20.0%	1= 3.4%	1= 1.7%	5= 5.0%	9= 5.9%
19. Foreign Merchants	0	0	0	2= 6.9%	3= 5.0%	4= 4.0%	4= 2.6%
20. Retailing	0	0	0	1= 3.4%	2= 3.3%	5= 5.0%	6= 3.9%

Table 3.3 Continued

	1809-19	1820-39	1840-59	1860-79	1880-99	1900-19	1920-39
21. Other Merchants	0	0	1=20.0%	0	3= 5.0%	5= 5.0%	9= 5.9%
22. Insurance	0	0	0	1= 3.4%	0	1= 1.0%	4= 2.6%
23. Stockbroking	0	0	0	0	2= 3.3%	6= 5.9%	2= 1.3%
24. Shipowning	0	0	0	0	2= 3.3%	8= 7.9%	15= 9.8%
25. Other Commerce	0	0	0	0	0	1= 1.0%	1= 0.7%
26. Newspapers	0	0	0	0	0	0	6= 3.9%
27. Publishing	0	0	0	0	0	0	0
28. Other Miscellaneous	0	0	0	0	0	0	0
29. Professionals – Law	0	0	0	0	0	0	1= 0.7%
30. Other Professions	0	0	0	0	0	0	0
31. Public Admin. & Defence	0	1=25.0%	0	0	0	0	0
32. Others	0	1=25.0%	0	0	0	1= 1.0%	1= 0.7%
Total	1	4	5	27	60	101	153

*Mfc. = Manufacturing.

Table 3.4: Non-landed Half-millionaires, 1809-1939

	1809-19	1820-39	1840-59	1860-79	1880-99	1900-19	1920-39
1. Coal Mining	0	0	0	1= 1.0%	7= 4.3%	18= 6.9%	15= 4.3%
2. Other Minerals	0	0	1= 3.7%	0	2= 1.2%	4= 1.5%	4= 1.1%
3. Iron & Steel	0	1= 4.2%	5=18.5%	11=11.5%	4= 2.5%	18= 6.9%	5= 1.4%
4. Shipbuilding	0	0	0	0	0	2= 0.8%	7= 2.0%
5. Engineering	0	0	0	1= 1.0%	10= 6.1%	11= 4.2%	9= 2.6%
6. Chemicals	0	1= 4.2%	0	0	8= 4.9%	8= 3.1%	10= 2.9%
7. Cotton Mfc.	0	2= 8.3%	1= 3.7%	7= 7.3%	14= 8.6%	4= 1.5%	12= 3.4%
8. Woollen Mfc.	0	0	1= 3.7%	1= 1.0%	6= 3.7%	7= 2.7%	9= 2.6%
9. Other Textiles	0	1= 4.2%	0	4= 4.2%	3= 1.8%	8= 3.1%	9= 2.6%
10. Construction	0	0	0	2= 2.1%	2= 1.2%	5= 1.9%	2= 0.6%
11. Other Mfc.	0	0	1= 3.7%	5= 5.2%	3= 1.8%	12= 4.6%	27= 7.7%
12. Brewing	0	1= 4.2%	2= 7.4%	1= 1.0%	10= 6.1%	15= 5.7%	22= 6.3%
13. Distilling	0	0	0	0	2= 1.2%	3= 1.1%	4= 1.1%
14. Tobacco	0	0	0	1= 1.0%	1= 0.6%	2= 0.8%	9= 2.6%
15. Foods	0	0	0	0	9= 5.5%	9= 3.4%	22= 6.3%
16. Banking	0	3=12.5%	6=22.2%	18=18.8%	19=11.7%	14= 5.4%	26= 7.4%
17. Merchant Banking	0	0	0	5= 5.2%	9= 5.5%	15= 5.4%	7= 2.0%
18. Other Finance	0	0	0	2= 2.1%	2= 1.2%	9= 3.4%	12= 3.4%
19. Foreign Merchants	1=33.3%	5=20.8%	3=11.1%	8= 8.3%	10= 6.1%	12= 4.6%	25= 7.2%
20. Retailing	0	0	0	1= 1.0%	6= 3.7%	9= 3.4%	11= 3.2%

Table 3.4 Continued

	1809-19	1820-39	1840-59	1860-79	1880-99	1900-19	1920-39
21. Other Merchants	2=66.7%	4=16.7%	4=14.8%	14=14.6%	12= 7.4%	40=15.3%	20= 5.7%
22. Insurance	0	1= 4.2%	0	2= 2.1%	0	1= 0.4%	9= 2.6%
23. Stockbroking	0	2= 8.3%	0	2= 2.1%	4= 2.5%	9= 3.4%	10= 2.9%
24. Shipowning	0	0	1= 3.7%	2= 2.1%	8= 4.9%	16= 6.1%	41=11.7%
25. Other Commerce	0	0	0	1= 1.0%	1= 0.6%	1= 0.4%	6= 1.7%
26. Newspapers	0	0	0	2= 2.1%	1= 0.6%	3= 1.1%	2= 0.6%
27. Publishing	0	1= 4.2%	0	0	3= 1.8%	2= 0.8%	0
28. Other Miscellaneous	0	0	0	0	0	0	1= 0.3%
29. Professionals - Law	0	0	0	4= 4.2%	3= 1.8%	3= 1.1%	4= 1.1%
30. Other Professions	0	0	0	1= 1.0%	1= 0.6%	1= 0.4%	4= 1.1%
31. Public Admin. & Defence	0	2= 8.3%	2= 7.4%	0	0	0	0
32. Others	0	0	0	0	3= 1.8%	1= 0.4%	5= 1.4%
Total	3	24	27	96	163	261	349

Table 3.5: Non-landed Lesser Wealthy, 1809-69

		1809-29	1850-69
1.	Coal Mining	2= 1.3	6= 4.1
2.	Other Minerals	0= 0	0= 0
3.	Iron & Steel	3= 1.9	2= 1.4
4.	Shipbuilding	1= 0.6	0= 0
5.	Engineering	1= 0.6	8= 5.4
6.	Chemicals	3= 1.9	3= 2.0
7.	Cotton Mfc.	4= 2.6	13= 8.9
8.	Woollen Mfc.	1= 0.6	2= 1.4
9.	Other Textiles	2= 1.3	2= 1.4
10.	Construction	1= 0.6	1= 0.7
11.	Other Mfc.	5= 3.2	11= 7.5
12.	Brewing	5= 3.2	6= 4.1
13.	Distilling	1= 0.6	3= 2.0
14.	Tobacco	0= 0	0= 0
15.	Foods	2= 1.3	1= 0.7
16.	Banking	23=14.9	25=17.0
17.	Merchant Banking	1= 0.6	4= 2.7
18.	Other Finance	2= 1.3	3= 2.0
19.	Foreign Merchants	11= 7.1	13= 8.8
20.	Retailing	1= 0.6	2= 1.4
21.	Other Merchants	37=24.0	22=15.0
22.	Insurance	2= 1.3	1= 0.7
23.	Stockbroking	6= 3.9	3= 2.0
24.	Shipowning	1= 1.3	4= 2.7
25.	Other Commerce	1= 1.3	2= 1.4
26.	Newspapers	0= 0	0= 0
27.	Publishing	0= 0	0= 0
28.	Other Miscellaneous	0= 0	0= 0
29.	Professionals – Law	12= 7.8	2= 1.4
30.	Other Professions	8= 5.2	1= 0.7
31.	Public Admin. & Defence	15= 6.5	4= 2.7
32.	Others	4= 2.6	3= 2.0
Total		154	147

Table 3.6: The Occupational Sector of Non-landed Millionaires, 1809-1939

	1809-19	1820-39	1840-59	1860-79	1880-99	1900-19	1920-39
1. Mfc.	1=100.0%	1=25.0%	2=40.0%	12=41.4%	23=38.3%	27=26.7%	44=28.8%
2. F-D-T	0	0	0	1= 3.4%	14=23.3%	19=18.8%	4-=26.1%
3. C/F	0	1=25.0%	3=60.0%	16=55.2%	23=38.3%	54=53.5%	61=39.9%
4. Publ.	0	0	0	0	0	0	6= 3.9%
5. Prof.	0	1=25.0%	0	0	0	0	1= 0.7%
6. Misc.	0	1=25.0%	0	0	0	1= 1.0%	1= 0.7%

Mfc. = Manufacturing
F-D-T = Food-Drink-Tobacco
C/F = Commerce/Finance
Publ. = Publishing
Prof. = Professions; Public Administration and Defence
Misc. = Miscellaneous

Table 3.7: The Occupational Sector of Non-landed Half-millionaires, 1809-1939

	1809-19	1820-39	1840-59	1860-79	1880-99	1900-19	1920-39
1. Mfc.	0	5=20.8%	9=33.3%	32=33.3%	59=36.2%	97=37.2 %	109=31.2%
2. F-D-T	0	1= 4.2%	2= 7.4%	2= 2.1%	22=13.5%	29=11.5 %	57=16.3%
3. C/F	3=100.0%	15=62.5%	14=57.9%	55=57.3%	71=43.6%	125=47.9 %	167=47.9%
4. Publ.	0	1= 4.2%	0	2= 2.1%	4= 2.5%	5= 1.9 %	3= 0.9%
5. Prof.	0	2= 8.3%	2= 7.4%	5= 5.2%	4= 2.5%	4= 1.5 %	8= 2.3%
6. Misc.	0	0	0	0	3= 1.8%	0	5= 1.4%

Table 3.8: The Occupational Sector of the Non-landed Lesser Wealthy, 1809-69

	1809-29	1850-69
1. Mfc.	22=14.3 %	48=32.7%
2. F-D-T	8= 5.2 %	10= 6.8%
3. C/F	85=55.2 %	79=53.7%
4. Publ.	0=0	0=0
5. Prof.	35=22.7%	7= 4.8%
6. Misc.	4= 2.6%	3= 2.0%

chemical manufacturing and cotton manufacturing each accounted, from the late nineteenth century, for five per cent or more of the non-landed total; at the half-millionaire level, the cohort percentages, for instance for cotton manufacturers, were higher still. In all the manufacturing trades accounted for about 40 per cent of all millionaires among the nineteenth-century cohorts after 1840, declining to about 26 per cent to 28 per cent in this century; their total among half-millionaires was somewhat lower, although in this century its total was higher. An interesting trend is apparent among the two lesser wealthy cohorts. There, the manufacturing percentage rose from only 14.3 per cent in 1809-29 to 32.7 per cent in 1850-69. The earlier figure indicates that the Industrial Revolution had produced very few deceased wealth-holders at the level £160,000-£500,000 down to the 1830s. Of the total of 154 early lesser wealthy among all the non-landed categories, only 22 were in any of the manufacturing trades — among them four cotton spinners, three each in ironmastery and chemicals and five in the miscellaneous manufacturing trades. By 1850-69, this sector had risen to 48 individuals out of 147, including 13 cotton manufacturers, eight engineering contractors, six colliery proprietors and 11 in miscellaneous manufacturing trades. A more detailed examination of the intervening cohorts at this level — those dying between 1830 and 1849 — could pinpoint the rise of manufacturing wealth here with greater accuracy.

The 'food-drink-tobacco' category has not been included with manufacturing proper. This is clearly arguable. It seems patent to this author at least that these trades are not normally thought of as part of the Industrial Revolution, which surely is by definition limited to the major areas of economic growth in manufacturing and industry. The fields in this category which were already productive of large fortunes in the early nineteenth century, like those of the brewer and maltster, were sociologically far closer to the pre-industrial society — indeed, to landed society — than to the new manufacturer. Mass production came much later.

The very substantial and ever-increasing share of the wealth structure occupied by these trades is a tribute to the unquenchable thirst, the universal sweet tooth and the tobacco-relieved nervous tension of the average Briton. Here, as much as in the City of London merchant banks themselves, a limited number of wealthy dynasties was the rule. Brewing produced the Charringtons, Watneys, Combes, Hanburys — the household names of beer; in distilling the names are perhaps less well-known, but only slightly less clannish. Sweets, biscuits and condiments encompass virtually all of the foodstuffs wealth-holders. Here again it is the Frys and Cadburys (those Quaker hedonists), Leas and Blackwells who predominate. With tobacco the picture is plainer still, for here it is the Wills, the Bristol cigarette dynasts, together with their relatives and business partners in Imperial Tobacco, who virtually monopolise the field. In fact, the Willses are (with the Rothschilds) the family with more wealth-holders than any other. Because of this concentration in a few wealthy dynasties, a number of towns where their works were located were partly over-represented in the geography of wealth. Burton-on-Trent, for example — the northern beer capital — produced more wealth-holders *per capita* than any other place in Britain, possibly excepting the City of London itself. It is probably the case that, except for beer (where possibly the opposite is true), great fortunes in these trades are possible only in a society already on its way towards affluence. A society constantly in Malthusian conflict with starvation does not worry about condiments or biscuits; the taste for cigarettes, or even for distilled spirits, is very much an acquired and a modern one. Because of this, the numbers and percentages of wealth-holders show a sharp upward trend from the late nineteenth century onward (although for whatever reason there is a slight decline, both at the millionaire and half-millionaire level, during the twenty years 1900-19). By 1920-39, however, the number of millionaire brewers was equal to the combined total of millionaire cotton and chemical manufacturers, the number of half-millionaire foodstuff makers was the same as the half-millionaire colliery magnates and shipbuilders put together. Among that cohort, there were 11 millionaire tobacco manufacturers, but only three iron- or steel-makers and one millionaire shipbuilder. The values of England were beginning to change.

Among the early lesser wealthy groups it is interesting to note that there were always a few examples drawn from these trades. Most were brewers — men like Samuel Whitbread, who committed suicide in 1815, leaving £200,000 — with two in the 'foodstuffs' category: a sugar-refiner and tea dealer. Little changed by 1850-69, when the numbers and percentages were almost identical. The flood would come later.

The majority of non-landed wealth-holders were men employed in finance and commerce. This is true of every cohort of the wealthy with two exceptions: in 1809-19 the single non-landed millionaire was a manufacturer (William Crawshay, the ironmaster); and in 1880-99, the number of millionaire industrialists and men in commerce and finance was equal. Of the 16 cohorts at the three levels of wealth studied here, commerce comprised an absolute majority among nine; in all the others (with the two exceptions just noted) it formed the plurality. The proportion of commerce is roughly the same at all levels of wealth; however, differences can be discerned if particular occupations within the commercial/financial sector are examined more closely. For example, there was a considerably higher percentage of merchant bankers among millionaires than among half-millionaires, while the situation is reversed among other (mainly discount and private) bankers, where half-millionaires are the more significant. (This is probably important for ascertaining in which particular fields the highest peaks of wealth could be obtained, and in which fields fortunes of somewhat smaller size could more readily be amassed.) Similarly the mercantile trades, especially 'foreign' and 'other' merchants, were more significant among half-millionaires than among millionaires — for example, no fewer than 40 'other' merchants were deceased among the 261 half-millionaires of the period 1900-19. However, all types of mercantile and financial wealth were well-represented among the very wealthy, and numbers here are only relative.

Among the two 'lesser wealthy' groups, there are several important differences at the level of particular occupations. Merchant banking is almost nonexistent (further evidence that successful merchant bankers tended to be *enormously* wealthy), while banking is well-represented; shipowners (increasingly more important at millionaire and half-millionaire levels) were few, but merchants — particularly (as with the half-millionaires) 'other' and 'foreign' merchants, were plentiful. A comparison of the two lesser wealthy cohorts reveals few significant changes over time, in contrast to the greatly increased importance of manufacturing at this level of wealth between 1820 and 1850.

Wealthy newspaper proprietors and publishers — who cannot in fairness be assigned elsewhere, and who have hence been categorised

separately — are very largely a product of the late nineteenth and
early twentieth centuries, when they begin to play a more significant,
but extremely limited role, in the total structure of wealth. Significantly,
only one wealth-holder in this area was deceased prior to the 1860-79
cohort. He was Andrew Strachan (1747-1831), the King's Printer,
who left £800,000. (Strachan's rights passed to his nephews, the
Spottiswoodes.)[12] From the 1880s on came the flood of wealthy
newspaper magnates, men like Edward Lloyd (1815-90), founder of
the *Illustrated London News*, and wealthy publishers like George
Smith (1824-1901) of Smith, Elder, publisher of *Jane Eyre*, Darwin,
Ruskin, Thackeray, Browning, Queen Victoria and the *Dictionary of
National Biography*.[13] Finally in the interwar period the probate
calendars record the genuine press lords, led by Alfred Harmsworth,
first Viscount Northcliffe (1865-1922), and his £5.2 million estate;
several of his brothers left enormous fortunes as well.

The last major occupational sector — the professions, public
administration and defence — is, curiously enough, among the most
interesting and historically significant of all. This is so because of the
rapid decline in its numbers after the 1840s — at least until the 1920s,
when the deaths of eight wealthy lawyers and other professionals again
increased its significance. The decline in this category after the early
nineteenth century occurred above all among those who earned their
fortunes in the public administration and defence sphere. Among the
lesser wealthy, where this trend is most perceptible, the percentage in
the professions, public administration and defence declined from 22.7
per cent in 1809-29 to only 4.8 per cent in 1850-69. The number of
wealthy lawyers or judges at this level dropped from 15 to four. Why
was this? This was the end of 'Old Corruption', the world of patronage
and place so synonymous with eighteenth-century British politics,
and which lingered on until the Age of Reform. Most typical of these
men, perhaps, was John Scott, 1st Earl of Eldon (1751-1838), the
famous Lord Chancellor (for 25 years), who left £707,000 plus much
land. Son of a Newcastle coal merchant, he was also a living example
of the other face of Old Corruption (and of the old order in England
generally), its relative openness to new men. Among Lord Eldon's
contemporaries who appear here and who provide a sense of the flavour
of this vanished world, are such men as Alexander Adair (*c*. 1739-1834),
army agent, who left £700,000; Sir Charles Flower, 1st Bt. (1763-1834),
government provision contractor and Lord Mayor of London, the son
of a cheesemonger in the Minories, who left £500,000; Charles, 1st
Baron Arden (1756-1840), brother of Spencer Perceval and Registrar

of the Court of Admiralty for 50 years, whose fortune totalled
£700,000; Charles Middleton, 1st Baron Barham (1726-1813), admiral
and placeman, who left £150,000; Sir William Wynne (£180,000 in
1816), official Principal of the Court of Arches and Master of the
Prerogative Court of Canterbury; Samuel Richard Fydell (1771-1868),
Receiver-General for Lincolnshire from 1794 to 1834, whose fortune
totalled £250,000; and the judge, Edward Law, 1st Baron Ellenborough
(1750-1818), who left £200,000. Anglican ecclesiastics were also
prominent among the very wealthy, men like Hon. William Stuart,
Archbishop of Armagh (1755-1822), fifth son of the Earl of Bute, who
left £250,000; George Pretyman Tomline (1750-1827), Pitt's tutor and
later Bishop of Winchester, whose estate totalled £200,000; and Charles
Manners-Sutton (1755-1828), Archbishop of Canterbury from 1805 to
1828, who left £180,000. Such ecclesiastical fortunes would be almost
inconceivable by the late nineteenth century: few sections of the British
wealth structures could have changed so radically. Many wealth-holders
who were essentially landowners also shared in the placeman's bounty.
Heneage, 4th Earl of Aylesford (1751-1812), was Lord Steward to HM
Household; he left £200,000. Hon. Brownlow North (1741-1820),
son of the 1st Earl of Guildford, later became Bishop of Winchester;
his fortune totalled £180,000. James, 4th Earl of Cornwallis (1742-
1824), held the Bishopric of Lichfield for over 40 years; he was also
Dean of Windsor and Dean of Durham; he left £200,000. Many others
held purely political posts and shared in the perks of office. The
extreme example of the possibility of a career open to talent in the
early nineteenth century was probably that of the younger son of a
none-too-wealthy Irish earl, Arthur, 1st Duke of Wellington (1769-1852),
whose personal fortune of £500,000 was wholly the product of his vast
parliamentary and foreign grants (£600,000 from the British parliament
alone), a tribute to his military victories.

Perhaps the primary importance of the occupational distribution of
the very wealthy lies in its essential and basic difference from the
national statistics of occupational employment or the occupational
factors in the national product among the whole population. The
reason for this is simple: the statistical indices of macro-economics are
influenced far more by labour-intensive than by capital-intensive
industries. One has merely to compare the role of banking and finance
in the occupational distribution of the wealthy with its place in the net
national product to appreciate this. The manufacturing, mining and
building sectors of the economy accounted for between 34.4 per cent
and 40.2 per cent of the total national income during the period

1831–1901, while the share of the trade and transport sector ranged between 17.3 per cent and 23.3 per cent.[14] The difference between the lead of manufacturing over commerce evidenced in these figures, and the lead of commerce over manufacturing in the statistics of wealth-holders reflects the distribution of working-class incomes in the whole population. National employment statistics demonstrate that the difference at the top was made up at the bottom: 'commercial occupations' accounted for only 1.4 per cent of all males employed in 1841, while the various census categories of industrial and manufacturing trades provided employment for 43.0 per cent of the total; in 1911 while commercial occupations still amounted to only 5.7 per cent of the male labour force, industry and manufacturing rose to 48.6 per cent.[15] More than anything else, perhaps, this is an indictment of the macro-economic approach in economic history to the understanding of nineteenth-century British elites and their relationship to the rest of society.

Similarly, Marxism also fails in its comprehension of the salient features of the Victorian British elite. Although in many of his writings Marx gave full weight to the importance of bankers and large-scale merchants as an element in the post-industrial bourgeoisie,[16] it can hardly be doubted that the interaction of industrial capitalists with their employees constitutes *per necessitum* the focal point of the class struggle; it is here that revolutions are made or aborted. But it is surely a logical fallacy to infer from the central importance of industrial capitalism in the dialectical process, the central importance of industrial capitalism for the bourgeoisie. Marx viewed mercantile capitalism as characteristic of an earlier and inferior stage of society than industrialism,[17] and by nature as being inherently representative of a more primitive state of society. As with macro-economics, such a perception may distort our knowledge of British elites.

Unusual sources of wealth were surprisingly rare. I have, for instance, never identified a single wealth-holder whose fortune was the result of an illegal activity or practice: but of course accurate information on this would be virtually impossible to come by.[18] There were no real-life Charles Augustus Milvertons or even Auguste Melmottes in Britain. On the other hand, as noted before, it is striking that the muck-raking American-style *exposé* of the sordid history of the great fortunes has no parallel in England: as we have seen, Samuel Smiles is much more in the English style than Gustavus Myers or Felix Lundberg.

Eccentric sources of wealth were more common, though they, too, were rare, and became rarer both as time went on and as one ascends the wealth scale. Among millionaires, a few well-trodden paths of wealth predominate. Especially after the mid-nineteenth century, career patterns became models of the Victorian straight and narrow in all their dimensions. For eccentricity or local colour, one has to look primarily − again − to the earlier wealth-holders, particularly the 'lesser wealthy'. Such careers have, I believe, more than a curiosity value, for they indicate something of the incredible diversity of the English *ancien régime* before it became solidified into hard occupational and class moulds by industrialisation. John Courtoy (or Courtois), who died in December 1818 'at an advanced age', leaving £250,000, was a *hairdresser* who, 'by dint of various extraordinary exertions in various ways, and through a most rigid economy in his expenditure . . . died immensely rich . . . Long well-known in the purlieus of St. Martins and the Haymarket, [h]is appearance was meagre and squalid, and his clothes, such as they were, were pertinaciously got up'.[19] An anecdote concerning Courtoy relates how, having attended the Court Room of East India House to vote as a stockholder, he was then asked to cut the hair of several of his fellow-stockholders! His executor was Charles Drummond, the banker.

There are no other careers quite so eccentric, but many unusual by later standards. The sculptor Joseph Nollekens (1737-1823) left £200,000, and it is interesting to record that the great artist J.M.W. Turner (d. 1851) left £140,000. Such artistic fortunes were not repeated until the mid-twentieth century. Miles Peter Andrews (1742-1814), a playwright who wrote *The Election*, inherited, of all things, a lucrative gunpowder manufacturing establishment at Dartmouth and left £175,000. James T. Broadwood (1772-1851) made his fortune of £300,000 by manufacturing pianos; William J. Chaplin (1787-1859), 'born in humble circumstances' in Rochester, built up one of the largest coach proprietorships in England, including 64 stage coaches worked by 1,500 horses. Obviously a man of enterprise, he promptly switched to railways, becoming chairman of the London and South-Western and director of several others.[20]

Unexpected, too, by later standards were the occupational descriptions given to many of the early wealth-holders. John Jones (d. 1817), who left £160,000, was a London apothecary; George Pratt (d. 1818), who left the same sum, was a 'meal man' (a dealer in meal, probably on government contract); Henry Hewetson (d. 1838), a half-millionaire, was a 'gold and silver laceman' at King Street, Covent

Garden. Thomas Gadd Matthews (d. 1860) was a 'dry salter' in Bristol; William Thwaytes (1746-1834), who left £700,000, is described in his will and other sources as a 'grocer' — in the parlance of the day — a large-scale wholesale tea merchant and foodstuffs dealer in London and a Jamaica planter; it was his tea which was thrown into the harbour at the Boston Tea Party.[21]

In a slightly different category are the unknown cases which remain in any sizable historical sample of names such as this. About two per cent of those leaving £500,000 or more, and a much higher percentage of the 'lesser wealthy', simply could not be traced in any source. Even their occupation is unknown to me. Their wills proved of little value in identifying them, which is the case generally; wills are almost never mini-autobiographies. It is not surprising, given the paucity of sources official or unofficial, that the historian should draw a blank with such early figures as John Baker of Lower Grosvenor Street, who died on 16 May 1818, leaving £500,000, or Thomas Allen, who died near Amersham on 15 November 1829, also leaving £500,000. But what about Lt.-Col. Ernest S. Halford (*c.* 1872-1932), occupation unknown, date and place of birth unknown, parentage unknown, who left £619,000? What about Thomas Pockington (1860-1935), described as a 'dealer in property and estates' in London, whose parentage or early career could not be traced, but who left a sizable legacy from his £790,000 to found a trust for fatherless boys of Acton and Shepherd's Bush? What of half-millionaires like Samuel Engels (*c.* 1845-1907), Herbert Edgar Reid (*c.* 1850-1914), or John Abbot (*c.* 1834-1917), of whom literally nothing whatever could be traced? What of the mysterious wealthy Anglican clergymen of the nineteenth century (who lacked any traceable careers as placemen or placemen relatives) like the Rev. Thomas Leman (1749-1826), worth £160,000; Rev. James Williams (1814-71), who left £500,000 and sold Tring Park to the Rothschilds; or the Very Rev. Thomas Parr Brymer (1797-1852), who left £350,000 — if they were the fools of sons who were placed in the Church, who were their fathers? I have not been able to learn.

Some Individual Trades

In order to give some idea of the human aspects of the wealthy in various occupations — those details which can transform an otherwise dry numerical study — I have chosen to concentrate on a smaller number of important occupations in each of the main employment sectors. In mining and minerals I have focused on coal mining. For manufacturing industry I will concentrate on those vital entrepreneurs of industrialisation, the chemical manufacturers (which, as a category, includes patent medicine and pharmaceutical makers) and cotton manufacturers. In the 'food-drink-tobacco' sectors, brewers will be examined; in commerce and finance, I will look at the merchant bankers and shipowners.

Coal Mining. A total of 51 colliery owners[22] left £500,000 or more between 1809 and 1939 — ten millionaires and 41 half-millionaires.[23] Very few immensely wealthy colliery owners died before the late nineteenth century: the first colliery millionaire (Joseph Love of Durham), died only in 1785; the first half-millionaire later still, in 1879 (Edward Joicey, of the famous Durham dynasty). The eight 'lesser wealthy' colliery fortunes which could be identified — two among the first cohort and six in the second — indicate the limits of wealth possible for colliery magnates in the early part of the century. Among these early wealth-holders, William Russell (1734-1817) and his son Matthew (d. 1822), of Brancepeth Castle, Durham, who left, respectively £280,000 and £220,000, were the only two early colliery magnates; the most significant of the later cohort were probably Joseph Straker (1784-1867) of Northumberland, a major shipowner, and the founder of a notable colliery dynasty; and the famous Welsh magnate Thomas Powell (1779-1863), founder of Powell Duffryn, who struck the famous four-foot seam at Duffryn in 1842; he left £250,000.[24]

At the other end of the scale were the ten colliery millionaires. Several of these, most notably David A. Thomas, 1st Baron Rhondda (1856-1918) who left £1,169,000 and served as Lloyd George's Food Controller in 1917-18, and James Joicey, 1st Baron Joicey (1846-1936), Chairman of the two largest County Durham coal companies (who left £1,520,000), are extremely well-known, but many others are not. For instance, such magnates as John Nixon (1815-99), chairman of the South Wales Coal Association, James F. Fyfe-Jamieson (1866-1929) of Glasgow's William Dixon and Co. (and a major petroleum investor)[25] or William E. Harrison (1875-1937), of the Staffordshire fields, possess only a local historical fame.

Indeed, considered as individuals among a group, the wealthy colliery-owners made little impact upon the course of history. Only one dynasty, the Joiceys, received a peerage in this period,[26] only a handful of others received baronetcies or knighthoods. The geographical spread of the colliery magnates among Britain's major coal fields was similarly diverse and variegated. Two millionaires, 14 half-millionaires, and three lesser wealthy colliery owners were magnates in the fields of Tyneside and Durham, by far the largest geographical concentration, but all of the other major coal fields of Britain produced their colliery wealth-holders.

In one facet of their social backgrounds, however, the colliery magnates present an extremely homogeneous picture. Virtually without exception, they were Anglicans. Of the eight millionaire, 32 half-millionaire and seven lesser wealthy colliery magnates whose religions could be traced, probably only two each among the millionaires and half-millionaires were known to have been dissenters.[27] One millionaire and four half-millionaires were Scots Presbyterians. All the rest were Anglicans; many of these were generous in their endowment of churches or in their Anglican philanthropy. The virtual Anglican monopoly among colliery magnates — anomalous among purely industrial pursuits — suggests one possible line of division between master and man. With Anglicanism went disproportionate Conservatism: although Liberal supporters and politicians there were, like Lord Rhondda and Sir Arthur B. Markham, 1st Bt. (1866-1916), a backbench Liberal MP for 16 years, who was known for his 'tremendous onslaught on Messrs. Werhner, Beit & Co.' during the Boer War, and his equally ardent support for Lloyd George's 1909 Budget,[28] the number of Conservatives was greater still, much greater than one would expect *a priori* given the industrial and non-conformist nature of their constituencies. Such men as William Thomas Lewis, later 1st Baron Merthyr (1837-1914), a half-millionaire who had the misfortune to be the Tory candidate in Merthyr Tydfil in 1880, or his son, the 2nd Baron (1866-1932), who contested both East Glamorganshire in 1892 and Merthyr Tydfil in 1895 — hereditary insanity not being confined to the old aristocracy — were much more typical. In some industrial towns where coal was king — Newcastle-on-Tyne being the prime example — there was a considerable nexus of old Anglican, Tory families, heavily involved in banking and commerce as well, who were sufficiently well-established to have become an accepted part of the landed gentry.

Most colliery wealth-holders, too, emerged from roughly the same economic backgrounds; they were the sons of fairly wealthy, sometimes exceptionally wealthy, colliery owners. Few were self-made men or intergenerationally mobile across occupations. A typical father was himself a colliery owner who left between £75,000 and £500,000 at death, though, among the final cohort studied here, a good many were second-generation wealth-holders, the sons of fathers who also appear in this study. There are two exceptions to this pattern. A number of colliery dynasties arose from backgrounds of mining engineers or engineering managers in the coal fields of landed aristocrats. The two prime examples of this were the Joiceys and the Lewises (the Barons Merthyr mentioned above). The father of Lord Joicey (d. 1936), was just such a mining engineer who was unlisted in the probate calendars when he died in 1856; he had been described as a mere 'millwright' on his marriage licence in 1837. Colonel John Joicey (1816-81), a relative who left £710,000, was the son of a 'colliery agent' who also left nothing at his death in 1848. The rise of this dynasty to a great wealth might almost take Samuel Smiles's breath away. Similarly, the father of Lord Merthyr was an engineer at the Plymouth Ironworks, Merthyr Tydfil, who left only £3,263 at his death in 1900 (when son must have already become very rich). Lord Merthyr in his youth walked two miles every evening to learn his mathematics lesson, his obituary records.[29]

There were, too, a handful of genuinely self-made men, even long after the Industrial Revolution had begun. Joseph Love (1796-1875), who died a millionaire, was the younger son of a working miner who began life as a pitboy. He opened a grocery and provision shop, eventually re-entering the colliery trade as an entrepreneur.[30] Similarly, John Nixon (1815-99), another millionaire, was the son of a tenant farmer at Barlow, near Newcastle.[31] Some magnates straddled the class borders. In that peculiar Scottish tradition of class-mixing, so alien to England, William Weir (1826-1913), who left no less than £2,220,000 at his death, was the son of a small farmer at Dunpark, near New Markland, yet his mother was the sister of William Baird, the greatest Scottish ironmaster and also a great colliery magnate. Weir eventually became principal partner in William Baird & Co., owning vast ironworks besides his colliery interests.[32] Such stories were, however, much more unusual in England, where normally a colliery magnate's family had been well-to-do for some generations. Again, there is here a sameness, a homogeneity, in the pattern, while few such men achieved national renown. The 'coal master', the bogeyman of so much left-wing diatribe in the early part of this century, remains a surprisingly vague creature. Indeed, the only colliery owner to whom a local habitation and a name was commonly given was Lord Londonderry, who was not a colliery owner in the strict sense at all.

Chemical Manufacture. In contrast to the relative homogeneity of the colliery owners, the picture presented by the wealthy chemical manufacturers is one of much greater heterogeneity. This was characteristic, first of all, of the very products they made. Four wealthy chemical manufacturers, including three millionaires, were makers and vendors of patent medicines, men who saw their chance in the Englishman's chronic indigestion and constipation, and took it; another made his millions in pharmaceuticals. Other chemical manufacturers made their fortunes in such unlikely areas as gelatine and glue (Robert Cox, 1845-99, of Edinburgh, who left £544,000), varnish (the partners John Noble (1813-90) and Thomas R. Hoare (1816-92) of London, both half-millionaires), photographic processing materials (Dr Joseph J. Acworth (1853-1927), a half-millionaire with Ilford Ltd.), and seedcakes (Arthur Earle (1839-1919)). Rich soap-makers were only slightly less numerous (and certainly more permanent) than their product's bubbles, starting with such millionaires as the great William H. Lever, 1st Viscount Leverhulme (1851-1926), and Joseph Watson, 1st Baron Manton (1873-1922), who won £34,000 at the Turf in 1921,[33] a year prior to obtaining his peerage from Lloyd George. But most wealthy chemical manufacturers were concerned in purely industrial chemicals or processes, for instance in the manufacture of alkali or in dyeing and bleaching for the textile industry.

The chemical manufacturers also differed from the colliery owners — who, as individuals, were, let us concede, a fairly dry bunch — in the number of colourful or larger-than-life entrepreneurs among them. Leverhulme was probably the most dynamic and, in business history terms, the most important. But he had several rivals in this respect. Sir Charles Tennant, 1st Bt. (1823-1906), whose great St Rollox works, capped by the famous Tennant's Peak, its immense smokestack which was the tallest structure in Glasgow, was a man of three unusual distinctions: he was the father of Margot Asquith; he was the father of children born 53 years apart (said to be a record in this respect for monogamous countries) — and he was the richest Scotsman of the nineteenth century, leaving the immense sum of £3,146,000 at his death. Each of the patent medicine or pharmaceutical manufacturers was notable or colourful in his way: Thomas Holloway (1800-83), the celebrated proprietor of 'Holloway's Pills' who endowed Holloway College for Women with £700,000, erected a sanatorium for 'the mentally afflicted of the lower-middle class', and left £596,000; James C. Eno (1828-1915), the millionaire vendor of 'Eno's Fruit Salts', whose birthplace and ancestry are completely unknown,[34] and whose grand-daughter, implausible as this may seem, is Lady Cripps, widow of Sir Stafford; Sir Joseph Beecham, 1st Bt. (1848-1916), of 'Beechams Pills' fame, whose son was Sir Thomas, the great conductor; Sir Henry Wellcome (1854-1936), who was born on the American frontier, made his £3 million by manufacturing the 'tabloid' form of drugs (the term was later applied to newspapers) and founded the Wellcome Medical Museum; and William G. Hughes (1873-1935), proprietor of Kruschen Salts.

The geographical venues of the wealthy chemical manufacturers were also widely dispersed among a wide range of urban areas. In so far as there was a capital of wealth-holding in chemicals, it was Liverpool and the Merseyside area. Merseyside, as we shall see later, was primarily a great centre of commercial wealth; chemicals were its leading manufacturing industry. Leverhulme, Manton and Beecham had their works nearby; so did much celebrated dynasties as those of Sir John T. Brunner, 1st Bt. (1842-1919) who left £906,000 and Ludwig Mond (1839-1909), who left £1,422,000, as well as soap kings like Frederick H. Gossage (1832-1907) and alkali magnates like Frank Gaskell (1853-1937). Manchester and other northern towns produced mainly industrial and textile chemicals; typical of their magnates were such men as the Leeds millionaire ammonia manufacturer and tar distiller Edward A. Brotherton, 1st Baron Brotherton, (1856-1930) and the Manchester bleacher and dyer Frederick Cawley, 1st Baron Cawley (1850-1937). Surprisingly, a number of chemical wealth-holders earned their fortunes in small south of England towns far removed from the smokestacks of the north. Such entrepreneurs included William Ranson (1826-1914), a manufacturing chemist of Hitchin, Hertfordshire, and Sir Richard P. Cooper, 1st Bt. (1847-1913) of Lichfield and Berkhamstead.[35] London was not particularly well-represented. Its only chemical millionaires were Wellcome and Frank Clarke Hill (1808-92), a rather elusive Deptford manufacturer who was also a notable shipbuilder and, in 1839, invented a steam carriage which ran to Sevenoaks and Hastings.[36] Perhaps the best-known Londoner in this category was a lesser wealth-holder, George Beaufoy (1796-1864), of the famous firm of Lambeth vinegar and acid makers.[37]

In religion, the chemical wealth-holders were as diversified as the colliery owners were homogeneous. Although Anglicans formed a plurality with six millionaires and 13 half-millionaires, adherents of Presbyterianism, Lutheranism, Methodism, Quakerism, Unitarianism and the Free Church of Scotland figure among them. German-born Ludwig Mond and his millionaire son, the 1st Baron Melchett (1868-1930) were Jews. With their originally Swiss Lutheran partners, the Brunners, they were representative of the important foreign, particularly Germanic element among the wealthy chemists, which included as well men like Christian Allhusen (1806-90), a Kiel-born Newcastle millionaire. For whatever reason, chemicals and soaps, like sweets and cocoa, had a strong attraction for dissenting entrepreneurs. The Quaker Reckitts of Hull, the famous starch manufacturers, are typical. Leverhulme started life as a Methodist. Even Scottish dissenters appear, in the persons of the White dynasty of Glasgow — John (1810-81), James (1812-84) and John Campbell, later 1st Baron Overtoun (1843-1908), all half-millionaires, all adherents of the Free Church of Scotland.[38]

With disproportionate non-conformity went disproportionate Liberalism. Again in contrast to the coal magnates, there appear to have been rather more Liberal supporters and members than Tories, although there was a good deal of transferral of allegiance in 1886 and again in the 1920s. Indeed, here there was often Liberalism with a vengeance. Sir John Brunner was an 'advanced' Liberal whose recent biography is entitled *Radical Plutocrat*.[39] Overtoun was a staunch Liberal supporter whose peerage came in 1893 from Gladstone. Lord Glenconner (1859-1920), Sir Charles Tennant's half-millionaire son, was a Liberal MP and Cabinet minister and, of course, Asquith's brother-in-law. Lord Melchett was similarly a Liberal MP and Cabinet minister under Lloyd George. His abandonment of the Liberals for the Tories in 1926 over Lloyd George's 'socialism' and to further promote Empire economic union was an important act, symbolising for many that two bourgeois parties in the circumstances of post-war England were one too many.[40]

But nearly as much as with the colliery owners, few wealthy chemical manufacturers were 'self-made men'. Some who were said to have been were, on closer inspection, no such thing. Lord Leverhulme, for instance, is often described as a 'self-made man' but, if that is so, he is the only one in history whose father left £58,000. Like Leverhulme, most were second- or third-generation scions of a prosperous, but not immensely wealthy family firm, who built up their inheritances into real fortunes. On balance they were somewhat poorer than the fathers of the colliery wealth-holders. Quite typical of the family progression here was Sir Charles Tennant, whose father had founded the family business and had left £76,000 at his death in 1838. Similarly, the father of John and James White had left £37,000, the father of Francis Reckitt (1827-1917), the starch millionaire, £14,000. Even the fathers of most of the immigrant wealth-holders were men of some means (as was the case generally with the fathers of immigrant wealth-holders). The fathers of Allhusen and Mond were merchants in Germany. But some self-made men there were. The father of Thomas Kenyon (1843-1916), a Manchester dyer and bleacher, was described as a 'colour-mixer' on his son's birth certificate; Holloway's, a baker and publican in Penzance. Perhaps to balance Mond, Brunner's father was Unitarian

Table 3.9: Venues of Cotton Wealth-holders

Millionaires:		Half-millionaires:	
1. Greater Manchester:		1. Greater Manchester:	
Manchester	1	Manchester	3
Other towns:		Other towns:	
Bolton	1	Oldham	12
		Leigh	2
2. Other Lancashire:		Rochdale	1
Blackburn	1	Bury	1
Wigan	1	Bolton	2
3. Derbyshire	3	2. Other Lancashire:	
		Accrington	1
4. West Riding:		Blackburn	1
Todmorden	2	Preston	3
Huddersfield	1		
		3. Derbyshire	6
5. Paisley	13	Nottinghamshire	1
Lesser Wealthy:		4. West Riding:	
1. Greater Manchester:		Todmorden	1
Manchester	4	Huddersfield	1
Other towns:		Other	1
Bury	1		
Heaton	1	5. Paisley	4
2. Other Lancashire:			
Blackburn	3		
3. Derbyshire	7		

minister and schoolmaster; Brunner's first job, at 15, was as an office-boy in a Liverpool shipping office.

Cotton Manufacture. With the cotton manufacturers, we reach the heart of the Industrial Revolution. 'Whoever says Industrial Revolution, says cotton', Eric Hobsbawm has put it[41] — and so it is widely believed. There were indeed a great many wealthy cotton manufacturers, who were among the most numerous of industrial wealth-holders. Twenty-four millionaires,[42] 40 half-millionaires, and 17 among the two lesser wealthy cohorts earned their fortunes in the making of cotton textiles. As Table 3.9 indicates, they were representative of all of the main textile centres of Britain, though not, surely, in the frequency one might imagine *a priori*.

There are two exceedingly surprising conclusions to be drawn from this table. One is the unimportance of Manchester (but not of the outlying towns within what was to become its conurbation); the other, the phenomenal number of wealth-holders in Paisley. Like the dog in the Sherlock Holmes story which did nothing in the night-time, Manchester — the great 'cottonpolis' of the nineteenth century — is notable chiefly for its paucity of cotton wealth-holders. In the entire period between 1809 and 1939, only one millionaire cotton manufacturer made his fortune in Manchester,[43] with only three others among the half-millionaires.[44] It is significant that — in contrast — four of the lesser wealthy were Manchester men, indicating perhaps, the scale of wealth which it was possible for a manufacturer to accumulate there.[45] As the table indicates, however, there were many more cotton wealth-holders in the outlying towns of Greater Manchester. Even so, only one other cotton millionaire earned his fortune here, the Bolton cotton spinner and MP John P. Thomasson (1841-1904). At the half-millionaire level, in contrast, there was a plethora of cotton fortunes, most notably in Oldham, with its 12 half-millionaires, certainly as high a ratio of population wealth as in virtually any town or industry in England.

Two other north of England cotton areas require some mention. Both are of great significance in British industrial history. These are the Derbyshire-Nottinghamshire cotton towns, especially Derby and Willersley, and the north Lancashire cotton rim, above all the town of Blackburn. Willersley and Blackburn are of great significance indeed, for there the two greatest, and wealthiest, of all the early cotton entrepreneurs had their works, Richard Arkwright (1755-1843)[46] and Sir Robert Peel, 1st Bt. (1750-1830), the father of the prime minister. Both were millionaires, among the very earliest *industrial* millionaires in British history. Peel, in particular, was exceedingly rich, said to be worth £1,500,000 by his death in 1830; in addition he was a considerable landowner, and, of course, a man bent — successfully, as it turned out — on founding a dynasty which genuinely merged with the old elite.[47] As is often pointed out, a really wealthy cotton magnate like the elder Peel might well have favoured the factory legislation which would have crippled the innumerable smaller men; the probate records graphically show that Peel was indeed worth at least twenty or thirty times as much as the *average* successful cotton manufacturer, and possibly a hundred times as much as the little fish.[48] Both Arkwright and Peel founded dynasties, with many wealthy descendants; yet as was typical of many middle-class families, their wealth was divided equally or nearly equally among their descendants, so that virtually no single one was immensely rich. Arkwright, for instance, left one half-millionaire son (Peter, d. 1866), but no fewer than six descendants dying among the lesser wealthy in the 1850-69 cohort alone, each worth about £300,000 or so. Two were rural Anglican vicars, as clearcut an example of the decline of entrepreneurship as one could wish. Much the same was true with the Peel dynasty; the prime minister, 2nd baronet and eldest son of the cotton millionaire, left £400,000 in personalty.

However, the most striking of all the centres of cotton wealth was neither Willersley nor Blackburn, but Paisley, in Renfrewshire near Glasgow. This was the business venue of one of the most remarkable of all British wealth dynasties, the Coatses, and also of their partners the Clarks, proprietors of the great sewing thread firm of J. & P. Coats, later known as Coats and Clarks. Prior to the First World War, J. & P. Coats was the third largest incorporated industrial firm in Britain, with a capital value of £11.2 million in 1905.[49] After the Rothschilds and the Wills family of Bristol's Imperial Tobacco Company, the Coatses produced more wealth-holders than any other in Britain: nine millionaires and three half-millionaires between the deaths of Thomas (1809-83), the giant figure of the firm's early history, and grandson Major John Alexander Coats, aged 40, in 1932. The wealthiest were George, 1st Baron Glentanar (1849-1918), who left £4,324,000, and William Allan Coats (1853-1926), who left £3,993,000; several others left more than £2 million.[50] The Clarks, in contrast, produced merely two millionaires and one half-millionaire. Coats or Clark, these dynasties followed the same pattern of factory-town industrial patriarch in the fathers and idle rich in the sons. When John Clark (b. 1827) — baptised into the United Presbyterian Church, founder of Newark, New Jersey's thread industry, Liberal turned President of the Paisley Liberal Unionists — died in 1894 leaving some £545,000, '. . . the blinds of the Clark Town Hall were drawn . . .', as a local obituary put it. Only a decade later, one of the younger Clarks was living the Edwardian high-life of yachting and gambling which the most distinguished man this family ever produced later summarised: 'My parents belonged to a section of society known as "the idle rich", and although, in that golden age, many people were richer, there have been few who were idler'.[51]

In certain respects, however, the Scottish Coatses and Clarks were not typical of the English cotton wealth-holders. Among them, as we have seen, there was a strong dissenting streak within the overarching framework of the Scottish religious structure: Thomas Coats (d. 1883) was a Baptist — of course unusual in Scotland — while several others were adherents of the United Presbyterian Church (although several were Church of Scotland). But most English cotton-manufacturers — contrary to all expectations — were Anglicans. This was not so clearly marked among the millionaires as among the half-millionaires: among the English millionaires, three were Anglicans, but dissent was well-represented by such notable figures as Congregationalist John Rylands (1801-88) of Wigan, who left £2,575,000; the Unitarian-turned-Anglican Strutts of Belper, and the Quaker Fieldens. But among the half-millionaires, 24 were Anglicans compared with nine for all other denominations (including the probable Roman Catholic — one of the few — Francis J. Summer (1807-84) of Glossop); among the lesser wealthy, 11 were Anglicans and only two dissenters.

The Anglicanism of most wealthy cotton manufacturers is not so surprising now as it would have been prior to the publication of John Foster's important Marxist work, *Class Struggle and the Industrial Revolution*,[52] with its microscopic study of the bourgeoisie in three northern towns, including the cotton (and engineering) centre Oldham. In general, Foster's conclusions regarding the wealthy bourgeoisie there are extremely sound, though it is not clear to me that the origins of many nineteenth century rich families lay (as he suggests) as far back as the seventeenth century;[53] many first or second generation self-made men were just that. Where perhaps Foster is most fundamentally wrong is in his assumption that wealthy nineteenth-century manufacturers *should* have been dissenters rather than Anglicans. This is, of course, not Foster's error alone: it was believed by Weber and Ashton and innumerable others. But, if the statistics here are to be believed, enterprise and business ability were disproportionately features of men brought up in the Church of England. This important topic must await another chapter for the full treatment it merits. A factor at work here, however, may be that the Industrial Revolution in Britain took place in the country-side, in remote areas and tiny hamlets close to running water for mills and agricultural raw materials, in places like Strutt's Belper, Peel's Blackburn or Arkwrights's Willersley, rather than in urban centres associated with dissent, Old or New.

Perhaps because of their Anglicanism, most cotton wealth-holders by a slight majority were Tories rather than Whigs or Liberals, though it must be said that many died in the late nineteenth century when most rich people had become Tories. The 1886 split in the Liberal ranks sent some into the Unionist party, for instance the former Bolton Liberal MP John R. Thomasson, and many of the Coats dynasty whose allegiances are known. Some, however, stood firm, for instance Sir

Thomas Glen-Coats (d. 1922), who was a Liberal MP from 1906 to 1910. At the half-millionaire level, too, the figures described as 'ardent' Liberals, like Eli Lees (1814-92) of Oldham, or Liberal MPs like Rt. Hon. John F. Cheetham (1835-1916), another Oldham spinner who served in Parliament in 1880-5 and 1905-10, or Lewis Haslam (1856-1922), a Bolton manufacturer who served between 1906 and 1922, are more than outnumbered by equally ardent Conservatives, more active perhaps in local than national politics and, of course, at the very top there was Peel.

As with the other occupational groups we have analysed here, few wealthy cotton spinners were 'self-made' in any sense, although probably more were genuinely second generation self-made men. Because the early cotton works could indeed be founded on the proverbial shoestring, some of the early figures had managed to rise from extremely humble backgrounds. William Yates (1739-1813), Peel's partner, for instance, who left £175,000, became a partner with £200 in capital; he had once been a cotton-mill apprentice.[54] Similarly, a somewhat later Manchester manufacturer, James Kershaw (1795-1864), was the son of a working man and started as a clerk; he left £300,000.[55] Such examples, however, were rare, probably precisely *because* the capital value of the early cotton works, and the wealth of the early cotton manufacturers, was so small. It was not until the late nineteenth century that very wealthy cotton spinners began to die in substantial numbers; they were mainly the second or third generation of their family firms and were the sons of prosperous but not really wealthy fathers.

Before turning from the cotton lords, we should draw attention to another interesting feature of their place in the structure of wealth: the fact that so few died during the last decade of this study, the 1930s. Only one millionaire and three half-millionaires died in this decade, two of whom were Coatses. Indeed, if the Coatses and Clarks are removed from the list, the number dying after the First World War is much reduced. The English cotton wealth-holders appear in the probate calendars mainly between 1875 and 1914.

Brewing. Leaving the wholly industrial or manufacturing trades for the intermediate category of food-drink-tobacco, our representative group for detailed examination here are the brewers (which includes certain related wealth-holders like maltsters and brewery sugar manufacturers). Brewing was one of the most significant and lucrative of all trades in the nineteenth century, and its entrepreneurs present many interesting and *sui generis* social and economic features. There were a great many of them — no fewer than 33 brewing millionaires, 50 half-millionaires and 11 lesser wealthy; unlike the colliery owners or even the chemical manufacturers, a great many were and are indeed household names, though far less is known to the ordinary man, or even to the economic historian, about their lives and careers.

As with the other groups we have examined, the geographical distribution of their business venues was extremely wide — wider, indeed, than with any of the previous groups. Virtually every British town of any consequence had its brewery dynasty, no matter what the predominant nature of its business or occupational structure. As is widely known, our present brewing companies and, *a fortiori*, those which existed in the last century, were themselves amalgams of the innumerable local breweries which had always existed in Britain: by and large, the numerous brewery wealth-holders were simply men whose businesses merged into local or even national combinations or ologopolies earlier than in many other fields. Even in the late nineteenth century, several cities had already produced more, and wealthier, brewing dynasties than others of comparable or greater size. In the first place there was London, with 12 brewing millionaires, 18 half-millionaires, and all 11 of the lesser wealth-holders. (Additionally, nearby towns like Ware, Hertfordshire; Plumstead, Kent; and Watford, Hertfordshire produced six more wealth-holders.) The great London dynasties included such well-known names as James Watney (1800-84) and his namesake son (1832-86); Sir Henry Meux, 2nd Bt. (1817-83); Spencer (1818-1904) and Charles E.N. Charrington (1859-1936); and Charles Combe (1836-1920), just to choose from among the many millionaires; or representatives of such famous dynasties as Robert Hanbury (1796-1884), Robert Courage (1830-93) and John Henry Buxton (1849-1934) among the half-millionaires. The most famous of the lesser wealthy brewers was unquestionably Samuel Whitbread, the Whig politician who committed suicide in 1815, leaving £200,000 (and much land); his descendant, another Samuel Whitbread (1830-1915), still left £680,000. Indeed, reviewing the names of the wealthy London brewers is rather like a five-minute tour of Britain's billboards and television advertisements. In fairness, however, this would be to exaggerate: there were London brewery wealth-holders whose names are forgotten. Who, for instance, now remembers Henry Gardner (1796-1879), who left half of his £600,000 to found a School for the Indigent Blind, Charles Beasley (1843-1923), of the North Kent Brewery, Plumstead, who was in 1879 appointed brewer to the Royal family or the many lesser wealthy figures like John Newberry (1750-1815)

Table 3.10: Business Venues of Brewing Fortunes

Millionaires:		Half-millionaires:	
London	12	London	18
Plumstead, Kent	1	Amersham	1
Ware, Herts.	1	Watford	1
Burton	6	Rickmansworth	2
Liverpool	3	Burton	6
Manchester	1	Liverpool	2
Bristol	1	Manchester	3
Newcastle	2	Bristol	1
Newark, Notts.	1	Nuneaton	2
Swansea	1	Leeds	2
Dorchester	1	Tadcaster, W.R. Yorkshire	1
Edinburgh	1	Sunderland	1
Dublin	2	Grimsby	2
		Brighton	1
		Shepton Mallet	1
Lesser Wealthy:		Birmingham	1
London	11	Eastbourne	1
		Yarmouth	1
		Ipswich	1
		Nottingham	1
		Edinburgh	1
		Dublin	1

or John (d. 1864) and Charles Farnell (d. 1865) of Isleworth?

The other disproportionately numerous centre of brewery fortunes was Burton-on-Trent in Staffordshire, with its six millionaires — compared to Manchester's one — and six half-millionaires (compared to Birmingham's one). The dynasties here are household names, too. Millionaires included Richard Ratcliff (1830-98), John Gretton (1833-98) who left nearly £3 million, Alfred O. Worthington (1844-1918), and the two men who gave their names to the 'beerage', Henry Allsopp, first Baron Hindlip (1811-87), (who left £558,000) and Michael A. Bass, first Baron Burton (1837-1909).

The remaining brewing fortunes were very widely distributed; this meant that while, for instance, Bristol and Edinburgh each produced one brewery millionaire, so did such towns as Dorchester, Swansea and Newark. Consequently, they vary in renown from the celebrated, like Edinburgh's William McEwan (1827-1913), or Warrington's Sir Gilbert Greenall, 1st Bt. (1806-94) to purely local figures like Newcastle's James Deuchar (1851-1927), Dorchester's Edwin Pope (1845-1928) and the Newark malt millionaire Arthur G. Soames (1854-1934) — who did, however, marry Peel's grand-daughter, and was the grand-father of Sir Christopher. The big population centres all produced their brewing magnates, although not, perhaps, in the number or quality one might expect. Manchester's millionaire Sir Edward Holt, 1st Bt. (1849-1928), or Bristol's Philip H. Vaughan (1829-1917), are typical. But the greatest brewing family fortune emerged neither from London, Burton or even Manchester, but — likely or unlikely as this may seem — from Dublin and belonged, of course, to the Guinnesses. This dynasty produced three wealth-holders between 1809 and 1939: Sir Benjamin (1798-1868), who left £1.1 million; Arthur, first Baron Ardilaun (1840-1915), whose fortune totalled £729,000; and Edward, first Earl of Iveagh (1847-1927), the owner of Kenwood and its paintings. Iveagh left £13,486,000, the second largest British fortune.

In religion, the brewery wealth-holders were as homogeneous as any group of wealth-holders. They were overwhelmingly, almost unanimously, Anglican. Among the millionaires, for instance, 26 were known to have been Anglicans, two adherents of the Church of Scotland (one of whom died an Anglican), while one was of Unitarian and another of Quaker descent, though they themselves, too, were almost certainly Anglicans. (One of these, for example, Vyell E. Walker (1838-1906), of an old Quaker family, was himself a Harrovian and Captain of the Gentlemen's cricket team; his six brothers were all famous cricketers.) Not merely were the wealthy brewers overwhelmingly Anglican, but they were generous and devout philanthropists of the Church, terms like 'staunch' or 'noble benefactor' frequently appearing in their obituaries. Even the Irish Guinnesses were adherents of — and princely contributors to — the Church of Ireland. Sir Benjamin, for example, erected St Patrick's Anglican Cathedral in Dublin at a cost of £150,000.[56] A Methodist or Baptist brewery millionaire is almost as inconceivable as a Methodist great landowner and, indeed, with its pre-industrial origins, its connotations of 'merrie England' and close association with Conservatism, the brewery trade as a whole was in many respects culturally and socially close to the old aristocracy, especially after the radical/dissenting/teetotaling nexus emerged in the mid-nineteenth century. There were — as is almost always the case — exceptions to this pattern: there was a strong Quaker element among the brewing dynasties which existed from the eighteenth century, like the Hanburys and the Buxtons,[57] although most of their descendants had long since gone over to the established Church by 1850. Only a handful of practising dissenting wealth-holders can be identified among the brewers: Robert Arthington (1823-1900), for instance, was a Leeds Quaker and left £550,000 to Baptist and other African missionary societies, the largest legacy ever left to foreign missions by a single man.[58] A real oddity was William P. Manners (1847-1915), an adherent of the strict Plymouth Brethren sect, who was one of the few men, and certainly one of the earliest, in British business history to take the managerial road to real wealth. The son of a Burton draper, he entered Worthington & Co. as an office boy, eventually becoming chairman and finally leaving £536,000.[59]

Not unexpectedly, there was a solid majority of Conservative supporters and members among the rich brewers, often elected in constituencies where they were among the chief employers of labour. Spencer Charrington, whose service as Conservative MP for Mile End in London's East End between 1885 and 1904 might seem an unfathomable riddle until it is realised that his great brewery stood there, is typical of this, as was the election of Sir Gilbert Greenall for Warrington at various times between 1847 and 1892. Some of the brewers, however, particularly the earlier ones, were Whigs or Whig/ Liberals, like Whitbread or Sir Edward N. Buxton 2nd Bt. (1812-58), whose family was close to Gladstone. The 1886 split affected many of these wealthy Liberal brewers, sending a good many to Unionism, for example Lord Burton or the Craig-Sellars. Thereafter, rich Liberal brewers were virtually unheard-of and, politically, the brewery magnates became even more solid than before. They themselves, or their close relatives, were often prominent among the most right-wing elements within the Conservative party — for instance the millionaire John Gretton, first Baron Gretton (1867-1947), a right-wing Tory MP for 47 years or Henry Page Croft (1881-1947), the prominent die-hard Conservative back-bencher and minister, who was named after his grandfather, the millionaire Hertfordshire maltster Henry Page (1812-94).

As with the other groups we have discussed, few wealthy brewers were self-made men. Indeed, if anything, the rate of intergenerational social mobility was lower among the brewers than among the other groups we have examined. Many fathers left sums in the hundreds of thousands, and some were millionaires. Many, but not all, were themselves brewers or engaged in related trades. Only a very few genuinely self-made men can be identified, like Manners or Deuchar, whose father, a publican, is unlisted in the probate records. The father of Edwin Pope was a landowner who left £50,000; the father of Admiral Sir Hedworth Meux (1856-1929), was the second Earl of Durham: in 1910 he inherited Meux's Brewery from a relative and changed his name. Even when the fathers of wealth-holders appear to have been quite small men, closer inspection shows them to have been rather more successful: Charles Beasley's father, described as a 'licensed victualler' on the son's birth certificate, managed to accumulate £45,000 by the time he died 45 years later. Henry Page's father, a baker, left £12,000 in 1852, certainly not a sum associated at the time with poverty. Most wealthy brewers were the heads of family firms, often generations old, but some were self-made men in the sense of having started their own firm: Beasley founded the North Kent Brewery in 1871; William Garton (1832-1905), founder of the Anglo-Bavarian Brewery at Shepton Mallet, was the son of a civil engineer; Sir John Robinson (1839-1929), like Garton a half-millionaire, was the son of a woolstapler and maltster; he developed the father's malting business into Nottingham's Home Brewery Company.[60] Overall brewing is preeminently a field where successful entrepreneurs and entrepreneurial response came from well-established firms.

Merchant Bankers. We turn lastly to representative financial and commercial trades. It is perhaps proper that we begin with the merchant bankers — that peculiar group of financiers engaged exclusively or almost exclusively in foreign or government loans. It is important to keep in mind that these classical houses of nineteenth-century finance did not include the discount or commercial bankers, nor all the private financiers, individuals engaged in private loan transactions, bill discounting, etc. City interests frequently overlapped, and it is probable that assigning many wealth-holders to one or another category of finance is a matter of opinion. The occupational category of finance thus includes much more than the merchant bankers or the discount bankers alone. Besides private financiers, it would include as well stockbrokers and insurance brokers, and it is important to keep this in perspective.

The merchant bankers were thus only a small part of the totality of financial wealth, but they were nevertheless a quite substantial group, with 29 male and two women millionaires, 35 half-millionaires and five lesser wealthy. It will be recalled, for instance, that there were only 24 cotton millionaires, including all the innumerable Coatses. As a group, the merchant bankers (and the rich financiers in general to a lesser extent) differ in several important and fundamental respects from all of the other occupational groups we have thus far discussed. Perhaps the most obvious difference is that they were all located, as businessmen, in the same place, in the City of London — indeed, in a specialised quarter of the City of London. A Manchester merchant banker or a Glasgow merchant banker is literally inconceivable; the closest approximation to one among the wealth-holders were perhaps the Brown family of Brown, Shipley, who had strong Liverpool mercantile connections and the Schusters, with their Manchester mercantile business.

The other immediate and striking difference between the merchant bankers and the other groups we have studied are their anomalous religious and ethnic origins. No Anglican majority here; no rivalry between Church and chapel. The merchant banking community in the City of London was overwhelmingly foreign and disproportionately Jewish, especially at the very top levels. Among the 31 millionaire merchant bankers, no fewer than 24 were Jews, four Anglicans, while one each belonged to the Church of Scotland, Greek Orthodoxy and Lutheranism. Among the half-millionaires, the foreign sects were considerably less numerous but still substantial: eight Jews, 16 Anglicans, five Lutherans, three Scots Presbyterians, one Greek Orthodox. Among the lesser wealthy, the religions of only two are known: one Lutheran and one Anglican.

Who were these men? We can distinguish several types. Let us begin with the Rothschilds, 'preeminent in finance throughout Europe', as their entry in *Burke's Peerage* states. Ten Rothschilds, including two Rothschild women, left millionaire estates between the death of Nathan Mayer (the founder of the English branch) in 1836, and 1939, plus another — evidently a poor relation — at the half-millionaire level.[61] Their individual fortunes were immense. Nathan, the progenitor, was widely believed to have left £5 million at his death, easily the largest personal fortune ever left in Britain up to that date. Several more left £2 million or more, plus great stretches of agricultural land and financial links throughout Europe and, indeed, the world. Their princely taste and styles of life, to say nothing of their princely friends, are too well-known to need any elaboration.

There were many other great Jewish merchant banking dynasties — and again it is worth making the point that many other varieties of finance, whether dominated by Jew or gentile, are not being considered here. Perhaps the most remarkable were the Sterns, virtually unknown and certainly unchronicled by historians, but at one time nearly as great as the Rothschilds. Like the Rothschilds, too, they began in Frankfurt as bankers. Their specialities included Portuguese and Turkish finance. The first two English heads of this house were Viscount (of Portugal) David (1807-77), who left £1 million, and Herman, Baron (again of Portugal) de Stern (1815-87), who left £3,545,000; their brother James (1835-1901) left £1.1 million. The next generation carried on with Sydney, 1st Baron Wandsworth (1845-1912), a 'lavish contributor to party funds' who received his peerage after only four years on the Liberal back-benches, and his cousin Herbert, first Baron Michelham (1851-1919), who gave £1 million as a wedding present to his son. They left, respectively, £1.6 million and £2.0 million. The Sterns suffered an almost unexampled case of entrepreneurial decline. The last to leave a vast fortune, Sir Edward, 1st Bt. (1854-1933), left only £666,000. He was 'the last prominent City man to go daily to his office in a horse-drawn carriage';[62] by the 1930s Stern Brothers, their business house, had become, in the words of one historian, 'little more than an office for the payment of the coupons on the loans they have issued in the past'.[63] Other prominent Jewish merchant banking houses among the rather confusing array of the 'Cousinhood' included the Raphaels, with three millionaires, the Franklins, Montagues, Samuels,[64] Bischoffscheims, Schiffs, Waggs and Hambros. Most remained faithful to their ancestral religion and played a notable part in Anglo-Jewish affairs. An exception were the Hambros, of Danish extraction, but Jews none the less, who were widely believed to be the Nordic descendants of Vikings.

Other foreign groups, though not as prominent and obvious as the Jews, were also well-represented. Just as the Rothschilds head the list of Jewish notabilities, so it is fitting that their great rivals, the originally Lutheran German-Danish Barings, ought to appear first among the other foreign groups. Baring millionaires included Thomas (1800-73) and John, 2nd Baron Revelstoke (1863-1929), who left £2.6 million; several others, like Sir Francis, 1st Bt. (1740-1810) appear among the half-millionaires or lesser wealthy. Their wealth, however, was not nearly so astonishing as that of the Rothschilds, and the great Baring Brothers crash of 1890 substantially reduced their fortunes, at least for a time: the first Baron Revelstoke, who died in 1897, left only £37,000, the Baring equivalent of begging in the streets. Yet the Baring impact on English society, whether in politics, colonial administration or as marriage partners for the older aristocracy, was probably considerably greater than the Rothschilds, doubtless because of the Barings'

Protestantism.

Several other notable merchant banking wealth-holders were also of German Lutheran extraction. Probably the most significant was William Henry Goschen (1793-1866), son of a publisher in Leipzig, and father of George Joachim Goschen, the famous late Victorian politician. He left £500,000. Wealthier were the Schroeders, who produced a multi-millionaire in Baron Sir John H.W. Schroeder, 1st Bt. (1825-1910). Frederick Huth (1777-1864), Alexander F.H. Kleinwort (1815-86) and Henry F. Tiarks (1832-1911), son of the Duchess of Kent's Lutheran chaplain, all half-millionaire merchant bankers, emerged from the same milieu.

An interesting and significant immigrant group among London's financial and commercial elite, to whom relatively little attention has previously been paid, are the Greeks. Like the Jews they profited from their international connections, often with the links provided by one family, in this case within the Levant and Middle East. Unlike the Jewish financiers, however, they were also engaged in mercantile activities like importing and trading as well as strictly financial pursuits, and they might with nearly equal justice have been assigned to the mercantile occupational categories. The best-known of these families were the Rallis, who are still prominent; others include the Vlastos and Corialegnos, to whom they were related. The title awarded to the multi-millionaire Sir Lucuis E. Ralli, 1st Bt. (1846-1931) illustrates their social acceptability. The final national group who might be mentioned are the Americans. Although George Peabody, because of his philanthropic activities, left just under £500,000 and cannot be included here, while the celebrated financiers Junius Spencer and his son John Pierrepont Morgan, who both left millionaire estates in England, are more properly considered Americans, Walter Hayes Burns (1838-97), J.P. Morgan's brother-in-law and the son of a New York dry goods merchant, lived and worked in London for decades and left £806,000. His daughter married 'Lulu' Harcourt.

Although as many as 18 of the merchant bankers were of British descent, even among these there were many with foreign connections. The Browns, of the famous firm of Brown, Shipley, were Scots-Irishmen who were merchants in Baltimore at the beginning of the nineteenth century, then cotton exporters in Liverpool and, later still, powers in the City. Sir William, 1st Bt. (1784-1864), left £900,000; several of his descendants were millionaires. Similarly the considerable fortunes of Michael George Herbert (1893-1932) and Sir Sidney Herbert, 1st Bt. (1890-1939), grandsons of Lord Herbert of Lea, were due as much to their American mother, a Rhode Island Gammell, as to their connections with Morgan, Grenfell. A number of merchant-banking wealth-holders were of Huguenot descent, although thoroughly Anglicised (and often Anglicans) after several centuries in Britain. The most famous of these was Rt. Hon. Henry Labouchere (1831-1912), the radical MP and editor of *Truth*, whose £550,000 fortune was largely the product of his Baring mother. Of similar descent was Francis C. LeMarchant (1843-1930), a millionaire with H.S. Lefevre & Co.

One of the very strangest of all business dynasties was that of the three Earls of Leven and Melville — respectively the 10th, 11th and 12th — who left vast fortunes at the turn of the century. Although of ancient lineage, they owned only 8,800 acres of land in the 1880s, and turned readily to London and to business life in an unusually direct way. That way was eased by the fact that the 9th Earl, who died in 1876, was married to the daughter of Samuel Thornton, the Evangelical banker. The 10th, 11th and 12th Earls were active full-time bankers in London, the 11th Earl, for instance — who left £1,220,000 in 1906 — being a partner in the American House of McCullough & Co. and later in Melville, Fickus & Co.[65] His son, the 12th Earl, who died in a hunting accident at the age of only 27, already had begun a career with Frederick Huth & Co., and left £670,000. The remaining merchant bankers — who are virtually all to be found below the millionaire level — who were of British descent present no clear pattern, although many had connections with Baring Bros. Among them were Charles Baring Young (1801-82), a Baring on his mother's side, and Charles Lloyd Norman (1833-89), Montagu Norman's father, a partner in Baring Bros. for nearly 40 years.

Politically, the merchant bankers present a contrasting and evolving picture. The mid-Victorian City was overwhelmingly Liberal, and among no grouping more so than the foreign bankers, with their need for cosmopolitan pacificism and their overwhelmingly foreign origins. Lionel de Rothschild, who left £2.7 million in 1879, was of course the first practising Jew to take his seat in the House of Commons, and of course he was a Liberal. Yet the attachment of this element to the Liberal party was never complete. Several Barings served as Conservative MPs, even relatively early in the century — the millionaire Thomas (d. 1873) in 1835-7 and 1844-73, for instance — and, perhaps more importantly, were strongly associated with Liberal Unionism and the drift to Conservatism during the last quarter of the century. Symbolically, millionaire Baron Ferdinand de Rothschild (d. 1898) was one of the original Liberal Unionist MPs; there were many others. By the late nineteenth century the City was as firmly Tory as it had been Liberal a generation before. A half-millionaire like the leading banker Henry H. Gibbs, first Baron Aldenham (1819-1907), Tory MP for the City of London in the early 1890s, father of the Vicary Gibbs who compiled the *Complete Peerage*, and leading member of the English Church Union, was highly representative of what the City had by then become. The Gibbses had originally become prosperous in the ignoble trade of guano — bird droppings from South America, used as fertiliser — and only later became notable and wealthy merchant bankers. By the First World War even so non-U a figure as Samuel Samuel (d. 1934), born in the East End, inevitably served as Tory, rather than Liberal MP for Wandsworth and Putney. Some Liberals remained, however. Most of these, like Samuel Montagu, 1st Baron Swaythling (d. 1911), were Jews who characteristically combined wealth with a social conscience. Yet they were a diminishing and, after 1918, irrelevant minority, as the City of London and the Conservative party became practically interchangeable terms.

In terms of their social origins, the merchant bankers were anything but 'self-made men'. Indeed, one often has the impression that a 'self-made' merchant banker would be one whose father was not a millionaire. This is, at first glance, rather paradoxical. The City has always been more genuinely open to new men, as many post-1945 examples prove, than perhaps any other sector of British business life; moreoever, in the case of the merchant bankers, a great many were immigrants. While these points are true, certain *caveats* are needed in their interpretation when considering the merchant bankers. Almost none of the immigrant merchant bankers were literally penniless when they moved to London, but were mainly the sons of established bankers abroad or, in the case of the Barings, of established cloth merchants in England. Since so many belonged to a small number of families, many were the sons and grandsons of those already very rich, like the later Rothschilds. Indeed, it is not possible to point to a single wealth-holding merchant banker who was, strictly speaking, a 'self-made man'. At best, some came from just above this level, from the lower end of the middle class. Lord Swaythling's father was a watchmaker and silversmith who left £12,000 in 1859; Samuel Samuel's a shell-and-curio shop proprietor in the East End who left £14,000 in 1870; the father of Henry F. Tiarks, as was noted, a Lutheran minister who left £8,000 in 1858. Yet in no single case, as far as can be ascertained, was there genuine poverty, a manual or low-clerical background. Such backgrounds were not uncommon among the City wealth-holders, but these were mainly found among the miscellaneous financiers and the merchants who could, on occasion, found an eminently lucrative business on little more than pluck and luck alone. For the peculiar world of the nineteenth-century merchant bank, with its vast web of international connections and necessarily profound knowledge of foreign conditions, its preeminently dignified and respectable aspect, and the astronomical sums with which it dealt, an established family network was, if not absolutely crucial, at least a great advantage, and few could realistically expect to establish this in a single generation.

Shipowning. The last occupational group we shall discuss here are the shipowners. They are a very numerous and powerful group, perhaps the epitome of nineteenth-century British commerce.[66] Like the merchant bankers, the wealthy shipowners differ in several material respects from the other wealth-holding groups we have studied. First and most obviously, they were to be found in seaports – and, disproportionately, in three or four of the greatest seaports, although a host of lesser ports were represented. In particular, Liverpool, with nine millionaire and 27 half-millionaire shipowners, is far in the lead, with Glasgow (four and 11), London (three and eight), West Hartlepool (two and two), and Hull (four half-millionaires) also well-represented. Seaports with one or two wealth-holders included not only the likes of St Ives, Whitby and Workington, Cumberland, but such great towns as Cardiff, Bristol and Middlesbrough. Cardiff, for instance, produced only two shipping wealth-holders, the millionaire Henry Radcliffe (1857-1921) and John Cory (1855-1931), a half-millionaire. It is more difficult to summarise concisely the world of shipping wealth in a Liverpool or Glasgow. There were, of course, numerous shipping dynasties – in Liverpool, the Ismays, Roydens, Bibbys, Brocklebanks, Bateses and Rankins, for instance, or in Glasgow the Burnses (Barons Inverclyde), Cayzers or Gardiners, or the Curries or Mackays (Earls of Inchcape) with wider regional interests, yet the majority of shipping wealth-holders, even in Liverpool or Glasgow, were one-man entrepreneurs whose families produced no other wealth-holders and are not particularly well-known, men like James H. Welsford (1863-1917) of Liverpool or Thomas Prentice (1856-1926) of Glasgow, half-millionaires who are typical of this type of shipowning wealth-holder.

Such men remind us that there are three characteristics which set the shipping wealth-holders apart from the other groups we have discussed. First is the relatively high rate of upward social mobility among these men, higher, in all likelihood, than among any of the groups we have discussed. To mention only some of the more striking examples of this, millionaire Sir Charles Cayzer 1st Bt. (1843-1916), of Clan Lines and Cayzer & Irvine, was the son of a schoolmaster in Limehouse who is unlisted in the probate returns; Walter Runciman, first Baron Runciman (1847-1937), the millionaire Chairman of Moor and Anchor lines and father of the namesake Cabinet minister, was the son of an employee of the Coast Guard service,[67] while half-millionaires James J. Welsford, Sir Thomas Sutherland (1834-1922) and John R. Harrison (1856-1923) were the sons, respectively, of a ship's steward, a house painter and a husbandman on a Cumberland farm. The most extraordinary instances of social mobility are, however, to be found among perhaps the three greatest names of all. Sir Samuel Cunard, 1st Bt. (1787-1865), founder of the famous firm which bears his name, was the son of a master carpenter of Philadelphia and Halifax, Nova Scotia. Sir Donald Currie (1825-1909), the great head of Castle Line and associate of Gladstone, who left £2,433,000, was the son of a Belfast perfumer and hairdresser who left £488; while the richest man of all, Sir John Ellerman, 1st Bt. (1863-1933) (who might equally well have been listed as a financier), was the son of a small corn merchant, who died when his son was nine years old, leaving £600. Many other similar examples can be found. Conversely, only a small minority were the sons of very wealthy men. Why was this? It seems that nineteenth-century shipping was one field where an entrepreneur could begin with one small vessel, carve out a special and prosperous route for merchandise or passengers, and with luck develop an immense fleet by discreet steps. The rough-hewn image of the nineteenth-century shipping magnate, made familiar by the 'Onedin Line' television series and similar portrayals, is not far removed from reality.

The second characteristic of the shipowners which sets them apart from many other groups is the very high percentage of Scotsmen, often of meagre background. These Scotsmen abounded not only in Glasgow and Edinburgh, but as internal migrants to Liverpool, London and abroad. Such great shipowners as Duncan Dunbar (1804-62), the earliest shipping millionaire, who was educated at Forres Grammar School and Marischal College, Aberdeen but who earned his fortune in London; Robert Rankin (1801-70), formerly of Mearus, Renfrewshire and later of Rankin, Gilmour of Liverpool; or James Lyle Mackay, 1st Earl of Inchcape (1852-1932), son of a small Arbroath shipowner whose business career began in Calcutta and whose immense world-wide interests saw him leave £552,000 in Britain and nearly £1.8 million in other parts of the Empire, are all examples of this. A significant number of other shipping wealth-holders originated in the extreme north of England – in border counties like Cumberland or the North Riding, and were often of Scottish descent.

The third characteristic of the shipping wealth-holders may appear paradoxical in view of these points. It was the great strides made by rich shipowners into the aristocracy and into titled and landed society. It is a commonplace view of late Victorian and Edwardian England that this was when foreign bankers, diamond magnates and newspaper lords finally arrived, in the Court society headed by the Prince of Wales. But it would be just as accurate to find an essential hallmark of the age in the gain of social respectability by rich shipowners. It was in Tranby Croft, the Yorkshire seat of Arthur Wilson, of the great Hull shipping dynasty, that the most famous of all the scandals involving the Prince of Wales took place, this time over the card table. The progress of the Wilson family towards social acceptability is symbolic of all shipping magnates. The father of Arthur Wilson (1837-1910) and his brother Charles H. Wilson, first Baron Nunburnholme (1833-1907), both half-millionaires, founded the firm only in the 1820s. By the late nineteenth century, it has grown into the largest private shipping firm in the world, with a capital value of £2.5 million. In 1871, Charles Wilson entered into what must be termed British new money's most astonishing marriage when he wed the niece of the great Duke of Wellington, the daughter of Wellington's youngest brother! Nunburnholme served as a Liberal MP for many years, remaining, curiously, a committed radical. Generally speaking, rich shipowners appear to have been decided winners in the marriage market. Sir William Nelson, 1st Bt (1851-1922), a Liverpool half-millionaire – and despite the fact that he was a Roman Catholic and the son of a man who had started life as a cattle salesman in Coldrinagh, Ireland – married his daughter to the second Duke of Westminster! There are a surprising number of such instances.

Similarly, a very striking percentage of wealthy shipowners acquired titles – occasionally peerages, but more typically baronetcies, which were lavished on them by the score. Inchcape acquired one of only two earldoms ever bestowed upon a businessman without notable political service (Iveagh, the brewer, was the other). Many, too, purchased sizable tracts of land, often long after it was strictly necessary for social acceptability. A half-millionaire Grimsby trawler owner named Sir George F. Sleight, 1st Bt. (1853-1921) – whose father was described in the 1871 Census as a 'fisherman', and who began life as a hawker of cockles – was at the time of his death probably the largest landowner in Lincolnshire.[68] Christopher Furness, first Baron Furness (1852-1912), the millionaire West Hartlepool shipowner, shipbuilder and Liberal MP, the seventh son of a grocer and provision merchant who had left £460, owned over 30,000 acres in northern England, was the patron of seven livings and the Lord of the Manor of Grantley, Yorkshire.[69] Again, many other such cases could be mentioned.

One reason for the relative success of the shipowners was their disproportionate Anglicanism (or, if Scots, Presbyterianism). Very few indeed were dissenters, although Lord Runciman was a devout Methodist, Charles W. Harrison (1854-1938), a millionaire Londoner, was the son of a dissenting minister and, most remarkably, there were even a number of Jewish shipping magnates, like John I. Jacobs (1856-1917), a London half-millionaire. The picture we have of a successful nineteenth-century shipowner is thus one of a pushing, rough-hewn, self-made man, but one likely to be Anglican or Presbyterian, and anxious to rise through thoroughly acceptable paths into social acceptability: a picture, of course, widely thought to be true of most nineteenth-century entrepreneurs but, as we have seen, untrue more often than not. Most wealthy shipowners were apolitical, but most who were partisan were likely to be Liberals. There was, however, a most notable shift towards Liberal Unionism among the wealthy shipowners during the 1880s, part of the generally disproportionate shift of commercial wealth towards Conservatism at this time, but also much as one might expect of men of this background as the Liberal party appeared to abandon its old individualism. Sir Donald Currie was one of the original Liberal Unionist MPs, despite his friendship with Gladstone, while such other notable magnates as Ralph Brocklebank (1803-92), Sir Edward Hain (1851-1917) and Thomas H. Ismay (1837-99) were known to have been staunch Liberal Unionists. It might finally be remarked that the wealthy British shipowners, in their typical characteristics, closely resemble the mercantile and pastoral pioneers of Australia;[70] it seems that this disproportionately Scottish, self-made, rather buccaneering type helped to build the Empire as well as trade overseas.

It is clear from the array of groups we have considered here that the very wealthy were not a homogeneous and unified whole, but demonstrated quite striking dissimilarities. Indeed, each of the occupational categories discussed here — as well as any of the others we might have analysed but did not do so in the space at hand — is unique with regard to the range of its social characteristics. This is true, too, not merely of occupational groupings, but of such other units as those defined by geography, social mobility, politics and religion. There is, in fact, only one thing and one thing only which linked the diverse men and groups in this chapter: their wealth. In all other respects, they are as variegated as any other set of 1,300 men.

From Old to New

There is another way of arranging the occupational categories of the wealthy which is also illuminating, and points to the ways in which secular changes in the economy affect the very wealthy. This consists of dividing the occupations of the wealthy into what might be termed 'old', 'intermediate' and 'new' trades, respectively those — very roughly — which became profitable before or during the Industrial Revolution, those which were profitable throughout the past two centuries and those which became profitable only during the past century. Much of the pattern disclosed by arranging the occupational categories in this way is not revealed until much later in the century than 1939; the cohorts of wealth-holders dying between 1940 and 1969 have not been brought into the discussion in the earlier part of this book, including this chapter, but they are discussed elsewhere.[71]

These divisions correspond, roughly, to the staple industries of the nineteenth century, plus landowning and finance in the case of the 'old' category, and to what may be termed the consumer-oriented trades, including large-scale retailing, among the 'new'. Between the cohorts deceased in the earlier part of the nineteenth century, and those deceased in the mid-twentieth century, the British wealth structure shifted strikingly from the 'old' to the 'new' trades.[72] For example, those classified among the 'new' trades accounted for about 13 per cent of all millionaire deaths in the years 1900-9, but for about 60 per cent of such deaths in 1960-9. The 'new' trades included such areas of business activity as food products like custard powder and soft drinks, electrical and other consumer goods, petroleum, newspapers and property development. Conversely, although the portion of wealthy landowners remains high, there is a marked decline in the number of older-style mercantile and financial fortunes, especially after the 1930s, for example among the bankers, stockbrokers, foreign merchants, shipowners and the like — groups which, as we have seen, were the very backbone of the nineteenth-century British wealth structure. Is this illusory, a statistical mirage produced by higher levels of estate duty avoidance and family settlements among those groups closer to the metropolitan sources of legal and financial advice in such matters? Has the 'managerial revolution' penetrated the City (and the older manufacturing trades) to a greater extent than elsewhere? Or is this a valid illustration of

Schumpeterian decline? Without a very great deal of private information about the men and families involved, it is difficult to say.[73] But it is obvious that technological change, alterations in patterns of consumer demand and preference, rising expectations and the replacement of men by machines, will all work to alter the structure of wealth. To the extent that this is so, the wealthy, no less than the poor, are the putty moulded by much larger and broader events.

The Geography of Wealth

If it was on the commercial or financial side of the Victorian business world that the great fortunes were disproportionately to be found, it would seem to be a corollary of this that the centre of wealth-making in nineteenth-century Britain was London and such commercial towns as Liverpool rather than the industrial towns of the north of England. This was indeed the case, although it would evidently be a gross over-simplification merely to identify London with commerce and the north with industry. Nevertheless, most top London fortunes were left by those in commerce or finance, while most of the northern fortunes — the rule here being considerably less hard and fast — were earned in manufacturing, despite the wealth of merchants in provincial trade centres like Liverpool, Glasgow and Leeds. Assigning each non-landed wealth-holder to the locality or conurbation in which his fortune was earned — where his bank, factory, mine or ships were located — a pattern of geographical distribution is indicated as favourable to London as the occupational distribution demonstrated the lead of commerce.[74] The results of this geographical classification of the wealth-holders are set out in Tables 3.11-3.13, which detail the number of millionaires, half-millionaires and lesser wealthy deceased in each geographical area by cohort.

The geographical distribution of wealth and income, particuarly the wealth and income of the elites, is a most important matter. For much of the nineteenth century it is, in my judgement, the central salient line of division in British society, rather than social class. So important is this matter, indeed, that I would prefer to defer the full discussion the subject deserves until my book on *Elites and the British Social Structure*, where it will serve as that work's central organising theme. Chiefly for that reason, the discussion here will be relatively brief. Despite the current academic fashionability of British local history and economic geography, there have been few works of

Table 3.11: Number of Millionaires, by Geographical Origin and Date of Death

Name	1809-58	1858-79	1880-99	1900-19	1920-39
1. City of London	4	14	11	34	34
2. Other London	1	2	9	13	24
3. Outer London			1	1	3
4. Greater Manchester		2	2	3	6
5. Merseyside		1	8	4	15
6. West Yorkshire		2	2	4	11
7. South Yorkshire					1
8. West Midlands			2	3	5
9. Tyneside		1	1	5	6
10. Clydeside		2	4	12	12
11. East Anglia		1	1		1
12. Bristol				6	6
13. South-west England			1		1
14. Other South England					
15. Ribblesdale	1		1		
16. Mid-Lancashire			1	1	
17. Notts-Derby-Belper	1	1	4	2	6
18. Other Midlands			2		2
19. South Wales	1	2	2	2	4
20. Teesside			1	1	4
21. Humberside				1	
22. Other North England					1
23. Edinburgh				1	3
24. Other Scotland		1			2
25. Belfast				1	1
26. Dublin		1			1
27. Other Ireland			1		
28. Nationwide		1	3	4	2
29. Foreign			2	1	5
				Unknown 1	

importance which treat geographical sectionalism as a factor in British local history and economic geography.[75] Yet the importance of sectionalism as a factor in British history is arguably as considerable an element in explaining the behaviour of men and groups during the past

Table 3.12: Number of Half-millionaires, by Geographical Origins and Date of Death

Name	1809-58	1858-79	1880-99	1900-19	1920-39
1. City of London	15	37	40	48	72
2. Other London	9	9	19	29	34
3. Outer London	1	1	3	4	6
4. Greater Manchester	1	11	15	16	21
5. Merseyside	2	10	8	24	25
6. West Yorkshire	2	4	3	15	21
7. South Yorkshire		3	3	6	5
8. West Midlands	2	2	3	5	14
9. Tyneside		3	7	17	16
10. Clydeside	1	6	11	17	28
11. East Anglia		1	2	3	4
12. Bristol	1	1	2	2	5
13. South-west England		1	3	2	5
14. Other South England			1		1
15. Ribblesdale	2		2	2	5
16. Mid-Lancashire			1	2	4
17. Notts-Derby-Belper		3	3	11	6
18. Other Midlands			6	4	5
19. South Wales	3	2		5	5
20. Teesside		2	2	3	2
21. Humberside				3	7
22. Other North England					4
23. Edinburgh			3	4	8
24. Other Scotland			2	6	4
25. Belfast			1	2	4
26. Dublin			1	3	
27. Other Ireland					
28. Nationwide		2	6	5	3
29. Foreign	6	1	10	13	24
Unknown	2	4	2	6	5

two centuries as class. For example, the advocates of electoral reform in 1830-2 were motivated perhaps as much by the desire to enfranchise the new towns of the north of England as by the desire to enfranchise the middle class. Virtually every reform or protest movement in

Table 3.13: Number of Lesser Wealthy, by Geographical Origins and Date of Death

Name	1809-29	1850-69
1. City of London	59	43
2. Other London	31	21
3. Outer London	2	1
4. Greater Manchester	6	14
4. Merseyside	2	5
6. West Yorkshire	2	
7. South Yorkshire		
8. West Midlands	4	4
9. Tyneside	2	3
10. Clydeside		3
11. East Anglia	4	1
12. Bristol	3	5
13. South-west England	3	1
14. Other South England		2
15. Ribblesdale		1
16. Mid-Lancashire		
17. Notts-Derby-Belper	3	7
18. Other Midlands	2	1
19. South Wales		1
20. Teesside		
21. Humberside		
22. Other North England		
23. Edinburgh		2
24. Other Scotland		
25. Belfast		
26. Dublin		
27. Other Ireland		
28. Nationwide		5
29. Foreign	14	10
Unknown	22	13

modern British history, as Donald Read demonstrates, from Wyvill in the 1780s to the Jarrow hunger marchers of the 1930s contained a strong sectional component — a region as well as a class may feel itself aggrieved.

That there are distinct and impressive regional differences in the venues of the wealth elites is evident from Tables 3.11-3.13. Among millionaires, London was the venue for between 39 per cent and 63 per cent of the total number in each cohort; among half-millionaires, for between 38 per cent and 64 per cent; while among the lesser wealthy London's lead was even clearer. The six conurbations making up the heart of industrial England in Lancashire and the West Riding accounted for no more than 25 per cent of the most favourable millionaire cohort, and for between 18 per cent and 27 per cent of the half-millionaire groups. As with the place of commerce in the occupational structure of wealth, London's lead, though less marked at the close of the nineteenth century, was never lost.

At the centre of London's wealth was the City, which was by itself in every period and at every level of wealth the single most important geographical unit, generally by several orders of magnitude over its nearest rival. Nearly all of the City wealth-holders were engaged in commerce: only five City millionaires, for example, cannot be readily assigned to a commercial Order among the SICs. Many of the City's wealth-holders obviously belonged to such celebrated financial and mercantile dynasties as the Rothschilds, Barings, Rallis, Sassoons, Gibbses, *et al.* But many others remain virtually unknown, and one important reason for the failure of economic historians to grasp the central importance of the City has been its relative neglect in business histories and industrial biographies. While everyone knows of the major figures of the Industrial Revolution, little attention has been paid to the careers of many of the City's wealthy men. Unnoticed are the vast, and typical City fortunes of such men as Richard Thornton (1776-1865), an insurance broker and Baltic merchant who boasted that his signature was 'good for three million' and left £2,800,000;[76] Hugh McCalmont (1809-87), a stockbroker and foreign merchant worth £3,122,000; and Giles Loder (1786-1871), a Russia merchant who left £2,900,000. Such men were among the very wealthiest in the country, wealthier by several dozen times than the majority of successful industrialists. G.K. Chesterton's shrewd observation that the wise man hides a pebble on a beach, a leaf in a forest, is perhaps best illustrated by the invisibility of many of the City's richest men.

London consisted of far more than the City, and its predominance in the British wealth structure was to a large extent the product of the variety and number of fortunes in its outlying districts. It is impossible to characterise these quickly. Brewing, retailing and shipping fortunes were the most numerous, including among them dynasties like the

Watneys and Charringtons, department-store owners like William Whiteley (1831-1907) and James Marshall (1806-93), art dealers like Sir Joseph J. Duveen (1843-1908) and shipowners like the Scruttons and Harrisons. Industrial fortunes were a minority, heavy industry represented by engineers and shipbuilders like John Penn (1805-78) of Greenwich, chemical manufacturers like Frank C. Hills (1808-92) and builders like Thomas Cubitt (1788-1855) and Edward Yates (1838-1907). Most of the remaining London wealth-holders were government placemen or London bankers.

Next to London, the most important conurbation was Greater Manchester. It included not only Manchester proper, but outlying industrial towns like Bolton, Bury and Oldham. Manchester will always remain a symbol and synonym for many things, from the doctrine of laissez-faire to the 'immizeration of the working class', but its importance as a centre of British wealth is simply belied by the available facts. This may seem difficult to credit, but − as we have seen − in the entire period between 1809 and 1914 only one Manchester cotton manufacturer left a millionaire estate, while only two others left fortunes in the half-millionaire class. Of all the Manchester wealth-holders deceased in the span of this study, only six were manufacturers or industrialists, while the remainder included seven cotton merchants, three bankers, a number of brewers and a newspaper proprietor. It is to the outlying towns of Greater Manchester that one must look to find the textile manufacturing and industrial fortunes in this conurbation. Such wealth was to be found in the smaller towns like Oldham, with its nine cotton-spinners and three machinery manufacturers among the wealth-holders, or among families like the Fieldens in Todmorden, the Peels in Blackburn or the Bulloughs in Accrington. In these smaller outlying towns, every wealth-holder without exception was a manufacturer or industrialist.

Liverpool, as the greatest of northern commercial cities, followed the London pattern in producing more wealth-holders than Manchester. Here only two of the local fortunes were earned in industry − both in soap manufacturing − and the bulk of Merseyside fortunes were earned by its foreign traders, shipowners and commodity merchants of various types. The West Yorkshire wealth-holders were mainly in the industrial SICs, among them such families as the Fosters, worsted manufacturers at the Black Dyke Mills and the Cunliffe-Listers (Barons Masham) silk-plush manufacturers. But the commercial life of the area was dominated by several old Anglican families based in Leeds, like the Fabers, Becketts and Oxleys.

Each of the remaining centres of wealth requires some comment. Until 1914 the West Midlands was relatively unimportant; its fortunes were mainly earned by ironmasters and colliery owners in the Black Country rather than by Birmingham men. On Tyneside the most lucrative sources of wealth were the coalfields of Durham and Northumberland and the engineering and shipping trades of Newcastle and Jarrow. Similarly, Clydeside rose to its leading place as a venue of wealth only among the cohorts deceased from 1880 onwards, on the basis of Glasgow's shipping and engineering, the nearby coal and iron seams and the sewing-thread families of Coats and Clark in Paisley. The situation in Bristol was unusual in that nearly all of its wealth-holders belonged to two families, the tobacco-manufacturing Willses and the Frys, the Quaker sweets manufacturers. There were virtually no fortunes here whose origins lay in the slaving and mercantile past of that town. Among the lesser towns and geographical areas, a considerable number of manufacturing and industrial fortunes were earned in much smaller localities, among families like the Claytons and Shuttleworths, the agricultural machinery manufacturers of Lincoln, the Arkwrights and Strutts in Derbyshire or the Patons and Thomsons, who made woollens in Alloa, Clackmannanshire. With the exception of East Anglia, where dissenters provided a number of local banking dynasties of great wealth, it was a rarity for a merchant or banker not trading in a large conurbation to accumulate a vast fortune, whilst in smaller towns the leading manufacturer was likely to be its wealthiest man.

The key question which must be asked of the occupational and geographical distributions outlined above is whether they were characteristic only of the very rich, or whether they were indicative of a more basic division within the whole of Victorian middle-class society. It will be here contended that the geographical and, by implication, occupational statistics offered here are the tip of an iceberg, very similar below the surface to the visible portion.

It is here that the Income Tax statistics, whose importance was discussed in Chapter 1, are most helpful. Among the remarkable returns in the Parliamentary Papers or in manuscript at the Public Record Office are several which touch directly on the question of the geographical distribution of business and professional incomes assessed under Schedule D of the Income Tax. Perhaps the two most relevant which might be discussed briefly here[77] are, first, the county breakdown of Schedule D assessments in 1812[78] and, second, the listing of assessments under Schedules A, B, D and E in each parliamentary constituency in the United Kingdom in 1879-80, which was printed in the

Parliamentary Papers in April 1882.[79] A comparison of these sources demonstrates the lead of London over the rest of the country among the middle class as a whole, a lead which persisted despite the growth of the new industrial towns.

In 1812, out of a total of £34.4 million assessed under Schedule D in the whole of Great Britain, £13.3 million, or 38.8 per cent of the national total, was assessed in London, Westminster or Middlesex. In contrast no more than £4,046,000, or 11.8 per cent of the national total, was assessed in the six industrial counties of Lancashire, Yorkshire, Warwickshire, Staffordshire, Northumberland and Glamorgan. The place of London in these figures, moreover, is almost certainly *understated* in several important ways: the assessment under Schedule D of £3.9 million, or 11.3 per cent of the national total, in the Home Counties of Essex, Kent and Surrey belonged for the most part, evidently, to industries located within the future municipal boundaries of London, or to London businessmen living and paying their taxes there. This alone is sufficient to bring the London total to just under half of the national total assessed under Schedule D.

It is probably not surprising that more than half of Britain's middle class income in 1812 should be the income of Londoners. What is perhaps more surprising is that the lead of London over Britain's other major urban areas persisted throughout the nineteenth century. In 1879-80, the 28 largest provincial towns – those with populations in excess of 100,000, whose combined population was 5,580,000 – were assessed under Schedule D for £78.7 million, while the ten London boroughs, whose population totalled 3,333,000, were assessed for £87.7 million.[80] The place of commercial as opposed to manufacturing wealth at this time may be seen more clearly, if the provincial trading centres like Liverpool – assessed at £11.0 million, more than any provincial city, including Manchester at £9,809,000 – Bristol, Edinburgh and Dublin, are considered apart from the manufacturing towns. There is of course no definite distinction between commercial and industrial towns, but were the predominantly commercial towns excluded, it seems likely that the assessment of the major provincial towns would be decreased by approximately three-sevenths. Moreover, as with the 1812 data, exclusive reliance on Schedule D excludes much other middle-class income assessed under Schedules A, C and E, and found more frequently in London than in the provincial towns. The amount assessed under Schedule E in 1879-80, for instance, *apart from* public office-holders (including the military and naval forces) was £5,934,000 among the ten London boroughs and £4,788,000 in

the 28 leading provincial towns. These totals would largely have
consisted of the income of limited business corporations and their
employees, as well as of non-business corporations such as churches.[81]

London's place among the leading British towns in 1879-80 was the
more remarkable since the provincial cities examined here were in 1881
67 per cent more populous than the ten London boroughs. Thus it
seems a plausible inference not merely that London possessed a larger
total business income than all of the chief provincial towns combined
but that its middle class was richer *per capita* and almost certainly more
numerous than in the provincial towns. The expansion of Britain's
industrial base in the post-Napoleonic War period made London relatively
less important in the wealth structure than it had been, but it still
remained considerably wealthier than the remainder of Britain's leading
towns combined. The assessment of the City of London in 1879-80
(£41,237,000) was twice that of Manchester and Liverpool combined.
And although it would be quite fallacious to infer more than a cautious
minimum concerning the occupational distribution of middle class
Londoners from the bald figures for their taxable incomes, it can with
considerable truth be asserted that where there was commerce, finance
or trade, money was made more readily than where there was manufacturing or industry. Standing above everything else there was London,
the fixed point around which the Victorian middle classes revolved.

Notes

1. *Standard Industrial Classification* (London, HM Stationery Office, 1958).
A subsequent revision of the 1958 Classification was made in 1973. This is not, in
my opinion, an improvement, and the 1958 system forms the basis of the analysis
here.
2. See B.R. Mitchell and Phyllis Deane, *Abstract of British Historical
Statistics* (Cambridge, 1971), Chapter II, esp. pp. 55-61, 73-4.
3. Ibid; see also Phyllis Deane and W.A. Cole, *British Economic Growth,
1688-1959* (Cambridge, 1969).
4. *Standard Industrial Classification*, p. 1.
5. The 24 Orders are: I. Agriculture, Forestry and Fishing; II. Mining and
Quarrying; III. Food, Drink and Tobacco; IV. Chemicals and Allied Industries;
V. Metal Manufactures; VI. Engineering and Electrical Goods; VII. Shipbuilding;
VIII. Vehicles; IX. Other Metal Goods; X. Textiles; XI. Leather and Fur;
XII. Clothing and Footwear; XIII. Bricks, Pottery, Glass, Cement, etc.; XIV. Timber,
Furniture, etc.; XV. Paper, Printing and Publishing; XVI. Other Manufactured
Goods; XVII. Construction and Civil Engineering; XVIII. Gas, Electricity and
Water; XIX. Transport and Communications; XX. Distribution; XXI. Insurance,
Banking and Finance; XXII. Professional and Scientific Services;
XXIII. Miscellaneous Services; XXIV. Public Administration and Defence.
6. The chief drawbacks of the S.I.C.s as they stand are the classification of

publishers of all kinds together with paper manufacturers in Order XV and the lack of a historical dimension in several categories, for instance Order VIII – to take an extreme case – under which coach-builders and manufacturers of aeroplanes would be classified as the makers of 'vehicles'. Some of the other more all-encompassing categories, for instance Order X – textiles, have been subdivided in a more usable fashion.

7. Though, naturally, if a wealth-holder genuinely earned his fortune through a professional career, he was assigned to it, e.g., Lord Eldon (d. 1838) the Lord Chancellor, who earned his £707,000 from the law.

8. What, for the purposes of this work, is a landowner? He is one whose family's income was wholly or chiefly derived from the land for at least three generations. All wealth-holders whose family had been in trade or the professions within the last three generations are counted with the appropriate non-landed occupational category. In the great majority of cases, there is no doubt that a landowner was indeed a proper landowner – for instance with eighth dukes, seventh earls or tenth baronets.

9. The periodisation here is slightly different from that employed elsewhere in this chapter, counting the period from 1809 until January 1858 as one cohort. This coincides with the replacement of the Ecclesiastical Courts with the secular probate registry.

The reasoning behind these figures is as follows: the total number of landowners possessing a fortune in landed wealth of £500,000 or more was clearly considerably greater than the number leaving estates of this size in the probate calendars. To estimate even in an approximate fashion their true numbers it is necessary first of all to make use of the figures for gross annual rental in Bateman's *Great Landowners*. It is necessary to ascertain the total valuation of the landowner's realty in terms of a multiplier of his Bateman income. This figure, that for 1883, would have varied over time, rising in the periods 1809-15 and 1837-79, and declining in the intervening period and after 1879. Equally obviously, the acreages in Bateman would have varied over time as the size of the landed holding of each owner altered. The trouble here is that there are no comprehensive figures for such changes in the acreages of landowners, and any estimate such as that attempted here cannot fully take this element into consideration. Nevertheless, if certain assumptions are granted, the global number of very wealthy landowners can be estimated in at least a preliminary way. These are:

(1) That the 'multiplier' of gross annual income to total landed wealth be taken as 33 for the periods 1809-15 and 1837-79, and 20 at other times.
(2) In the absence of any comprehensive date, the acreage given in Bateman be taken as holding continuously throughout the entire period 1809-26. (Clearly this is less true for the last years of the period in question, 1918-25, than previously.)
(3) That during the period 1898-1925 when both personalty and unsettled realty were included in the probate valuations it is assured that 20 per cent of the total number of wealthy landowners then deceased left their landed property in an unsettled form, and was hence counted in the calendar valuation. (See Arthur Arnold, *Free Land* (London, 1880), p. 26, cited in F.M.L. Thompson, *English Landed Society in the Nineteenth Century* (London, 1963), p. 67.)

The next step is to determine a minimum Bateman gross annual rental which, multiplied by 33 or by 20, would bring that landowner into the millionaire or half-millionaire class. This would have varied during the periods of high and low landed income, viz:

	Millionaire £	Half-millionaire £
High income (1809-15, 1837-79)	30,000+	15,000-30,000
Low income (1815-37, 1880-1925)	50,000+	25,000-50,000

(E.g., £30,000 in the upper left-hand box multiplied by 33 equals £1 million.)

According to Bateman, the total number of incomes in each class was:

30,000+	15,000-30,000
161	225
50,000+	25,000-50,000
66	210

Assuming, as most economists did, that one-thirtieth of the total number of wealthy landowners died each year, during each of the periods of high and low rental, and change in the probate law, the number of wealthy landowners deceased was as follows:

	1809-15	1815-37	1837-79	1880-97	1898-1925
Millionaires	32	48	225	36	62(-20%= 50)
Half-millionaires	45	145	315	126	196(-20%=157)

Two further amplifications remain. First the figures above must be rearranged by the periodisation adopted throughout this work: and second, from these figures must be subtracted the number of landowners who do appear in the probate calendars as wealth-holders of personalty or unsettled realty. In the figures below, the number in brackets represents that when both these steps have been taken and the probate calendar landed millionaires are subtracted:

	1809-58	1858-79	1880-99	1900-19	1920-5
Millionaires	181(179)	117(114)	38(28)	34(14)	11(5)
Half-millionaires	349(338)	165(149)	137(122)	106(78)	34(25)

These figures, it cannot be emphasised too strongly, are extremely tentative global estimates. The exactness of the numbers lends a spurious air of certainty to them. However, if Bateman is accurate — and it is — one could be surprised if these figures were very wrong.

Finally, it must be pointed out that these are the figures for wealthy landowners' lands, and do not take into account their personal holdings or, on the other hand, their debts.

10. See W.D. Rubinstein, 'Wealth, Elites and the Class Structure of Modern Britain', *Past & Present* (76) 1977 and 'The Victorian Middle Classes: Wealth, Occupation and Geography', *Econ. Hist. Rev.*, 2nd ser., XXX (1977).

11. For those who think this claim overstated, I can only state here that this topic will be explored by me in a future book. For the purposes of this and other chapters in this book, it is sufficient merely to dissect the wealthy alone to see what this meant for them.

12. C.H. Timperley, *A Dictionary of Printers and Printing* (London, 1839), p. 918.

13. *The Times*, 8 April 1901; *Dictionary of National Biography Supplement*.

14. Deane and Cole, *British Economic Growth*, Table 37, p. 166.

15. Mitchell and Deane, *Abstract of British Historical Statistics*, p. 60.

16. E.g., Chapter 6 of *The Eighteenth Brumaire of Louis Bonaparte* in Karl Marx and Friedrich Engels, *Selected Works in One Volume* (London, 1968) Ch. 11, pp. 150-65.

17. George Lichtheim, *Marxism, A Historical and Critical Study* (London 1961), Pt 4, Chapter 3, 'Bourgeois Society', esp. pp. 155-9.

18. Very few wealth-holders earned their fortunes in 'immoral' trades, such as slave-trading or plantation-owning based on slavery. Most of these were at the 'lesser wealthy' level. Three exceptions were Henry Davidson (1771-1827), a West India merchant and plantation owner who left £500,000, David Lyon (1754-1827), Jamaica merchant and planter, who left £600,000 and James Ewing (1775-1853), West India merchant and later banker in Glasgow, who left £500,000. No English millionaire ever made his money from the slave trade or the employment of slaves.

19. *Gentleman's Magazine*, 8 December 1818, p. 644.

20. J. Boase, *Modern English Biography* (Truro, 1901).

21. Information supplied to me by the Clerk to the Clothworker's Company, London (June, 1973).

22. 'Colliery owners' as the term is used here, exclude virtually all landowners who, incidentally, received coal mining royalties (e.g., Lord Londonderry). A 'colliery owner' in our sense received the bulk of his income from his coal mining enterprises. Very few owned any land at all, apart from what they acquired after they had become wealthy.

23. In addition, there was one woman colliery millionaire, Miss Emily M. Easton (1818-1913), sister of the half-millionaire John Easton (1803-80), of Nest House, County Durham and Layton Manor, N.R.

24. *The Dictionary of Welsh Biography Down to 1940* (London, 1959), p. 1146.

25. One of the few significant facts to come to light in the obituaries of Fyfe-Jamieson was that he was a classmate of Stanley Baldwin's at Harrow!

26. Rhondda's peerage was essentially for his political services. He was a long-serving Liberal MP.

27. Among the millionaires, Joseph Love (d. 1875), a Methodist, and Edward Davies (d. 1898), a Calvinistic Methodist; among the half-millionaires, Joseph Evans (d. 1889) of Prescot, Lancashire, a Congregationalist, and J.H. Love (d. 1935) Joseph Love's son.

28. *The Times*, 7 August 1916.

29. *The Times*, 28 August 1914.

30. *Durham Advertiser*, 26 February 1875.

31. *Dictionary of National Biography*; Boase, *Modern English Biography*.

32. *The Times*, 23 September 1913; *Burke's Landed Gentry, 1937 ed.; Directory of Directors.*

33. *Complete Peerage, Supplementary Volume.*

34. 'The Story of James Crossley Eno', *Beecham Group Magazine, c.* 1965; source provided by Beecham Group Ltd. (January 1973).

35. Cooper was also a leading stock-breeder and 'practically erected Frinton-on-Sea'. (*The Times* 4 August 1913.)

36. N. Dews, *History of Deptford* (1893).

37. He left £250,000. On the family, see Barbara Kerr, 'The Beaufoys of Lambeth', *History Today*, xxiii (1973).

38. A nephew who became managing director of J. & J. White, William J. Chrystal (1854-1921), left £1,139,000. I did not succeed in tracing his original

religion.

39. Stephen E. Koss, *Sir John Brunner, 1842-1919: Radical Plutocrat* (Cambridge, 1970).

40. *The Times*, 29 December 1930.

41. E.J. Hobsbawm, *Industry and Empire* (London, 1969), p. 56.

42, There was one woman millionaire among cotton manufacturers, Mrs Enriquetta Rylands (d. 1904) the third wife and widow of John Rylands, the cotton multi-millionaire. She left £3,607,000, the largest fortune left by a British woman before the 1950s. It was she who erected the famous Rylands Library in Manchester.

43. The millionaire was Edward R. Langworthy (1796-1874), who served as Mayor of Salford in 1848-9 and 1850-1 and left £1,200,000. Langworthy was born in Chiswick, of all places, the son of a London merchant in the packing trade. He also spent some time in South America at the beginning of his career.

44. They were: Thomas Worthington (d. 1839) (whose estate was almost certainly worth far less than £700,000; this matter was discussed in a previous chapter); Thomas Ashton (1818-98) - there were no Manchester cotton half-millionaires in the 60-year interim − and John E. Prestwich (1848-1932).

45. On this see V.A.C. Gatrell, 'Labour, Power and the Size of Firms in Lancashire Cotton in the Second Quarter of the Nineteenth Century', *Econ. Hist. Rev.*, 2nd ser., XXX (1977).

46. Richard Arkwright was the son of Sir Richard Arkwright (1732-92), inventor of the spinning frame, who is said to have left £500,000, though prior to the start of this study.

47. Arkwright and a number of other early cotton entrepreneurs also acquired much land, which was unusual for nineteenth-century entrepreneurs. (This topic is further explored in the chapter below on landowning.) On the purchase of land by the Arkwrights see E.L. Jones, 'Industrial Capital and Landed Investment. the Arkwrights in Herefordshire, 1809-43' in E.L. Jones and G.E. Mingay, (eds.), *Land, Labour and Population in the Industrial Revolution* (London, 1967).

48. On the wealth of the typical industrial entrepreneur, see W.D. Rubinstein in *Econ. Hist. Rev.* and *Past and Present*. It *seems* as if the typical successful cotton manufacturer left about £100,000.

49. Chris Cook and Brendan Keith, *British Historical Facts, 1830-1900* (London, 1975), p. 253.

50. The millionaire Coatses, besides those noted above, were Archibald (1840-1912), James (1841-1912), Peter (1842-1913), Sir James, 1st Bt. (1834-1913), Sir Thomas Glen-Coats, 1st Bt. (1846-1922), Daniel (1844-1922), William Hodgson (1866-1928) and Andrew (1862-1930).

51. Kenneth Clark, *Another Part of the Woods* (London, 1974) p. 1. His parents 'took no part in public affairs, did not read the newspapers and were almost entirely without the upper-class feeling of responsibility for their tenants. My father gave so little time to his business interests that in the end he lost more than half his fortune'. (Ibid.)

52. John Foster, *Class Struggle and the Industrial Revolution* (London, 1974).

53. Ibid., p. 12.

54. Stanley Chapman, *The Early Factory Masters* (Newton Abbot, 1967), p. 91.

55. Boase, *Modern English Biography*.

56. *Dictionary of National Biography*.

57. But some of the brewing dynasties occasionally cited as Quakers had never been anything but Anglicans, e.g., the Grettons.

58. Boase, *Modern English Biography*.

59. *The Times*, 23 February 1915.

60. *Nottingham Evening News*, 11 March 1929.

61. This total does not include several foreign Rothschilds leaving immense estates in Britain, nor several of their close relatives (like Lord Rosebery) who left millionaire estates, nor several who have left fortunes since. The other millionaire Rothschilds were Baron Mayer (1818-74), Sir Anthony 1st Bt. (1810-76), Lionel (1808-79), Baron Ferdinand (1839-98), Alfred Charles (1842-1918), Leopold (1845-1917), Nathaniel, 1st Baron Rothschild (1840-1915), Hon. Nathaniel (1877-1923), Miss Alice (d. 1922) and Baroness Emma (1844-1935).

62. *The Times.* 18 April 1933.

63. Paul H. Emden, *The Jews of Britain* (London, n.d. [1942]), p. 543.

64. This Samuel is the millionaire Samuel Samuel (1855-1934), who headed M. Samuel & Co. (now Hill Samuel). He was the brother of Marcus Samuel, first Viscount Bearsted (1853-1927), who founded Shell Petroleum and left £4 million. They are not to be confused with, e.g., the family of Herbert Samuel the politician, some of whom changed their names to Montagu. *They* headed Samuel Montagu & Co. A certain genealogical skill is required here; when in doubt, consult Chaim Bermant, *The Cousinhood* (London, 1970).

65. *The Times*, 23 August 1906.

66. There was one woman shipping millionaire, Dame Fanny Houston (1857-1936) widow of Sir Robert P. Houston, 1st Bt. (1853-1926), a millionaire shipowner who escaped death duties by moving to Jersey. Dame Fanny – who had previously been married to Sir Theodore Brinckman and the 9th Lord Byron – made a free gift of £1.5 million to the British Treasury in 1926 in lieu of death duties on her husband's estate; she still managed to leave more than £1.5 million. On her remarkable career, see Alan Jenkins, *The Rich Rich* (London, 1977).

67. *The Times* obituary notes the 'working-class conditions of his early days' (*The Times*, 14 August 1937). See also his autobiography *Before the Mast and After*.

68. *The Times*, 19 March 1921.

69. *The Times*, 11 November 1912; *Dictionary of National Biography Supplement*.

70. See W.D. Rubinstein, 'Top Wealth-holders of New South Wales, 1817-1939', *Australian Economic History Review* (1980).

71. W.D. Rubinstein, 'Men of Property: Some Aspects of Occupation, Inheritance, and Power among Top British wealthholders' in Philip Stanworth and Anthony Giddens (eds.), *Elites and Power in British Society* (Cambridge [1974]), pp. 148-54.

72. There are detailed occupational and cohort tables in ibid., pp. 149-53.

73. Some of these themes will be discussed further in the chapters on wealth-holders as businessmen and on post-1945 wealth.

74. I have been guided in this division of Britain into geographical units by T.W. Freeman's *The Conurbations of Great Britain* (Manchester, 1959). Most of these divisions are self-explanatory, but some require comment. 'Other London' corresponds to the LCC, (excluding as the LCC did, the City of London). 'Outer London' includes such towns in Essex or Berkshire as Bocking and Reading. 'Clydeside' includes the mineral fields of Lanarkshire, Renfrewshire and Ayrshire, as well as Greenock. 'Mid-Lancashire' chiefly consists of Wigan and St Helens and the surrounding mineral areas. 'Ribblesdale' comprises Preston, Accrington, Blackburn and Burnley. 'Nottingham-Derby-Burton' also includes the outlying mineral deposits and local cotton works.

As with the assignment of wealth-holders by occupation, much in these tables is necessarily arbitrary. Nevertheless, in the great majority of cases there can be no question of a wealth-holder's proper venue – a Rothschild

belongs to the City, Sir Charles Tennant to Glasgow, for instance.
Several types of wealth-holders however, could not be assigned to a particular
locality and hence are *excluded* from these tables, most notably foreign
merchants trading abroad, multiple retailers with branches in various towns and
contractors and builders not exclusively in local trade. Thus the number of
wealth-holders in Tables 3.11-3.13 is lower than in the discussion of occupation.
Landowners are also *excluded* from these tables.

There is a time-honoured pattern whereby a family begins in a small way in
the provinces and then transfers its business to London as it expands. With few
exceptions this is not reflected in the data here. Most families experiencing this
pattern had moved to London at least a generation before they produced a
wealth-holder; their wealth-holders were Londoners maintaining few if any links
with their place of origin.

Previous research on the geographical distribution of personal wealth or
income in Britain is remarkably sparse. E.J. Buckatzsch, 'The Geographical
Distribution of Wealth in England, 1086-1843', *Econ. Hist. Rev.*, 2nd Ser., III
(1950-1), used only Schedule A (the tax on rents) of the Income Tax for the
nineteenth century. A.D.M. Phillips and J.R. Walton, 'The Distribution of
Personal Wealth in English Towns in the Mid-nineteenth Century', *Transactions
of the Institute of British Geographers*, 2nd ser., LXIV (1975) employs the
Assessed Taxes to reach, broadly, the same conclusions as here. See also
W.D. Rubinstein, 'Victorian Middle Classes'.

75. Perhaps the only work devoted to sectionalism as a persistent theme
in modern British history is Donald Read's *The English Provinces, c. 1760-1960,
A Study in Influence* (London, 1964). See also H.J. Dyos, 'Great and Greater
London: Notes on Metropolis and Provinces in the Nineteenth and Twentieth
Centuries', in J. Bromley and E.H. Kossman, (eds.), *Britain and the Netherlands*
(The Hague, 1971), pp. 89-112.

76. See W.G. Hoskins, 'Richard Thornton: A Victorian Millionaire', *History
Today* (1962), p. 578. Professor Hoskins discovered Thornton and his immense
estate 'by pure chance in the official index of wills [at Somerset House], for
1865, while looking for an impecunious artist'.

77. There is a fuller discussion in W.D. Rubinstein, 'Victorian Middle Classes',
pp. 617-19.

78. P.P. 1814-15, X, 'Account of Duties Arising From Profits'.

79. P.P. 1882, LLI, 'Parliamentary Constituencies (Population)'.

80. Ibid.

81. It is, unfortunately, not possible to establish the geographical
distribution of public office-holders assessed under Schedule D, but this would
plainly add still further to the lead of London. The 1882 Parliamentary return
only details (at the end of each country division) a global figure for all such
office-holders. For England and Wales this amounted to £14 million; for
Scotland, to £292,000; for Ireland, to £896,000.

4 SOCIAL MOBILITY AND INHERITANCE

Going Up

In this chapter, two related topics will be treated. First, the social origins of all British wealth-holders will be traced, with particular emphasis on identifying the instances and frequency of 'self-made men' among all non-landed wealth-holders. In the second part, the subsequent history of the great fortunes, after the death of the wealth-holders themselves, will be discussed, and the chief patterns of inheritance among the wealth-holders' heirs and descendants will be ascertained. It must be noted that landowners are excluded from either part of the discussion, although the sons of landowners or farmers whose wealth was earned in a non-landed field will be included.

The probate material is ideally suited to the study of intergenerational social mobility, and it is no coincidence that both of the previous researchers who notably employed this material have centred chiefly on this topic.[1] The probate data is well-suited to this topic for several main reasons. First, the universe of the wealthy – those whose origins are to be traced – is known in an objective and comprehensive manner, and thus is less open to criticism than any list of, for example, famous businessmen,[2] or men who appear in *Burke's Landed Gentry*, where the vagaries of editorial choice invariably affect the accuracy of the list's intentions. Among such lists, the less famous businessmen, or the less well-known sections of the landed gentry, are apt to be ignored. Second and more importantly, one can compare this (objectively-defined) list of wealthy men with the social status of the fathers of each, taking as the basis of one's comparison either the valuation of the estate of the father, or the father's occupational or place in the social hierarchy. The former type of comparison was employed by the two previous researchers in this field. For an accurate and full assessment of the social origins of an individual probably both types of information are necessary. Occupational definitions are frequently ambiguous or misleading by themselves: there are vast differences in wealth between a successful and unsuccessful 'merchant' or 'manufacturer', and conversely there are some occupations, for instance Anglican clergymen, whose members often possess very little wealth or income but undoubtedly high status and standing in the community.

To reach the ideal and include information on both the wealth and occupation of the father is in practice very difficult. In particular, it is often virtually impossible without the most laborious of searches to trace the date of death of the father, the *sine qua non* of ascertaining his valuation.[3] By and large, information on the occupation or social status of the father is much more readily available, either in the son's obituary or from official birth certificates and marriage licences. Alternatively, high status and at least middle-class standing may be inferred from the son's attendance at a public school or university, or from such biographical data as the fact that the father was a Justice of the Peace or Deputy-Lieutenant.[4]

In this study, involving many hundreds of individual names, data on both wealth and occupation of the father could be compiled only for the millionaires. For the half-millionaires and the lesser wealthy, comprehensive data was compiled only for the father's occupation, although wherever the father's date of death was known his valuation was also traced.[5] Among the half-millionaires, valuations were traced for approximately 60 per cent of the fathers. Among the lesser wealthy this figure is far lower, both because many fathers died prior to 1809 and because there is far less biographical information on these figures.[6]

There are two central aims of any exercise in the tracing of social origins, particularly where the criteria for determining the parameters of the study are frankly based, as here, on wealth. First, we wish to determine the extent to which wealth tends to reproduce itself. Second, and this is not quite the converse, we wish to learn the extent of upward social mobility and especially the instances of 'self-made men'. The first part of this exercise is much easier than the second, and important aspects of the topic will be treated in the latter part of this chapter. The second important aspect of this topic, the tracing of upward social mobility, is far more difficult and riddled with a number of major pitfalls which the researcher must keep carefully before him.[7]

First, there is in general a lack of accurate biographical information on 'self-made men' or, stated perhaps more carefully, it is invariably easier to trace those men whose origins were wealthy, affluent or merely comfortable, than to trace those who began poor. Clearly, all those whose fathers were titled, well-known members of the landed gentry, occupants of high positions in the professional world such as bishops or judges or were otherwise eminent, present no problem to the researcher. The same applies, though with considerably less force, to the sons of businessmen, who would typically be listed in the local directories and (at least after the mid-nineteenth century), in newspaper obituaries. For the sons of the poor, however, there are no such sources, and the researcher must fall back on the official documents — birth certificates and marriage licences, or census data — or on accounts of the wealth-holder's career in obituaries, all of which present problems of interpretation.[8]

Second, this chapter offers a comparison of father and son. Wherever a likely non-paternal source of wealth is known, most typically from either grandfather[9] or the father-in-law, this has been noted in the data below, but such a list can hardly exhaust all the possible sources of legacy. In the great majority of cases, however, there is little question but that the father's wealth and occupation was the key, and probably the exclusive element in any inheritance coming to the son. Since the discussion focuses on inheritance from father (or other relative) to son, in this treatment of social mobility those wealth-holders who 'married the boss's daughter' or rose through some element of luck or chance rather than through strict ability alone, are also included as instance of self-made men. This can be made clear in the discussion, but the ambiguity of classifying such cases remains.

Furthermore, and more importantly, the criteria for accurately terming a wealth-holder 'self-made' are inherently ambiguous and alter with the changing structure of Britain's economy and national income since the Industrial Revolution. There is no clear-cut definition of a 'self-made man', even in the popular mind. The term seems to be used both for those who rise from poverty to wealth, and also for those who rise in a field in which they had no previous family connections or contacts. These two uses of the term are evidently quite different, the former implying a greater degree of mobility than the latter. In terms of wealth and occupation in the present study, probably it would be generally agreed that those men whose parents were working class, or who knew poverty in their early years, could fairly be termed 'self-made men'. Conversely, no one could claim that a man whose father left, say, £100,000 could be 'self-made'. The ambiguity arises in determining where to draw the line between the clear-cut instances of working-class and solid middle-class (or higher) origin. There is a grey area between these two classes, including within it the sons of shop-keepers, farmers, clerical, service and lower professional workers — clergymen, particularly dissenting clergymen, schoolteachers, commercial travellers, bank clerks and the like — who probably until 1914 earned between £100 and at most £400 per annum and who typically left estates between £1,000 and £10,000.[10] The millionaire sons of such men may or may not be properly accounted as 'self-made'. To leave a fortune of £1 million starting from scratch in the nineteenth century was an astonishing achievement. It was the equivalent of saving £25,000 per year for 30 years at rates of interest prevailing during much of the nineteenth century, at a time when a country doctor considered himself well-paid on £500 a year,[11] a level of saving exclusive of consumption or expenditures (other than expenditure on freeholds, consumer durables or luxury items like works of art which would be included in the probate valuation or, of course, on reinvestment in one's business or in other shares), exclusive of the effect of trade recessions which might in the space of a few months wipe out the gains of twenty years, or of charity, *inter vivos* gifts or estate duty avoidance. Given the class barriers which undoubtedly existed after the early nineteenth century,[12] for even a single individual to rise from working class to wealth-holder in the course of one working lifetime is so phenomenal as almost to strain credence, and to rise even from the lower part of the middle class is a remarkable feat. Yet there are several dozen apparently well-verified examples of just such an extraordinary feat. Perhaps the central biographical question, then, is what the father (or other relative) leaves to the son, either in the form of a legacy, or allowance or gift before death, or in the form of elite educational opportunities, purchase of commission or apprenticeship, or partnership in the family firm or entrée into another. A father from the lower-middle class who dies young, leaving many children and large debts, may well have left his son nothing beyond his good name, even where his estate valuation amounts to several thousand pounds.[13]

There is in addition a wider dimension of this question, namely how the figures of probate valuation or occupation should be interpreted in the light of the distribution of wealth in British society. Prior to the Estate Duty Act of 1894 there are, so far as I am aware, only two tables in the Parliamentary Papers detailing the number of estates probated at each level of wealth. One has been set out in Chapter 2; the other, and much less useful one, which appeared in the Parliamentary Papers for 1843, listed the 'Total Number of Wills and Extracts [sic] of Administration Sent to the Legacy Duty Office' in 1839.[14] Combining the data in this table for London and provincial probates, and for wills and administrations, the total number of probates at each level of wealth in 1839 is set out in Table 4.1.

It will be noted that there is no data here for those estates valued at between zero and £20. In 1839 there were 182,000 male deaths and 177,000 female deaths in England and Wales,[15] of which perhaps two-fifths were deaths of minors. Even if only a small percentage of all estate-leavers were women — perhaps 20 per cent — it is clear — as we

Table 4.1: Number of Estates at Each Level of Wealth, 1839

Amount (£)	Number	Percentage
20-100	4,941	23.3
Under 200	3,206	
Under 300	1,862	
Under 450	1,844	50.3
Under 600	1,443	
Under 800	1,233	
Under 1000	1,057	
Over 1000	5,596	26.4

saw in Chapter 2 — that in 1839 only a minority of all adults left any estate at all.[16] It would appear that only about 14 per cent of all deceased adult males left property worth £20 or more.[17] In 1796, it was estimated that no more than six per cent of all persons (including minors) who died in England and Wales left any estate, while in 1873 this figure had increased only to eight per cent of the total.[18] The numbers leaving a substantial estate were clearly minute: my own impression of English society is that until about 1870 anyone leaving more than about £10,000 was, except in London, a very prosperous member of his community, while anyone with about £50,000 or more was definitely rich. In most circumstances, it would be improbable to term the son of a man leaving £10,000 or more in this period as 'self-made', or to describe his background as other than comfortable. Beginning about 1870 it would seem that there was a substantial increase in the number of estates at all levels of wealth, matching the increase in the number of very large estates which has been noted at this time in Chapter 2. An estate of £10,000 was now customarily that left by a successful small businessman,[19] while the factory owner, banker or prosperous barrister probably left at least £50,000. This was the level of wealth, for example, of businessmen-politicians like John Bright (£86,289 in 1889), Joseph Chamberlain (£125,000 in 1914), William E. Forster (£81,574) or Lord Ritchie of Dundee (£116,000 in 1906). This increase had occurred, moreover, without any significant change in the price index, which stood broadly at the same level in 1870 as 1913.[20] By 1913-14, when there were 164,000 male deaths in England and Wales of persons over 21, 77,998 persons left any estate.[21] Assuming that 20 per cent of all estates were left by women, about 41 per cent of all adult men left estates, 0.6 per cent of them — just 3,712 — above £10,000.

The Social Origins of Millionaires

This changing wealth distribution in English society must be kept in mind when assessing the wealth left by the fathers of all non-landed millionaires, the sole group for whom wealth as well as occupational statistics have been traced. In Table 4.2 is given the number of non-landed millionaires' fathers' estates. It is clear from this table that the great majority of non-landed millionaires emerged from backgrounds of affluence or real wealth, from among the top 0.6 per cent of all deceased male estates in 1913-14 or far higher still. Yet a minority of non-landed wealth-holders apparently emerged from backgrounds far less affluent, with many fathers having apparently left no British estate at all. Within the group whose fathers left between zero and £10,000 were many different strata of wealth, and it would be wrong, without further evidence, to assert from the figures in Table 4.2 that a fifth or more of the total number of non-landed wealth-holders started life poor. Most of the persons in the lower part of Table 4.2 were small businessmen or farmers rather than manual or low clerical workers, and a number of these were clearly men whose very small fortunes were probably no indication of their true status in the business world, but which was the product of either substantial estate duty avoidance or *inter vivos* gifts, or of late business reverses. A notable example of this was James Kitson (1807-85), father of James Kitson, 1st Baron Airedale (1835-1911), millionaire locomotive manufacturer. The senior Kitson left only £100, yet had served as Mayor of Leeds in 1860-2.[22] Another example is Theophilus Brotherton (1824-79), a Manchester cotton manufacturer and father of the chemical manufacturer and millionaire Edward A. Brotherton, 1st Baron Brotherton (1856-1930), who is unlisted in the calendars.

More light is shed upon this subject from a breakdown of the occupations or social status of the fathers of the millionaires. This is done in Table 4.3. The categories in this table are those also employed when examining the occupations of the fathers of the half-millionaires and lesser wealthy. These tables are ordered according to eight basic categories of fathers' status. The 'wealth-holder' fathers — those who left £500,000 or more — are given separately. (This group may also be regarded as the most successful of the business groups.) Those fathers who were businessmen but who left less than £500,000 have been divided into three groups. The 'Business I' category includes those who

Table 4.2: Valuations of the Estates of the Fathers of Non-landed Millionaires, by Dates of Death of the Sons

Valuation (Lower Limit) £	1809-58	1858-79	1880-99	1900-19	1920-39
2 million	0	5	1	5	11
1 million	0	0	2	7	25
500,000	2	3	7	7	16
250,000	0	2	5	8	14
100,000	0	4	9	14	14
50,000	0	1	6	13	8[f]
25,000	0	1	6	5[d]	10
10,000	0	1[c]	1	6	11[g]
3,000	0	3	5	4	10[h]
1,000	0	0	3	2[e]	3
0	1	3	2	5	4
Unlisted[a]	0	2	7	11	20
Total Traced	3	25	54	87	146
Unknown	5	4	1	4	3
Foreign	1	1	3	8	5
Irish/Scottish Unknowns[b]	0	1	2	1	1

Notes:

a 'Unlisted' estates are those in which, although the date of death in question is known, no estate valuation is listed. The 'unknown' class consists of those whose fathers' dates of death are unknown and could not be traced.

b These are Irish estates proved before 1858, for which no probate records exist, or Scottish estates proved 1824-75, for which only the manuscript source (I.R.27) in Edinburgh exists and which could not be traced for this research.

c The father of Francis Wright (d. 1873) left £18,000, but his grandfather left £100,000.

d H.L.B. McCalmont (d. 1902) was the son of a barrister who left £44,000, but his great-uncle left him the bulk of his £3 million fortune.

e Edwin S. Bowlby (d. 1902) was the son of an Anglican vicar who left £4,000. His maternal grandfather left £500,000, and this man's brother was the millionaire William Hodgson (d. 1886), son of a brewery sugar manufacturer.

f The father of James Fyfe-Jamieson (d. 1929) left £90,000; his mother was a close relative of the Baird colliery family.

g The father of Gerald H. Craig-Sellar (d. 1929) left £12,000; his maternal uncle was the brewery millionaire T.V. Smith (d. 1906).

h The father of Sir Alexander H. Brown (d. 1922), who died aged 32, left £5,000. His grandfather left over £500,000. Francis, 5th Baron Latymer (d. 1923 — he was a banker, not a landowner, whose peerage was called out of abeyance after 340 years) was the son of an Anglican vicar who left £6,000. His mother was a member of the Coutts banking family.

Table 4.3: Occupations of the Fathers of Non-landed Millionaires, by Dates of Death of the Son, and Percentages

	1809-58	1858-79	1880-99	1900-19	1920-39
1. Wealth-holder[a] (Businessmen)	1=11.1	8=25.0	10=21.3	19=19.6	51=34.9
2. Business I	2=22.2	6=18.8	16=34.0	35=36.1	34=23.3
3. Business II	1=11.1	3= 9.4	13=27.7	12=12.4	19=13.0
4. Small Business		5=15.6	4= 8.5	6= 6.2	11= 7.5
5. Landed I				1= 1.0	1= 0.7
Landed II			2= 4.3		
Farmers	1=11.1	2= 6.3	3= 6.4	3= 3.1	3= 2.1
6. Professionals Upper	1=11.1	2= 6.3	2= 4.3	·3= 3.1	3= 2.1
Professionals Lower			4= 8.5	4= 4.1	8= 5.5
7. Workers/ Shopkeepers	2=22.2	2= 6.3		7= 7.2	12= 8.2
8. Foreign – Established	1=11.1	1= 3.1	3= 6.4	7= 7.2	3= 2.6
Poor					1= 0.7
Unknown				2= 2.0	
Total Known	9	32	47	97	146
Unknown			2	2	2

Notes:
Percentages refer to those of the total known only.
a   The apparent slight discrepancy between this category and its counterpart in Table 4.2 is accounted for by the fact that in one case the grandfather's valuation, which was over £500,000, is used here.

were substantial or wealthy businessmen, but below the wealth-holder class. In wealth terms, it consists of those fathers known or thought to be worth between £50,000 and £500,000. 'Business II' are the prosperous businessmen of medium rank — equivalent to those leaving between £10,000 and £50,000. 'Small business' includes those entrepreneurs — apart from small shopkeepers — who owned small or moderate local concerns. In wealth terms it would include businessmen worth less than £10,000. Most of the figures in this group are small manufacturers or merchants.

The 'Landed' fathers have been divided into two classes. In the first group are the sons of large landowners, who owned 5,000 or more acres in Bateman. The 'Landed II' class contains the few cases in which the father owned 1,000-5,000 acres. The class of 'Farmers' consists of tenants and small yeomen. The 'Professional' category has been divided into 'Upper' and 'Lower' halves. Among the former are higher Anglican clergymen, barristers, solicitors, doctors, estate agents, engineers and others whose peak yearly earnings were probably above £400 per annum in the period up to 1914. The 'Lower Professionals' include all ordinary Anglican and all dissenting clergymen, clerks, schoolteachers, lower government officials and such oddities as a 'hairdresser and perfumer',[23] all with likely peak earnings between £100 and £400 per annum.[24] The 'Shopkeeper and Working Class' category consists of fathers who were small shopkeepers, manual workers or agricultural labourers, as well as those wealth-holders whose fathers' occupation is unknown, but who were themselves definitely known to have begun in poverty. The 'Foreign' class consists of the fathers of immigrants, and is divided between those who were poor and those who seemed to be at least moderately successful.

Interpreting the precise degree of social mobility among millionaire fathers in Tables 4.2 and 4.3 is not a straightforward matter, for the reasons noted above. What is clear and indisputable, however, is that the great majority of non-landed millionaires emerged from backgrounds of affluence or real wealth, while only a small minority were the sons of men without means or from manual or low-clerical occupations. Among the millionaire cohorts, a minority ranging between 18.5 per cent and 35.6 per cent of those known in Table 4.2 (and between 11.1 per cent and 34.9 per cent of those known in Table 4.3) were themselves the sons of wealth-holders, and moreover the tendency for the very wealthy to have themselves sprung from very wealthy backgrounds became increasingly common between 1880 and 1939. The majority of non-landed millionaires, although not perhaps the sons of enormously rich fathers, nevertheless came from backgrounds which would surely have been considered wealthy by the average Englishman, and which were among the top 0.1 percentile of Britain's wealth distribution. Nearly a majority of non-landed millionaires whose fathers' valuations are known were the sons of men who left £100,000 or more. In the period 1920-39, for example, 54.8 per cent of the non-landed millionaires whose fathers' probate valuations are known were the sons of men in the £100,000 class or above. Broadly speaking, the most important qualification for achieving millionaire status in Britain has been to have had a wealthy father.

Yet an important minority of non-landed millionaires apparently did emerge from backgrounds far less affluent. The precise extent of this, as noted above, is not crystal-clear. Taking the most narrow definition of the limits of this class – those who began in poverty or in the working class – only 15 millionaires could be described as self-made men, no more than 4.8 per cent of the known total.[25] At the widest definition, however, which would count, besides these men, all sons of shopkeepers, farmers, lower professionals and small businessmen (worth less than £10,000), this total rises to 78 individuals – 24.8 per cent of the total.[26] Probably the most reasonable verdict on this matter would include as self-made those fathers who were shopkeepers,[27] lower professionals,[28] smaller farmers[29] – though there is room for doubt here – and the very smallest businessmen,[30] but not those businessmen worth more than £3,000 or £4,000.[31] This would eliminate only about ten fathers, bringing the revised number of 'self-made men' to 21.6 per cent of the non-landed millionaire total – still far higher than the number who actually began poor.

Before turning to the half-millionaires, a word is perhaps in order about the curious status of those millionaires whose fathers were foreigners. Contrary to all expectations, and perhaps to the British experience in more recent times,[32] only one such immigrant began life poor, Bernhard Baron (1850-1929), the Jewish tobacco manufacturer who was born in poverty in Brest-Litovsk and left £4 million. All of the other immigrant millionaires without exception, including the Rothschilds and Rallis, came from families who were already well-established abroad, or were the sons of men of some standing and status, such as the German-born shipbuilder Sir Emil Robert Ropner, 1st Bt. (1838-1924), the son of an officer, either in the Prussian army or customs force. Most such immigrants whose families were already engaged in commerce merely extended to Britain the network of their activities.

The Social Origins of Half-millionaires and Lesser Wealthy

The half-millionaires present rather more difficulties than do the millionaires, since fathers' valuations were not available to supplement the information on their occupation in about one-third of the cases. Consequently, there are inevitably many ambiguities in assigning a businessman to his proper category, and there are more unknowns than among the millionaires. In Table 4.4 the occupations of the fathers of the half-millionaires are set out. The half-millionaire class clearly contains a smaller percentage of fathers who were themselves wealth-holders than was the case among millionaires, but it is noteworthy that this segment of half-millionaire fathers becomes of increasing significance with each cohort group. On the other hand, the percentage of half-millionaires from the two top business groups below £500,000 is

Table 4.4: Occupations of the Fathers of Non-landed Half-millionaires, By Dates of Death of the Son, and Percentages

	1809-58	1858-79	1880-99	1900-19	1920-39
1. Wealth-holders	1= 2.5	9=11.0	13=11.4	41=18.2	66=21.2
2. Business I	16=40.0	28=34.1	38=33.3	66=29.3	86=27.6
3. Business II	10=25.0	14=17.1	30=26.3	40=17.8	72=23.0
4. Small Business	1= 2.5	8= 9.8	19=16.7	28=12.4	18= 5.5
5. Landed I	2= 5.0	1= 1.2	1= 0.9	2= 0.9	2= 0.6
Landed II	3= 7.5	2= 2.4	1= 0.9	0	1= 0.3
Farmers	2= 5.0	6= 7.3	5= 4.4	10= 4.4	5= 1.6
6. Professionals Upper	2= 5.0	4= 4.9	8= 7.0	12= 5.3	16= 5.1
Professionals Lower	0	0	1= 0.9	6= 2.7	12= 3.8
7. Workers/ Shopkeepers	3= 7.5	10=12.2	7= 6.1	21= 9.3	35=11.2
8. Foreign Established	1	4	7	7	7
Poor				2	
Unknown	1	2		3	2
Total Known (British only)	40	82	114	226	313

more significant than among the millionaires, and the total percentage of half-millionaire fathers from these three categories is higher than the number of millionaire fathers from these classes between 1809 and 1879, and in 1920-39, and is only slightly lower in the two remaining periods. At the other end of the scale, the percentage of half-millionaires emerging from working-class or shopkeeper background is somewhat higher than among the millionaires – for instance, 11.2 per cent of British-born half-millionaires deceased between 1920 and 1939 came from this stratum, compared with 8.2 per cent of the millionaires deceased in the same period. Taking the wider definition of self-made men, the total percentage among small businessmen, farmers, lower professionals, working-class/shopkeepers and lower foreign fathers amounts to 24.6 per cent of the total (199 of the total of 809 individuals). The number emerging from working-class or poor backgrounds is however much lower, no more than 47-52 such individuals – 5.8 per cent to 6.4 per cent of the total – higher than among millionaires, but still minute.[33] And as with the millionaires, the number of foreign-born half-millionaires with humble beginnings is surprisingly small. Only two such cases are definitely known: Julius Caesar Czarnikow (1836-1909), who came without means from the German principality of Sondershausen, worked for a brokerage firm in the City and established the sugar brokerage firm of Czarnikow's, the source of his fortune of £774,000; and the celebrated art dealer Sir Joseph J. Duveen (1843-1908), the son, of all things, of a Jewish blacksmith in Zwolle, Holland.[34]

Turning to the two groups of lesser wealthy (Table 4.5) it is striking that definite knowledge is lacking on the origins of so many of these figures, particularly those deceased in the period 1809-29. As noted above, there are no official documents to fall back upon. The self-made portion would appear to be insignificant, but certainly this is a considerable understatement of the degree of social mobility among these two groups, since there are so many unknowns, and the unknown portion, as noted above, is likely to contain many more self-made men than those readily identified. The evidence for the three sons of wealth-holders deceased during the period 1809-29 is also less definite than is the case at a later date: these three were John Langston (d. 1812), the son of a London banker who died in 1795, 'said to have been worth half a million sterling',[35] John Elwes (d. 1817), illegitimate son of the celebrated miser and MP John Elwes (d. 1789), who is thought to have left £800,000[36] and, in a different category, Frederick, Duke of York (1763-1827), fifth son of George III (Frederick left £180,000 in personalty). Among the 'Business I' fathers of wealth-holders deceased in this period, the valuations of only two are definitely known, and the relative grading of the others was ascertained from biographical sources. The large number of 'Upper Professional' fathers included the bishops, tax farmers, East India Company officers and other Government officials and patronage recipients who, as has been explained, loomed so large in the occupational structure of the wealthy at this time. The known examples of self-made men consist only of Edmund Hill (d. 1809), a gunpowder manufacturer who began as a journeyman breeches maker,[37] William Yates (1739-1813), one of Peel's original partners as a cotton manufacturer, who began as a cotton mill apprentice, Matthew Kerrison (d. 1827), apparently a merchant in London, who was 'born in an inferior station' and was 'without the advantages of education',[38] and the hairdresser John Courtoy (d. 1818). (It will be seen that in none of these cases is the precise occupation of the father known.) The farmer's son was William Jones (1757-1821), Manchester banker and uncle of Lord Overstone, who left £250,000. Among the lower professionals were several lesser clergymen, Anglican and

Table 4.5: Occupations of the Fathers of the Lesser Wealthy, by Dates of Death of the Son

	1809-29	1850-69
1. Wealth-holders	3	12
2. Business I	16	30
3. Business II	13	19
4. Small Business	0	4
5. Land I	4	2
Land II	5	2
Farmers	1	1
6. Professionals Upper	20	3
Professionals Lower	4	1
7. Workers/ Shopkeepers	4	3
8. Foreign Established		2
Poor		1
Unknown		1
Unknown	64	58
Total Known (British only)	70	77

dissenting.

Among the lesser wealthy deceased in the second period, 1850-69, there would appear to be even less social mobility than among those deceased in 1809-29, with only three men known to have begun poor, in addition to one foreigner of working-class origin,[39] while on the other side, there were 12 sons of wealth-holders and 49 from the two top business groups below £500,000.[40] As with the lesser wealthy of the earlier period, however, there are simply too many unknowns, particularly among the merchants and brokers of London, to accept this depiction unquestionably.[41] It is not unlikely, and, indeed, quite probable, that there was considerably more intergenerational social mobility among this cohort group than the figures indicate.

In terms of chronology, certain patterns of relative openness present themselves from the data for millionaires and half-millionaires. It would appear that those deceased in the period 1880-99 — and who were born, in the main, between 1805 and 1840 — came less frequently from humble backgrounds than was the case among any other cohort group. This was so for both millionaires — among whom there is not a single example of a father from the working class/shopkeeper category — and the half-millionaires, although the anomalously large number of unknowns among the half-millionaires may well conceal some instances of extraordinary mobility. If, however, the figures for this cohort are accurately expressed, this need not seem surprising, for as Harold Perkin has noted, the immediate effect of the Industrial Revolution was to establish a virtually impassable barrier to upward mobility,[42] and this is the cohort which would have been the most affected. Subsequently, it would seem, the population from other than the solid middle class and above accommodated itself, as it were, to the barriers erected around the year 1825. The two cohorts deceased between 1900 and 1939 show a much higher rate of upward social mobility.

The Rise of Self-made Men

In terms of occupation, self-made men appear to rise much more often in the Industrial/Manufacturing S.I.C.s than in commerce or finance. Among the millionaires, for example, of the 78 men whose fathers were small businessmen or below, only 16 earned their fortunes in transport, commerce or finance, although the greatest of all fortunes, Sir John Ellerman's, was earned in finance and shipowning by the son of a corn factor who left £600. The predominance of industry is perhaps not surprising, since the great City houses were in general either extensions of provincial mercantile businesses or founded by foreigners whose origins, as has been shown, were not often humble. Conversely, many of the manufacturing trades in the north of England were indeed founded on the proverbial shoestring,[43] or were greatly enlarged from very small beginnings by the founders' sons. Many self-made men, although there is no hard-and-fast rule here, earned their fortunes in fields that were new, or, within the framework of an old-established business, by methods substantially different from those which typically prevailed before. Examples of this would include such men as Alfred Harmsworth, 1st Viscount Northcliffe (1865-1922), who revolutionised the British press — the son of a failed barrister whose estate is unlisted in the probate calendars — and Northcliffe's equally important predecessor Edward Lloyd (1815-90), who began working at 12, opened his first press at 15, and founded the *Illustrated London News* in 1842;[44] or such men as Thomas Holloway (1800-83), the son of a baker and publican in Penzance whose famous pills were publicised by spending up to £50,000 per year on advertising;[45] the railway contractor Thomas Brassey (1813-70), son of a farmer in Cheshire; or John J. Sainsbury (1844-1928), founder of the supermarket chain, whose father was a worker in the frame and ornament trade in Lambeth.[46] Within the established fields, men of obscure origin tended to pioneer some new technique or mode of business, for example Robert Fleming (1845-1933), the 'pioneer of the investment trust', son of a Dundee shopkeeper;[47] James Buchanan, 1st Baron Woolavington (1849-1935), whose fortune of £7,150,000 was the product of the new demand he created in England for Scotch whisky; or indeed Ellerman himself, whose financial dealings included property speculation and 'takeovers' of a type not seen again on that scale until after the Second World War.[48]

There were also numerous examples of self-made men rising in long-established trades, in many respects the most extraordinary type of success. For example, John Reddihaugh (1841-1924), the son of a weaver-smallholder near Bradford whose estate is unlisted at Somerset House, was apprenticed to a tailor and began at the age of 21 to deal in a small way in woollen waste products, becoming one of the most important woollen merchants in Bradford. He left £1,653,000.[49] The textile industry was particularly open to new men, with such figures as Edward Langworthy (1796-1874), cotton millionaire and Mayor of Salford; Ernest H. Gates (1873-1925), the son of a bricklayer who eventually acquired the Saltaire worsted mills and left £938,000 at the age of 51; or Alfred Hood (1863-1929), a Liverpool cotton broker and the son of a labourer in a cotton factory, being examples of extraordinary success even at a very late date in the development of the textile industry. Nevertheless, on the whole, it is a probable fact that self-made men rose in new trades or lines of business, at the fringes of established society.

Comparison with Other Industrial Societies

The final, and in many ways most interesting question which must be asked concerning this subject is the comparative one: is the rate of intergenerational social mobility among British wealth-holders high or low compared with other industrial societies? This is not an easy question to answer, for even in the United States wide-ranging and detailed studies of intergenerational mobility among *wealth-holders* have never, so far as I am aware, been undertaken. With the exception of France,[50] Europe is a complete blank; and, indeed, the English probate material may well be unique in the sense of covering an entire nation for over 150 years.

Nevertheless, a number of studies of social mobility among American businessmen and wealth-holders have appeared, and they might usefully be summarised here. It is imperative to realise that studies of *businessmen* alone necessarily *overstate* the proportion of self-made men, by excluding all of the 'idle rich' who inherited their means but took no direct part in management. Furthermore, all studies of 'famous' businessmen or 'well-known' millionaires almost certainly also overstate the amount of social mobility, by focusing on the small number of entrepreneurs whose success stories are famous — for instance the Rockefellers and Carnegies — and typically omitting the less famous millionaires who may have begun in much more affluent circumstances. Nor must it be forgotten that the lower boundary of the American millionaire class is considerably below even the half-millionaire class among British wealth-holders, and it is presumably easier, *ceteris paribus*, to scrape into the lower rungs of the American millionaire class in the course of a single lifetime than into the British. These studies may be summarised as follows:

(1) Of 1,464 businessmen appearing in the *Dictionary of American Biography*, according to C. Wright Mills, only 10.4 per cent came from lower-class backgrounds, while 25.9 per cent had origins in the lower-middle class. Mills divided the American business elite into seven generations by date of birth. The generation born 1820-49 contained both the highest percentage of lower and lower-middle class origins, respectively 13.4 per cent and 28.6 per cent. For the most recent generation in his study, born in 1850-79, the two percentages were, respectively, 11.2 per cent and 18.1 per cent.[51]

(2) Pitirim Sorokin's early, and by more recent standards, primitive study of American millionaires and multi-millionaires found that 38.8 per cent of such men deceased between Colonial times and 1925 had 'started life poor', while 29.7 per cent began 'rich'.[52] Turning to then-living American millionaires, Sorokin noted a trend towards 'the wealthy class of the United States . . . becoming less and less open, and more and more closed, and tending . . . to be transformed into a caste-like group',[53] as the number beginning in poverty had dropped to 19.6 per cent while those with wealthy backgrounds had increased to 52.7 per cent. Of the 228 fathers of then-deceased millionaires, only 16 — 7 per cent — had been workingmen. Of the others, 56 had been farmers, with 119 merchants, bankers, etc. The remainder were professionals. Of 248 fathers of then-living millionaires, only four had been workingmen.[54]

(3) Professor Edward Pessen's recent study of top wealth-holders in four large eastern cities during the Jacksonian period (as determined by tax returns), concluded that only about two per cent had been born poor, while about six per cent were of 'middling economic status'.[55] Conversely, about 95 per cent of New York City's 100 wealthiest persons were born into 'families of wealth or high status or occupation', and similar percentages were found in Boston and Philadelphia. Pessen also found no difference between the social origins of his top wealth-holders and the 'lesser rich' of these cities.[56]

(4) William Miller's well-known study of American business leaders of the 1901-10 period found that only five per cent of his total of 179 were of 'lower family status' origins.[57] The fathers of only two per cent of this group had been workers, while 79 per cent had been businessmen or professionals. Another well-known study of the 'Industrial Elite of the 1870s' found that the fathers of 8 per cent of the total of 194 such men had been workers.[58]

(5) For business leaders of the 1920s there is F.W. Taussig and C.S. Joslyn's immense *American Business Leaders*. Collating 8,749 replies to a questionnaire among persons listed in *The Registry of Directors* for 1928, they found that 11.1 per cent of the business leaders aged 50 or more, and 10.5 per cent of those younger, were the sons of labourers. The sons of businessmen and professionals amounted to, respectively, 58.6 per cent and 13.4 per cent of those aged 50 and over, and 68.3 per cent and 12.5 per cent of those under 50.[59]

What emerges from these studies, clearly, is how little the 'self-made' components of non-landed millionairedom in Britain differ from that among Americans, especially when the *caveats* about the likely accuracy of the American studies are recalled.[60] Such a conclusion must surely be surprising. If there are good reasons why this conclusion is perhaps not so paradoxical as it might seem, I believe they may lie in part in the nature of inheritance in Britain, and this matter will be discussed below.

Coming Down

If the field of the social origins of the wealthy is ill-explored ground, that of the disposition of the great fortunes in the course of subsequent generations is *terra incognita*. When this subject is touched upon at all, it is generally in the context of a wider discussion of the decline of British entrepreneurship after the mid-nineteenth century, and without any specific reference to the question of inheritance.[61] Even the most time-honoured pieces of folk wisdom are empirically untested. Are younger sons of landowners, finding themselves without substantial means, really compelled to enter business life? Is there a perpetual movement of the sons of business magnates into the landed gentry? Or does inherited wealth simply continue to grow from one generation to the next?

The disposition of property from one generation to another according to the wills of the wealthy is a crucial and hitherto ill-explored source for coming to grips with some of these issues. The issues, indeed, are crucial, for if equal division rather than primogeniture is the rule among wealthy businessmen (as opposed to landowners), then much of the incentive for the sons and grandsons of wealthy men to remain in business life would be gone: in the case of millionaires and half-millionaires, they would be wealthy enough to be idle.

For information on this point, the wills of a substantial number of non-landed wealth-holders deceased between 1858 and 1899 were read to ascertain the disposition of property among the various heirs.[62] In all, 66 millionaire and 123 half-millionaire wills were included in this particular study. The results are quite striking, and indicate that equal or nearly equal division among the heirs of the top business or professional wealth-holders was very generally the rule: among the 59 cases where a millionaire left his property to a principal heir of a succeeding generation,[63] for example, only 14 left more than 80 per cent to one heir,[64] while in 37 cases less than 60 per cent of the property went to a single heir.[65] Among half-millionaires, of the 102 cases in which the chief heir was of a succeeding generation, again 78 of these heirs received less than 60 per cent of the total property. In a substantial number of cases, the principal heir received less than one-third of the total inheritance, indicating that the testator divided his property with scrupulous concern for equality.

There is much supportive evidence for the proposition that non-landed wealth-holders tended to divide their property equally. A systematic tracing of all the probate valuations of all the male descendants of non-landed wealth-holders whose genealogies appear in works like *Burke's Peerage* and *Burke's Landed Gentry* reveals much the same story: second, third, fourth and fifth sons, second, third and fourth grandsons, and even younger great-grandsons commonly left as much, or more, than eldest sons, with virtually no discernible trends at all in this patterning.[66] Furthermore, very few if any of these descendants of wealth-holders left sums which were, for their time and place, less than very substantial, less than, say £25,000 prior to the First World War. The great majority of wealth-holder descendants, even very distant ones, thus possessed at least £500-£1,000 per annum or more (and generally far more) necessary to situate them within, at the very least, the upper middle class. Nine of the 15 *fifth* and *sixth* sons of millionaires left £250,000 or more, implying an income greater than the proverbial £10,000 a year.

This conclusion has at least three important historical corollaries. First, it is important in situating the distance in sociological self-perception which separated the wealthy business and professional elite of nineteenth-century Britain from the landed elite, even in cases where businessmen were as wealthy as the great dukes and earls; even, indeed, in cases where they acquired titles and purchased substantial landed estates. Second, and more subtly, it must be noted that few of the descendants of the very wealthy *improved* upon the size of their ancestors' estates. Only a handful of the dozens of sons and grandsons of the half-millionaires — to take one example — employed the £100,000 or more which they probably inherited to build the vast fortune which such initial capitalisation would surely bring with even a minimal degree of risk-taking or ambition. This strongly suggests that the incentives to continue in the entrepreneurial paths of the founder of the dynasty's fortunes simply disappeared. Third, and following from this, it is more than likely that most of these sons and grandsons simply lived upon their interest, invested unimaginatively in blue chip stocks and consols, and in turn left little more than they inherited. Among the great-grandsons of all the wealth-holders traced here, only five left £500,000 or more. As George Orwell noted, 'For long past [before 1940] there had been in England an entirely functionless class, living on money invested they hardly knew where, the "idle rich", the people whose photographs you can look at in the *Tatler* and the *Bystander*, always supposing that you want to'.[67] The substantial fortunes of the younger sons of the wealthy may have constituted the precondition for failure among many nineteenth-century business dynasties. This was not a case of shirtsleeves-to-shirtsleeves, but of stately home-to-villa. This point is borne out by a fuller examination of the lesser wealthy: of the 134 non-landed wealth-holders deceased in the period 1809-29, only eight ever produced later members with really vast fortunes; among the 138 such men deceased in 1850-69, 24 did so. The great majority of these families moreover, disappeared from the genealogical works dedicated to recording the most successful instances of the acquisition of undoubted status.[68]

However, a further crucial refinement is needed in our interpretation of entrepreneurial decline, for in a majority of cases where descendants did leave £500,000 or more, these families were engaged either in banking or merchant banking, or in the production of alcoholic beverages, particularly brewing. It is probably true to say that in these two fields entrepreneurship could be most readily combined with dynastic pretention and acceptance by the older aristocracy. In these fields one was not, as was normally the case in manufacturing or industry, compelled to surrender any except the most nominal participation in business life prior to full social acceptance. Moreover, the successful banking and brewing dynasties intermarried much more freely with the landed aristocracy during the nineteenth century.[69] These banking and brewing families did this without diminishing their entrepreneurial ability: among brewers, for instance, their record of successful industrial organisation, as well as their early and widespread employment of steam technology, was second to none.

It is a strange but none the less true fact, that whenever historians discuss the decline of British entrepreneurship during the nineteenth century, they have in mind entrepreneurship among manufacturers and industrialists, and essentially ignore the world of commerce and finance. It is, at any rate, assumed that the question of entrepreneurial decline will identically concern all business groups. Yet among commercial dynasties (as among brewers) persistent entrepreneurial success continuing among later generations of a wealthy dynasty is much more common than among industrial dynasties. It is worth noting, for instance, that Winchester graduates were much more than twice as likely to enter one of the commercial or financial trades than manufacturing or industry, a ratio which persisted without substantial alteration between 1820 and 1922.[70] Families like the Rothschilds, Barings, Barclays, Goslings or Gladstones,[71] or the Whitbreads, Charringtons and Hoares have never severed their connections with business life despite the acquisition of great wealth and high status, although such industrial dynasties as the Peels, Arkwrights, Strutts and Cunliffe-Listers quickly did so. For industrialists and manufacturers the road from wealth to status was always a one-way street.

When considered in the light of these facts, the 'haemorrhage of talent' in British society since the mid-nineteenth century appears to be more selective and more ambiguous than if considered a natural consequence of the British status system and class structure. First, the all-important wherewithal for the withdrawal from business — the equal distribution of the property of the original wealth-holder — is there, as well as the magnet provided by the attractions of aristocratic society. Second, in certain particular fields, especially banking and brewing, there has been no withdrawal from business. But even granting that over a wide area of British economic life this phenomenon has occurred, need it have been, as is often alleged, disastrous to Britain's economic development? This is the question D.C. Coleman asks,[72] and he answers it by pointing out what is perfectly obvious but has consistently been overlooked, that the withdrawal of older families from the business world provides the opportunity for new men.[73] It is this observation that provides the link with the first section of this chapter. Is it not likely that the newer areas of enterprise in the economy will be developed by self-made men? Something of the sort appears to be the case for the wealth-holders discussed in this chapter. What is certainly true is that any unsubtle and overgeneralised account of the decline of British entrepreneurship must necessarily over-simplify a subject of great difficulty and subtlety, and that the decline of British entrepreneurship may not be due to the decline of the entrepreneur.

A final point about the development of great fortunes down the generations must be noted: there is simply no tendency for fortunes to increase in size to the really vast scale which might have been expected had they been kept intact, reinvested wisely, and allowed to grow. Take as an example, the fortune of a fairly run-of-the-mill mid-Victorian millionaire like, say, the shipowner Duncan Dunbar (1804-62), who left £1.5 million. Had his fortune been allowed to grow and accumulate at 7 per cent a year, it would have doubled every ten years. By 1912, 50 years after its founder's death, it would have been worth no less than £48 million — the greatest personal fortune in Britain and probably among the half-dozen greatest personal fortunes in the world. Thereafter its geometric growth would resemble an avalanche — or whatever metaphor suggests itself to one's literary sense.

Early in the 1920s the Dunbar fortune would have passed the £100 million mark; the accession of Queen Elizabeth II 30 years later would have seen it worth more than three-quarters of a billion. Growing like some monstrous slime from outer space, the 1960s would have witnessed it passing the £2 billion mark, the 1970s the £3, 4 and 5 billion level. By the early 1980s the £6 billion Dunbar fortune, competing only with the wealth of the OPEC oil princes in its magnitude, should doubtless form the book's centrepiece — only, instead of the 7 per cent annual growth rate we postulated of the founder's fortune, the Dunbar estate would now, surely, be increasing at 15 per cent to 20 per cent *per annum*, possibly even more, and should easily touch £10 or even

£20 billion before many of us have tasted death.

It goes without saying that this example is entirely fictitious. Indeed, if today's heirs of Duncan Dunbar, the mid-Victorian millionaire, or of the fortunes of such other bona-fide millionaires of the day as Samuel Eyres (1793-1868), William Henry Forman (1794-1869) or Francis Wright (1806-73) are either very rich or even socially prominent, they manage to keep this fact very quiet. No Victorian business millionaire, not even a Rothschild or Lord Overstone (whose last traceable wealthy heir died in 1944), has ever kept his fortune intact to the extent necessary to build up, across the generations, the vast, super-rich fortune of a kind depicted here in the case of Duncan Dunbar. There are many reaons for this.[74] No businessman, and certainly no heir or descendant of any businessman, is clever or lucky enough to make continuing and continuously successful investments. Death duties and other forms of taxation take their toll — sometimes generation after generation, more usually every few generations. But, most importantly, and as the evidence in this chapter confirms, there is an irresistible and automatic method whereby the wealth of the great plutocrats regresses to the mean, to use the term of the economist. It is called having children, and so long as any rich man leaves more than one descendant, his wealth is divided up rather than kept intact.

Notes

1. Josiah Wedgwood, *The Economics of Inheritance* (London, 1929) and Professor Colin Harbury and his associates, e.g. in C. Harbury and D.W.W.N. Hitchens, *Inheritance and Wealth Inequality in Britain* (London, 1979).

2. See, for example, the list of British entrepreneurs in Charles P. Kindleberger, *Economic Growth in France and Britain 1851-1950* (New York, 1960), pp. 128-31, based on *Fortunes Made in Business* (London, 1883).

3. Something must be said here of the actual process involved in tracing the valuation of the father. If the date of death is unknown the researcher must go through each of up to 70 or more probate calendars, from the year before the birth of the son (for he may be posthumous) to a date at which it may safely be assumed that the father must be dead. This is possible only for Englishmen and Welshmen after 1858, as before 1858 there is no central index containing valuations, and the manuscript index which does exist at the Public Record Office is not available on open shelf. (An index of Canterbury Court names is on open shelf, but it is not in strict alphabetical order.) There are, furthermore, questions of identification whenever the father has a common name, and, after all, the father may not be listed in the calendars. In practice it is not possible to trace more than at most ten names per day, and then only for the period after 1858.

There is a description of this exceedingly laborious process in Harbury and Hitchens, *Inheritance and Wealth Inequality in Britain*, pp. 11-37. The methods employed by these researchers were essentially identical to those used by myself, and it is difficult to see any other way in which such a study could be undertaken.

4. There are also a number of cases in which the father's date of death (and hence his valuation) is known, but in which his occupation is not known.

5. Even so, the occupations of the fathers of many early half-millionaires could not be traced.

6. There is in particular a lack of newspaper obituaries on the earliest figures. It was not until the mid-nineteenth century at the earliest, that provincial newspapers offered full obituary coverage of local businessmen.

7. On the general subject of social mobility, see Reinhard Bendix and Seymour Martin Lipset, (eds.), *Class, Status and Power* (London, 1967), a useful collection of essays, especially Part V, 'Social Mobility'. On social mobility in England the classic work is D.V. Glass, (ed.), *Social Mobility in Britain* (London, 1954) and on elite groups see Philip Stanworth and Anthony Giddens, (eds.), *Elites and Power in British Society* (Cambridge, 1974).

8. In America, many self-made men advertise this fact; in Britain, few do. The pages of *Burke's Landed Gentry*, and particularly the post-1914 editions which contain many erstwhile businessmen, bristle with genealogies bordering on the legendary, and implying a meaningful connection with the medieval gentry. During the period between 1880 and 1940, perhaps only two British wealth-holders were popularly known to have risen from poverty: Lord Nuffield and Sir Thomas Lipton. On the other hand, many widely known 'self-made men' were nothing of the sort.

9. In several cases the father, dying young, predeceased *his* own father, who died leaving a much larger fortune than the father. Such cases have been noted.

10. This figure is based on research undertaken in 1974-5 by the author for the Social Science Research Council Project on 'Wealth and Social Origins of British Elite Groups, 1880-1970' for the University of Lancaster, under the direction of Professor Harold Perkin.

11. W.J. Reader, *Professional Men* (London, 1966), p. 200.

12. Harold Perkin, *The Origins of Modern English Society, 1780-1880* (London, 1969), esp. Chapter VI and pp. 307-8.

13. There was a surprisingly large intergenerational flow between the lower part of the middle class and the upper working class. See Thomas Fox and S.M. Miller, 'Occupational Stratification and Mobility' in Bendix and Lipset, *Class, Status and Power*, pp. 574-81, esp. Table 5, p. 578. On the other hand, the amount of downward social mobility from the very highest level of English society to the working class was just about nil, in the case of the study which has attempted to measure it, among Winchester graduates born between 1820 and 1922, and the authors of the study suggest that the few such examples of this are purely voluntary, e.g., a convinced socialist who works on the factory floor. See T.J.A. Bishop and Rupert Wilkinson, *Winchester and the Public School Elite* (London, 1967), Chapter 2.

14. P.P. 1843, XXX, 603.

15. B.R. Mitchell and Phyllis Deane, *Abstract of British Historical Statistics* (Cambridge, 1962), p. 34, 'Population and Vital Statistics II'.

16. Of course, many of the others were not literally penniless. Apart from those leaving between zero and £20, one suspects that the heirs of working men owning only cash and chattels simply winked at the formal probate process.

17. Based on Table 4.1, as well as the population figures above. It should be remembered that land and settled personalty would have been excluded from these figures.

18. Anthony J. Camp, *Wills and Their Whereabouts* (London, 1974), p. xxxviii.

19. Cf. George Orwell, *Coming Up For Air* (London, 1939), of Grimmett, the prosperous grocer in Little Binfield, who died about the time of the First World War. 'But from what I know of him – not to mention that slapping tombstone in the churchyard – I bet he got out while the going was good and had ten or fifteen thousand quid to take to heaven with him.' (p. 198.)

20. Mitchell and Deane, *Abstract of British Historical Statistics*, pp. 472-3, 'Prices. 3'. The overall Rousseaux Index stood at 110 in 1870, 106 in 1913.

21. P.P. 1914, XXXVI, 320.

22. The senior Kitson 'built up a modest business that was the forerunner of the great works of (Lord Airedale)'. *Dictionary of National Biography, Supplement 1911-20.*

23. He was James Currie (1797-1851) of Belfast, the father of the millionaire shipowner Sir Donald Currie (1825-1909) and his brother the half-millionaire Donald Martin Currie (1837-1920). There is no reference to James Currie's occupation in any published source, and this required a good deal of detective work to track down.

24. In a limited number of cases those ostensibly belonging to the Upper Professional class have been assigned to the Lower Professional category as the evidence warrants. Most notably this was done with the failed barrister Alfred Harmsworth (d. 1889), whose estate is unlisted, the father of Lord Northcliffe and his brothers.

25. The 15 'self-made' millionaires were: Thomas Cubitt (1788-1855), the great builder, the son of a carpenter; Joseph Love (1796-1875), colliery owner, son of a working miner, and who began life as a pitboy, William R. Sutton (1836-1900), carrier, son of a barman in a pub, Sir Walter Scott, 1st Bt. (1826-1910), engineering contractor, son of a labourer; Sir William P. Hartley (1846-1922), jam manufacturer, son of a locksmith; John Reddihaugh (1841-1924) and John J. Sainsbury (1844-1928), on whom see below; Sir Joseph Hood, 1st Bt. (1863-1931) solicitor and tobacco company deputy-chairman, the son of a wheelwright; Sir Alexander Grant, 1st Bt. (1864-1937), biscuit manufacturer, the son of a railway guard; John A. Crabtree (1886-1935), who manufactured electrical switchgear, the son of a joiner; and Sir Howell J. Williams (1859-1939), building contractor, son of a slatemason.

Those also known to have begun in poverty included, besides Bernhard Baron (1850-1929) – on whom see below – Samuel Lewis (1837-1901), money-lender, a Jewish orphan who began as a commercial traveller; George Herring (1835-1906), financier, whose first job was as 'carver in a boiled beef shop in Ludgate Hill' and got his start as a successful bookie (*The Times*, 3 November 1906); and Arthur Keen (1835-1901), ironmaster, an orphan who began as a clerk.

26. Several fathers just above the £10,000 mark had sons who might well be considered 'self-made'. The most important were Lewis Samuel (1794-1859), a watchmaker and silversmith in London, who left £12,000. He was the father of Samuel Montagu (sic), 1st Baron Swaythling (1832-1911), the great merchant banker, who left £1,146,000. Swaythling began in business in 1853 on £3,000 borrowed from his father. (See *Dictionary of National Biography, Supplement 1911-20.*) The second, and perhaps even clearer case, is that of Marcus Samuel, 1st Viscount Bearsted (1853-1927) – no relation to Lord Swaythling – the founder of Shell Transport and Trading, who left £4 million. His father was Marcus Samuel (1799-1870), described in the probate calendars as an 'East Indian and general merchant', who left £14,000. In reality even this description is overstated, and Bearsted's story is one of the great romances of British business, for Marcus Samuel was the owner of a shell and curio shop in Houndsditch. On a business trip to Japan to search for shells for the family

business, Bearsted discovered a new method of cleaning out the holds of petroleum ships, which previously could only be used on one leg of a voyage because of the filth remaining after the petroleum had been cleared out. Hence Royal Dutch – Shell – named after a small shop in the East End of London. (See M. Henriques, *Lord Bearsted* (London, 1956).) Bearsted's brother Samuel Samuel (1855-1934), who developed the merchant bank M. Samuel, left £1,517,000.

27. These included: Joseph Morrison (d. 1804), innkeeper, father of James Morrison (1789-1857), textile warehouseman and merchant banker; Edmund J. Sutton (d. 1860), pawnbroker, father of Thomas M. Sutton (1848-1933), pawnbroker; James Dunn (1781-1863), grocer, father of Sir William Dunn, 1st Bt. (1833-1912), retail merchant in South Africa and financier in London; Frederick Beasley, 'licensed victualler', father of Charles Beasley (1843-1923), brewer; and John Fleming, shopkeeper (1807-73), father of Robert Fleming (1845-1933), investment banker. (Robert Fleming's grandson was Ian Fleming, creator of James Bond.)

28. These included: Nathaniel Clayton (d. 1827), of Lincoln, steam packet master, father of tractor manufacturer Nathaniel Clayton (1811-90); James Craig (1792-1868), estate bailiff, father of James Craig (1828-1900), the Ulster distiller; Walter Runciman (d. 1877), of the Coastguard service, father of Walter, 1st Baron Runciman (1847-1937), shipowner; James Riddell (d. 1867), photographer, father of George A. Riddell, 1st Baron Riddell (1865-1934), newspaper proprietor, George Henderson (1818-89), printer's reader, father of Alexander Henderson, 1st Baron Faringdon (1850-1934), stockbroker; William Haslam (d. 1878), bell-hanger (sic), father of Sir Alfred S. Haslam (1844-1927), refrigeration engineer; Rev. William Tate (1773-1836), Unitarian minister, father of Sir Henry Tate, 1st Bt. (1819-99), the sugar refiner; and John Keene (d. 1892), father of John H. Keene (1864-1931), insurance broker. The estates of most of these are unlisted. Henderson left £2,839, Tate £300, Keene £370.

29. These include: John Brassey (1778-1831), father of Thomas Brassey (1805-70), railway contractor; Giles Loder (1754-1834), father of Giles Loder (1786-1871), Russia merchant; William Ewing (1772-1853), father of Sir Archibald Orr-Ewing, 1st Bt. (1818-93), chemical manufacturer; William Palmer (1788-1826), father of Samuel Palmer (1820-1903), biscuit manufacturer; and William Watson (1828-1912), father of Sir William G. Watson, 1st Bt. (1861-1930), dairy retailer.

30. This category would include such men as Benjamin Eyres (d. 1837), a Leeds woollen manufacturer, who left £3,000, father of Samuel Eyres (1793-1868), who left £1,200,000; Josiah Fielden (1748-1811), cotton manufacturer who left £200, father of Thomas Fielden (1791-1869), who left £1,300,000 and Thomas Holcroft (1794-1865), unlisted cement manufacturer, father of Sir Charles Holcroft, 1st Bt. (1831-1917), ironmaster and colliery manufacturer, who began as an office boy.

31. No doubt this limit would have to be altered over time to take account of inflation and the changing levels of wealth-holding.

32. Compare, e.g., the lowly origins of the post-World War II property speculators, many of whom were the sons of Jewish immigrants. See Oliver Marriott, *The Property Boom* (London, 1967), esp. Chapters 4 and 5.

33. The self-made half-millionaires include Robert Jones (d. 1809), brandy merchant, who 'left Gower . . . fifty years ago to escape the grasp of the parish officers', (*The Times*, 22 November 1809); Seth Smith (1791-1860), builder; William Joynson (1802-74), paper manufacturer, who began as a 'poor and uneducated journeyman' (D.C. Coleman, *The British Paper Industry* (London, 1957), p. 242); Wynn Ellis (1790-1875), wholesale silk merchant; Henry Moses (1791-1875), warehouseman, who began as a 'slopseller'; Charles McGarel

(1781-1876), sugar merchant, the son of a cobbler; John Leschallas (1791-1877), builder, son of a carpenter; Richard Durant (1791-1878), silk merchant, son of a fuller; Sir Charles J. Freake, 1st Bt. (1814-84), builder, son of a publican; Robert Donaldson (1827-85), iron merchant, son of a market gardener; Abraham Laverton (1819-86), woollen manufacturer, son of a weaver; William Richardson (1811-92), machinery manufacturer, who began as a handloom weaver; John Maple (1815-1900), founder of the furniture store, who began as a shop assistant; John Lawson Johnston (1839-1900), inventor of 'Bovril', the food substitute, the son of a worker in a gunpowder factory; Edward Hulton (1838-1904), newspaper proprietor, son of a weaver; Frederick Gordon (1848-1905), shipowner, son of a shipwright; Edward Yates (1838-1907), builder, who began as a ditch-digger; Harris Lebus (1852-1907), cabinet manufacturer, who was the son of a cabinet worker; Thomas Kenyon (1843-1916), dyer, son of a colour-mixer; Henry J. King (1850-1920), son of a labourer, and himself a financier in London; William Morton (1837-1921), shoe manufacturer, son of a cowkeeper; Sir Thomas Sutherland (1834-1922), shipowner, son of a house painter; John Ross (1836-1923), foreign merchant, son of a blacksmith; John Robinson Harrison (1856-1923), shipowner, son of a husbandman; James D. Williams (1853-1925), mail order merchant, the son of a shop floorwalker; Sir James Duncan (1855-1926), son of a crofter in Fifeshire and himself a foreign merchant; Thompson Jowett (1863-1926) steel spring manufacturer, the son of a blacksmith; George Edwin Lowe (1851-1927), meat retailer, the son of a sawyer; Sir Thomas J. Lipton, 1st Bt. (1850-1931), tea merchant and food retailer, the son of an Irish labourer in Glasgow; Robert Rowley (1846-1936), hosiery manufacturer, the son of a carpenter; John T. Hedley (1853-1937), occupation unknown, the son of a stoker; John T. Linsley (1861-1936), wine merchant, the son of an engine fitter; and Henry Johnson (1866-1938), rayon manufacturer, the son of a silk thrower.

34. *The Times*, 24 April 1909; 26 June 1908.
35. *Gentleman's Magazine*, February 1812, p. 196.
36. Thornton Hall, *Romances of the Peerage* (London, 1914), p. 245.
37. *Gentleman's Magazine*, November 1809, p. 1,085.
38. Ibid., May 1827, p. 477.
39. They were: William J. Chaplin (1787-1859), the coach proprietor, who was 'born in humble circumstances' (Rev. A. Winnifrith, *Men of Kent*); Joseph Kershaw (1795-1864), a Manchester cotton manufacturer whose father was a worker. He began as a clerk; John Ashbury (1806-66), a Manchester railway carriage manufacturer who began as a wheelwright; and the famous Nova Scotia-born shipowner, Sir Samuel Cunard, 1st Bt. (1787-1865), son of a mechanic in Philadelphia.
40. Two of those included here in the wealth-holder class inherited from non-paternal sources. They were Joseph Neeld (1789-1856), the great-nephew and heir of the millionaire goldsmith Philip Rundell (d. 1827), and William M. Innes (1778-1860), who inherited the estate of his cousin Jane Innes, the daughter of an Edinburgh banker, who left £800,000 in 1839.
41. There are, for example, virtually no biographical records at all kept by the London Stock Exchange of its members. These men were seldom if ever noticed in obituaries.
42. Perkin, *The Origins of Modern English Society*, Chapter V.
43. Stanley Chapman, *The Early Factory Masters* (Newton Abbot, 1967), Chapter 7.
44. *The Times*, 9 April 1890.
45. J. Boase, *Modern English Biography* (Truro, 1901), Volume II, p. 1,515.
46. *J.S. 100: The Story of Sainsburys* (Sainsbury's Centenary Booklet, 1969), p. 9.

47. *The Times*, 2 August 1933.

48. Marriott, *The Property Boom*, pp. 115-16.

49. *Wool Record*, 23 October 1951; *Yorkshire Observer*, 10 October 1924. Wedgwood *(The Economics of Inheritance*, p. 138n2) notes with amazement the facts of his career.

50. Adeline Daumard *et al., Les Fortunes Français Aux XIXe Siècle* (Paris, 1973), does not touch specifically upon social mobility, but there are plans to do so in future work. (P. 111n2.)

51. C. Wright Mills, 'The American Business Elite: A Collective Portrait', *Journal of Econ. Hist.*, 1945.

52. Pitirim Sorokin, 'American Millionaires and Multi-Millionaires', *The Journal of Social Forces*, Vol. III (1926), p. 636.

53. Ibid., p. 635.

54. Ibid.

55. Edward Pessen, 'The Egalitarian Myth and American Social Reality: Wealth, Mobility, and Equality in the "Era of the Common Man" ', *American Hist. Rev.*, October 1971, p. 1,012.

56. Ibid., p. 1,013. Pessen's findings may not, however, be useful as a generalisation about America as a whole at that time. See Robert Gallman, 'Trends in the Size Distribution of Wealth in the Nineteenth Century, Some Speculations' in Lee Soltow (ed.), *Six Papers in Size Distribution of Wealth and Income* (New York, 1969), p. 28. Pessen's erroneous comments on British wealth-holding in this period should also be noted ('The Egalitarian Myth', p. 1,012).

57. William Miller, 'American Historians and the American Business Elite' in William Miller (ed.), *Men in Business* (New York, 1952), p. 326.

58. Frances W. Gregory and Irene D. Neu, 'The American Industrial Elite in the 1870s' in Miller, *Men in Business*, p. 202.

59. F.W. Taussig and C.S. Joslyn, *American Business Leaders* (New York, 1932), Table 27, p. 116.

60. It is surprising that no one has as yet analysed the lists of living American millionaires, including over 7,000 individuals, compiled by two New York newspapers in 1892 and 1902 and reprinted with an introduction by Sidney Ratner, *New Light on the History of Great American Fortunes* (New York, 1953). I know of no historical study of wealth in America which confounds the view of relatively low social mobility.
On this subject generally, see Edward Pessen (ed.), *Three Centuries of Social Mobility in America* (Lexington, Mass., 1974).

61. On this subject a useful recent summary is P.L. Payne, *British Entrepreneurship in the Nineteenth Century*, (London, 1974).

62. Most of these were wills of top wealth-holders which were described in considerable detail in the 'Wills and Bequests' column of the *Illustrated London News*.

63. In seven cases millionaires left their property to an heir of the same generation as himself, generally the widow. This property would soon pass again and so in these cases the long-term effects cannot be inferred.

64. Generally a son or grandson; the heir in these cases may, of course, have been an only child.

65. For fuller statistical data as well as a discussion of the sources and their limitations, see W.D. Rubinstein, 'Men of Property' in P. Stanworth and A. Giddens, (eds.), *Elites and Power in British Society* (Cambridge, 1974).

66. See ibid., for statistical evidence.

67. 'The Lion and the Unicorn', Part One, 'England, Your England' in *The Collected Essays, Journalism, and Letters of George Orwell*, vol. II (London,

1968), p. 90. Orwell goes on to note that members of this class were 'simply parasites, less useful to society than his fleas are to a dog'.

68. What happened to the descendants of these men is something of a mystery: some families must have died out (but where did the money go?) or have become impoverished, but certainly only a small minority acquired land or a title. Probably most became part of the great London upper-middle class.

69. This is based largely upon my examination of the careers of the major company chairmen in the study by Stanworth and Giddens (see Chapter Six below). See also, e.g., Dean Rapp, 'Social Mobility in the Eighteenth Century: the Whitbreads of Bedforshire, 1720-1815', *Econ. Hist. Rev.*, 2nd ser., XXVII (1974).

70. Bishop and Wilkinson, *Winchester and the Public School Elite*, Chapter 10, pp. 64-9. On the more ready acceptability of 'middlemen' by the gentry, see also Roy Lewis and Angus Maude, *The English Middle Classes* (New York, 1950), pp. 52-3.

71. One of William E. Gladstone's lesser-known sons, Henry Neville Gladstone (1852-1935) spent his life as a foreign merchant in Calcutta, eventually receiving a peerage in 1932 (Baron Gladstone of Hawarden) and leaving £473,000.

72. D.C. Coleman, 'Gentleman and Players', *Econ. Hist. Rev.*, 2nd ser., XXVI (1973), p. 110.

73. Ibid.

74. For an excellent discussion of this phenomenon in the American context, see 'Are the Rich Getting Richer? Trends in U.S. Wealth Concentration' and the other essays in Stanley Lebergott, *Wealth and Want* (Princeton, 1975), as well as other works by this sensible and sensitive economist.

5 SOCIAL BEHAVIOUR: RELIGION, POLITICS AND HONOURS

This chapter will discuss three important aspects of social behaviour among the top wealth-holders: their religious affiliations and the impact of religion upon entrepreneurial behaviour; their political service and loyalties; and honours — peerages and knighthoods — received. As with the previous chapters, only non-landed wealth-holders will be considered here; landowners will be discussed in Chapter 7.

Religion: The Weber Thesis and British Entrepreneurship

The connection between religious belief and entrepreneurial behaviour is a most significant issue in the social sciences. The link between the two was first raised, of course, by Max Weber, who argued that there was a salient causal connection between Protestantism and entrepreneurial performance in a capitalist economy. The Weber Thesis, which first appeared in print in 1904,[1] is unquestionably the most famous and widely-discussed theory proposed by a sociologist in this century. Weber's contention was that what he termed 'modern rational industrial capitalism, idiosyncratic of our Occidental culture complex, was distinctly different from earlier forms' of capitalism such as the mercantile or trading capitalism of the early modern period;[2] this was largely due to the emergence of a 'rational anti-traditional spirit'[3] in modern times. He pointed to what he termed the 'this-worldly ascetism' of Calvinist-derived sects like the Quakers and Baptists, sects which 'engendered a methodical regulation of life'[4] in striking contrast to the attitudes of Catholicism, Lutheranism or Anglicanism.[5]

It is safe to say that virtually every economic and social historian of Britain writing in the last 30 years has accepted that there is at least some merit to the Weber Thesis in its post-1760 British context.[6] Anglicanism plays the role which Weber ascribed in the Reformation period to Catholicism while Protestant non-conformity plays the role of Calvinism. It is thus widely believed that a greatly disproportionate number of entrepreneurs, innovators and successful businessmen flourishing in Britain from the early/mid-eighteenth century to 1914 at least, were Protestant dissenters — Quakers, Unitarians, Baptists, Independents, Presbyterians, Methodists or Huguenots — rather than adherents of the Church of England, and that an important reason for their success lay in the teaching and beliefs of their churches.[7] Michael Flinn, for instance, has taken this association as established: 'I propose', he wrote in his essay *Social Theory and the Industrial Revolution*, 'for the purposes of this paper (in common with most historians of the Industrial Revolution) to take a substantial disparity between the proportion of non-conformists in society and the proportion who were successful entrepreneurs as an assumption basic to any further argument'.[8]

The Weber Thesis is, then, an empirical proposition about social behaviour that may be tested empirically, and clearly must be so tested before its validity can be confirmed or refuted. It is an interesting commentary on the present state of economic history that, to the best of my knowledge, only one previous attempt has been made to count heads in this manner. This was Everett E. Hagen's analysis of 92 of the entrepreneurs and inventors mentioned in T.S. Ashton's *Industrial Revolution*.[9] He succeeded in tracing the religious affiliations of 71 of which 41 per cent of the Englishmen and Welshmen were dissenters, and 58 per cent were Anglicans.[10] Of the 20 Scotsmen in his sample, the religions of 12 were traced, and of these four were Anglican and the remainder either Presbyterians or dissenters. The key question is whether dissenters are overrepresented compared with their total percentage in the British population.

On the face of it, there can be little doubt that dissenters represented a very small percentage of the total population. The general consensus of opinion is that in the late eighteenth century no more than about seven per cent of the total English and Welsh population were dissenters.[11] This was before the very substantial increase in the size of Wesleyan and Wesleyan-inspired sects which began in the late eighteenth century. By the mid-nineteenth century, the number of people attending — if not holding official membership in — the various dissenting sects was far higher, probably exceeding the number of Anglican attenders by mid-century. According to Harold Perkin's reworking of the figures of the 1851 religious census, 19.7 per cent of the total English and Welsh populations attended Anglican services on 30 March 1851, while 20.2 per cent attended non-Anglican (including Roman Catholic) services.[12]

The fifth of the population attending Anglican services in 1851 is indicative of the ambiguous position of the Established Church in

England and Wales. For Anglicans (as for Old Dissent), the eighteenth century had been a time of numerical decline. A recent historian of modern English religious history, A.D. Gilbert, has noted that for the Church of England, 'the period 1740-1830 was an era of disaster, for whereas the Church of England had controlled something approaching a monopoly of English religious practice only ninety years earlier, it was on the point of becoming a minority religious Establishment. There may even have been an *absolute* decline of conformist practice during this period, despite the rapid expansion of English society'.[13] The percentage of the English and Welsh population over 15 attending Easter Day communion services was only 9.9 per cent in 1801 and 8.1 per cent in 1851, substantially lower than even the Religious Census figures.[14] On the other hand, then as now, the majority of the population probably regarded itself as in some sense 'C of E', even if this became manifest only at the rites of passage. Eighty per cent of the English and Welsh population marrying in 1851 did so with the benefit of Anglican rites, and even in 1901 this percentage was still about two-thirds.[15]

Scotland and Ireland reveal different patterns. Before the wave of Irish migration, and prior to the splits within the Church of Scotland which began in 1843, the overwhelming majority, probably over 90 per cent, of the Scottish population were adherents of the Church of Scotland. The Scottish population totalled about 10 per cent of the United Kingdom and 14 per cent of the British total populations in 1831 and 1841; in addition, about five per cent of the total British population were adherents of the Presbyterian churches of Ireland, Wales and England. In Ireland, about 80 per cent of the population was Roman Catholic, or about 25 per cent of the entire United Kingdom population in the 1830s; and perhaps 15 per cent to 20 per cent after the Famine.[16]

A percentage breakdown of the main religious denominations of the United Kingdom would therefore find that in the early nineteenth century about 60 per cent of the total United Kingdom population was nominally Anglican (with the observant percentage considerably lower), about 25 per cent Roman Catholics, about 15 per cent Presbyterians, about four per cent to five per cent dissenters, with much less than one per cent members of non-British immigrant sects like the Jews or Lutherans. By the mid-century, these figures were, respectively, about 55 per cent, 15 per cent, 15 per cent and 15 per cent (with non-indigenous sects still under one per cent). It is these figures to which any statistics on entrepreneurial success must be compared.

The probate data on wealth-holding happily offers perhaps the only objective and comprehensive series which permits a valid test of the Weber Thesis. The absolute need for an *objective* and *comprehensive* test of entrepreneurial success is indicated by the instructive manner in which Hagen's findings, I believe, can be shown to fail.[17] On the face of it, Hagen's findings seem to show that dissenters were indeed enormously overrepresented among Industrial Revolution innovators — 41 per cent of the English and Welsh sample compared with about five per cent and 15 per cent of the United Kingdom population in *c*. 1800 and 1850. There is, seemingly, a most substantial gap here which can probably only be accounted for by something like Weber's hypothesis. Hagen's findings are, however, open to serious, and, I think, fatal questioning on several grounds, and in particular on two counts which vitiate his whole enterprise.[18] In taking his names from Ashton's work, he has omitted all merchants and financiers, all shipowners and warehousemen and all bankers, tracing only industrial and manufacturing innovators (and, anomalously, seven innovators in agriculture). It must be said that this is quite commonly done among historians of this subject except when it suits their convenience to mention a Quaker banker or two. We shall see the consequences of this below. Worse still, there is a basic ambiguity running through Hagen's definition of 'innovators'. Is this a list of entrepreneurs or inventors? The two classes are, of course, conceptually quite distinct, and endless confusion has surely been the result of blurring the distinction between the two. The Weber Thesis concerns capitalist enterprise, and hence entrepreneurs; any reference to 'inventors' or 'innovators' who were not successful businessmen — though not without intrinsic interest — is simply not relevant. Time and again, however, writers on the Weber Thesis confuse the two categories, sliding from one to the other without the slightest pause. It is well-known however that many key inventors, for example James Hargreaves and Samuel Crompton, were incompetent or luckless as businessmen.[19] Turning again to Hagen's findings, one will see how few of his innovators were in fact successful entrepreneurs. To the best of my knowledge — and eliminating the already-wealthy landowners like Lords Leicester and Townshend — only a comparatively few were successful businessmen and only a handful died rich. Probably only four were worth in excess of £500,000; perhaps fewer than ten others studied by Hagen were worth more than £100,000 at their deaths.[20] The majority of these men — the key 'innovators' of the Industrial Revolution — died in moderate circumstances or were in actual poverty at their deaths. Even as a first approximation to an accurate assessment of Weber, Hagen's work here is lacking in conceptual clarity.

For any empirical test of the Weber Thesis to be valid, it must include successful entrepreneurs and only entrepreneurs, chosen on an objective and comprehensive basis. It is here that the probate sources are most helpful, for they provide just such information. Wealthy men (apart from landowners, not considered in the discussion here) and wealthy men alone are enumerated – the categories of inventor and entrepreneur are not mixed. The probate data is objective rather than reputational and the many little-known but highly successful businessmen of the time appear no less (and rather more) than the most celebrated figures. Furthermore, taking wealth at death as the criterion for measuring success favours, as it were, the prudent, the thrifty, the puritanical, over the spendthrift and extravagant. If there is a bias built into the nature of the data, it takes the form of overcounting those with a puritanical lifestyle compared with those whose lives were a round of conspicuous consumption, extravagant display and gambling, and presumably a disproportionate number of these were dissenters. Finally, it might be noted that the number of men in this study exceeds the number in Hagen's by twelve times.

Before turning to the evidence itself, something must be said of the problems associated with the collection of data and the conventions which have been adopted here. Tracing a man's religious affiliation is much more difficult than any other salient social characteristic assessed in this work, particularly as we are not concerned with his religion at death, but his original or familial religion, and a substantial number of unknowns remain, especially at the lower levels of wealth. Information on a man's adult religion may often be gleaned from his burial service or a similar source, but data about his childhood or original religion must often be inferred from such sources as the man's, or his parents' marriage licence – which states the name of the church or chapel where the marriage occurred – from attendance at a denominational school or university, etc., as well as from direct statements of religious identity, as in newspaper obituaries.[21]   An interesting problem of bias arises from this last factor. There were no local London newspapers until the late nineteenth century; almost all of the good ones were in provincial towns, especially in the north. In so far as religious affiliation was not distributed in a random geographical manner – and it was not – this will affect the findings. In fact, since there were proportionately more dissenters and fewer Anglicans in the north than in London, the known dissenting portion will be overstated and the Anglican portion understated. I am convinced that this has in fact occurred.

Table 5.1: Original Religions of Wealth-holders, by Year of Birth Cohorts

Religion	1720-39	1740-59	1760-79	1780-99	1800-19	1820-39	1840-59	1860-79	1880-99	Totals
Millionaires:										
1. Anglicans	1=100%	4=100%	2=40%	10=67%	25=57%	36=49%	12=39%	2=50%	0	92=51%
2. Dissenters	0	0	1=20%	3=20%	7=16%	11=15%	4=13%	0	0	26=15%
3. Church of Scotland	0	0	0	2=13%	9=20%	10=14%	5=16%	2=50%	0	28=16%
4. Roman Catholics	0	0	0	0	0	0	0	0	0	0
5. Jews	0	0	2=40%	0	4= 9%	13=18%	9=29%	0	0	28=16%
6. Lutherans	0	0	0	0	0	3= 4%	0	0	0	3= 2%
7. Greek Orthodox	0	0	0	0	0	1= 1%	1= 3%	0	0	2= 1%
8. Others	0	0	0	0	0	0	0	0	0	0
Column Totals	1=0.6 %	4= 2%	5= 3%	15= 8%	45=25%	74=41%	31=17%	4= 2%		179
Unknowns (by religion) = 19										
Half-millionaires:										
1. Anglicans	2= 50%	11= 85%	13=62%	37=61%	56=57%	94=54%	38=48%	9=75%	0	260=56%
2. Dissenters	0	1= 8%	1= 5%	12=20%	17=17%	28=16%	11=14%	0	0	70=15%
3. Church of Scotland	1= 25%	1= 8%	4=19%	4= 7%	16=16%	33=19%	13=16%	1= 8%	1=33%	74=16%
4. Roman Catholics	0	0	0	2= 3%	0	2= 1%	3= 4%	0	0	7= 2%
5. Jews	0	0	2=10%	5= 8%	5= 5%	11= 6%	11=14%	2=17%	2=67%	38= 8%
6. Lutherans	0	0	0	0	0	0	0	0	0	0

Table 5.1: Continued

Religion	1720-39	1740-59	1760-79	1780-99	1800-19	1820-39	1840-59	1860-79	1880-99	Totals
Half-millionaires:										
7. Greek Orthodox	0	0	1= 5%	1= 2%	2= 2%	4= 2%	3= 4%	0	0	11= 2%
8. Others	0	0	0	0	2= 2%	2= 1%	1= 1%	0	0	5= 1%
Column Totals	3= 1%	13= 3%	21= 5%	61=13%	98=21%	174=37%	80=17%	12= 3%	3= 1%	465
Unknowns (by religion) = 114										
Lesser Wealthy:										
1. Anglicans	18= 82%	29= 67%	16=62%	37=70%	8=89%	1=50%				109=70%
2. Dissenters	1= 5%	7= 16%	5=19%	7=13%	1=11%	1=50%				22=14%
3. Church of Scotland	1= 5%	4= 9%	4=15%	5= 9%	0	0				14= 9%
4. Roman Catholics	1= 5%	0	0	0	0	0				1= 1%
5. Jews	0	1= 2%	1= 4%	2= 4%	0	0				4= 3%
6. Lutherans	0	2= 5%	0	0	0	0				2= 1%
7. Greek Orthodox	0	0	0	2= 4%	0	0				2= 1%
8. Others	1= .6%	1= .6%	0	0	0	0				2= 1%
Column Totals	22= 14%	44= 28%	26=17%	53=34%	9= 6%	2= 1%				156
Unknowns = 128										

Table 5.2: Dissenting Denominations, by Birth Cohorts (Percents of Totals for all Religions)

	1720-39	1740-59	1760-79	1780-99	1800-19	1820-39	1840-59	1860-79	Totals
Millionaires:									
Congregationalist	0	0	0	0	1= 2%	4= 5%	0	0	5= 3%
Baptists	0	0	0	0	0	0	2=7%	0	2= 1%
Quakers	0	0	1=20%	1=7%	3= 7%	4= 5%	0	0	9= 5%
Unitarians	0	0	0	1=7%	1= 2%	2= 3%	0	0	4= 2%
Independents	0	0	0	0	1= 2%	0	0		1= 1%
Methodists	0	0	0	0	0	1= 1%	1=3%		2= 1%
Others (+ Dissent Unidentified + Probable Dissent (including Huguenots))	0	0	0	1=7%	1= 2%	0	0		2= 1%
Half-millionaires:									
Congregationalists	0	0	0	0	7= 7%	5=3%	3=4%	0	15= 3%
Baptists	0	0	0	0	1= 1%	4= 2%	1=1%	0	6= 1%
Quakers	0	1=8%	0	5=8%	3= 3%	10= 6%	1=1%	0	20= 4%
Unitarians	0	0	0	3=5%	2= 2%	1= 1%	2=3%	0	8= 2%
Independents	0	0	0	0	0	1= 1%	1=1%	0	2= 4%
Methodists	0	0	0	0	1= 1%	0	0	0	1=.2%

Table 5.2: Continued

	1720-39	1740-59	1760-79	1780-99	1800-19	1820-39	1840-59	1860-79	Totals
Half-millionaires:									
Others (+ Dissent Unidentified + Probable Dissent (including Huguenots))	0	0	1= .2%	3=5%	3= 3%	6= 4%	3=4%	0	16= 3%
Presbyterians in England	0	0	0	1=2%	0	1= 1%	0	0	2=.4%
Lesser Wealthy*									
Quakers	1=5%	3=7%	2= 8%	3=6%	1=11%	0			10= 6%
Unitarians	0	1=2%	0	1=2%	0	1=50%			3= 2%
Methodists	0	0	1= 4%	1=2%	0	0			2= 2%
Other Dissent, etc.	0	3=7%	2= 8%	2=4%	0	0			7= 4%

* Other denominations, no examples.

Just to be as fair to Weber's contentions as possible, in Tables 5.1-5.2, anyone with a *traceable* dissenting grandparent has been counted as a dissenter even if that person was known to have been an Anglican.[22] Tables 5.1-5.2 detail the original religion of non-landed wealth-holders, by year of *birth* cohort, down to those deceased in 1914 (*not* 1939). These tables thus differ in two respects from most of the other tables of the social or economic characteristics of the wealth-holders in this work: they are arranged by birth rather than death cohorts (which are more relevant), and they stop in 1914 (rather than 1939) after which the *original* religion of the wealth-holder becomes less relevant to his economic performance and considerably more difficult to trace.[23]

It will be seen from Table 5.2, detailing the individual dissenting denominations, that the number of wealth-holders among most of the sects is quite small and, among some cohorts, nil. To be sure, some denominations are overrepresented. In particular, the Quakers — as one might expect — are quite dramatically overrepresented, making up about five per cent of the total of wealth-holders compared with under one-tenth of one per cent of the English population. On the other hand, some groups are slightly underrepresented including, surprisingly, the Baptists, who made up about one per cent of the population. The Methodists were grossly underrepresented. They were, of course, much newer than the sects of Old Dissent and, by and large, drew their adherents from a lower social stratum. Nevertheless, there were successful Methodist millowners and Methodist colliery owners, like the family of Sir Josiah Guest and, if religious persuasion is important, there should have been many more.

In reviewing the place of dissent in the light of this evidence, one is continuously struck by the extent to which, generally speaking, our common impression of dissenting predominance in business life is based upon a rehearsal of names trotted out again and again, whose importance in the total picture is thereby exaggerated. When one has named the most celebrated Quaker dynasties, like the Gurneys, Peases, Barclays and Cadburys, one has virtually exhausted the roll-call of Quaker wealth; in contrast to the Anglicans, there are very few names of those who were just as wealthy but unknown.

Old Dissent — the Baptists, Quakers, Unitarians, etc. — was thus the predominant element among the dissenting wealth-holders throughout the period; only a handful of wealth-holders were Methodists. There were few surprises among the wealthy dissenting wealth-holders, and most have been well-served by historians. Most of the dissenters were in industrial or manufacturing trades, though particularly prominent among the food-drink-tobacco categories were the Congregationalist Willses (tobacco) and the Quaker biscuit and sweets dynasties like the Cadburys, Frys and Palmers. Among the commercial dissenting wealth-holders, however, was Lord Overstone, son of a Unitarian minister-turned-banker, and the famous and important Quaker bankers like the Gurneys, Peckovers and Barclays. Important figures among the dissenting industrial wealth-holders include the Huguenot silk and rayon manufacturing Courtaulds, the Quaker cotton Fieldens, the Congregationalist cotton manufacturer John Rylands (1801-88) and the Unitarian locomotive builder James Kitson, 1st Baron Airedale (1835-1911). Methodists included W.H. Smith (1825-91), the great wholesale newsagent and politician. A number of rather bizarre dissenting sects were represented, especially among the half-millionaires. The lead merchant Selwood C. Riddle (1836-1908) was a member of the Catholic Apostolic Sect; most curious of all (although he died in 1915 and hence does not figure in these tables), William P. Manners (1847-1915) rose from clerk to head the brewers Worthington & Co., despite membership in the strict Plymouth Brethren Sect. All in all, the splendid variety of dissenting sects to be found in nineteenth-century Britain — Invingites, Sandemanians, followers of the Countess of Huntingdon, and so on — seem to have produced few men with vast fortunes.

It must be obvious from even a casual perusal of Tables 5.1-5.2 that the dissenting proportion of non-landed wealth-holders is simply nothing like that suggested by Hagen or, indeed what one might have expected in light of the Weber Thesis. In fact, except for the dramatic overrepresentation of Jews and other migrants, the percentages bear a virtual random sample resemblance to the denominational percentages of the time — assuming that Jews and Catholics have changed places. The majority at each level of wealth were Anglicans, while Church of Scotland and dissenting adherents are also almost precisely as one would expect on a purely random basis. It is also noteworthy that the percentage of wealthy dissenters *increases* over time, which presents some difficulties to those who seek to explain the origins of the Industrial Revolution in terms of dissenting entrepreneurs. Extrapolating these figures backwards to the early eighteenth century would probably show even fewer wealthy dissenters than are indicated here. Equally interesting is the fact that some groups are not equally distributed up and down the wealth scale, in contrast to other groups, which are. In particular, the Jewish percentage is consistently higher at the richest levels, a fact important to the best interpretation of these findings. It is significant, too, that there are not more dissenters among the earlier 'lesser wealthy' groups, which would counter the superficially plausible argument that dissenters, being 'new men', had not yet had the time to amass really vast fortunes. Nor should it be forgotten that only non-landed wealth-holders are included here. If one adds the great landowners to the figures presented in this evidence — and many historians now regard them as essentially capitalists of the land[24] — the Anglican percentage rises still further, to something like 90 per cent to 95 per cent of the English total.

Apart from the Anglicans and dissenters were the Jewish, Roman Catholic and Greek Orthodox wealth-holders. Mention has already been made of the important role of the Jews at the centre of British financial and commercial life. The number of Jewish wealth-holders was far greater than their proportion in the population: with the exception of the Quakers, no other group was so overrepresented. The Jewish percentage of the wealth elite peaked just before the First World War, when over a fifth of all non-landed millionaires were Jews: at the time Jews accounted for no more than 0.3 per cent of the total population and, even in London, for no more than three per cent of the inhabitants. Virtually every Jewish wealth-holder was in a commercial or financial pursuit. Only three Jewish wealth-holders were industrialists, the great chemical manufacturer Ludwig Mond (1839-1909) and his son, Alfred Mond, 1st Baron Melchett (1868-1930), and the ironmaster Sir Bernhard Samuelson (1820-1905). All of the others were bankers or merchant bankers, stock or insurance brokers, foreign merchants or retailers, generally in the City of London, although such provincial families as the Behrenses, the Manchester cotton merchants, do appear. Although there had been a considerable amount of intermarriage with gentiles, few wealthy Jews left their ancestral faith. Two prominent Jewish wealth-holders who did do so, however, were David Ricardo (1772-1823), as successful at stockbroking (he left £500,000) as at founding political economy, and the stockbroker Ludwig E.W.L. Messel (1847-1915), the great-grandfather of Lord Snowdon. After the First World War the Jewish portion of the wealth elite — and the concomitant influence of Jews on political life — declined considerably, as political and economic conditions adverse to foreign trade and finance manifested themselves. This state of affairs persisted until after the Second World War.

Catholicism produced few wealth-holders. Even Ireland's wealthy were mainly Protestants, for example the Guinnesses — devout members of the Church of Ireland — or the many Presbyterian industrialists in Ulster. In England the only notable Catholic dynasty was the Hultons, newspaper proprietors in Manchester and London. Although Catholicism won many adherents in the middle class and always retained some in the aristocracy, there was virtually no Catholic penetration among the non-landed wealthy.[25]

In contrast, the profile of the Greek Orthodox wealth-holders is much like that of the Jews. All of them were related members of the Ralli-Vlastos-Schillizzi family of foreign merchants and bankers. Like the Jews, they generally remained true to their religious heritage. In the inter-war period, they possibly fared better than the Jews, since their trade routes to the Levant and the Middle East were less affected by events than were the Jews' with the continent.

In the light of the limited role of dissent compared with Anglicanism, what patently requires a fresh examination is not dissent but Anglicanism, especially as opportunity and career patterns for ambitious young Anglicans led away from business life into the civil service, the military and imperial service, into teaching, the universities, the higher professions and, indeed, the Church. Very little is known about distinctly Anglican attitudes toward business life, of Anglican patterns of character-training apart from the public schools, or of Anglicans' preferences for their fellow Anglicans as partners or clients. Some patterns are, however, evident from a closer examination of the religious distribution of the wealth-holders. 44 per cent of all commercial millionaires were Anglicans, while only seven per cent of commercial millionaires were dissenters (30 per cent were Jews; 15 per cent Church of Scotland adherents). Of the manufacturing millionaires, 52 per cent were Anglicans, 23 per cent dissenters, 33 per cent members of the Church of Scotland. Of the millionaires in the food-drink-tobacco occupational categories, 70 per cent were Anglicans, 24 per cent dissenters, two per cent adherents of the Church of Scotland. Similar percentages were found among half-millionaires and the lesser wealthy. Anglicans, then, succeeded more often in commerce and finance, and in foodstuffs (mainly as wealthy brewers), less often in manufacturing. Despite these generalisations there was certainly no dearth of wealthy Anglican manufacturers, like Arkwright (cotton), Peel (cotton), Stephenson (locomotive manufacturing), Brassey (railway contracting) or Armstrong (armaments and engineering). But most Anglican wealth-holders were in finance, particularly private banking, like the Smiths, Cunliffes, Becketts and Denisons, or in retailing or mercantile activities.

One important question is the extent to which Anglican wealth-holders were influenced by the Evangelical movement or by the various species of muscular Anglicanism so prevalent in Victorian society.

There are, indeed, many indications in the obituaries or biographies of Anglican businessmen that aspects of their religious beliefs were deeply-felt. Many built local churches or contributed to their restorations; for a few religion seemed a pervasive part of their outlook. Samuel Cunliffe-Lister, 1st Baron Masham 'very nearly went into the Church'; Sir Daniel Gooch, the locomotive engineer, was a 'strict Anglican'; Edmund D. Beckett, 1st Baron Grimthorpe, ecclesiastical barrister and banker (who left £2.1 million in 1905), designed and built churches.[26] But there is little evidence that religious training, or deeply held beliefs, figure strongly among the Anglicans in this study. Only one wealth-holder was a member of the famous Clapham Sect.[27] Few were known to have been Evangelicals and, indeed, it seems likely that Evangelicalism as a possible motivating force behind Anglican entrepreneurship has been exaggerated, whatever the importance of this movement for English society as a whole. The power and influence of Evangelicalism certainly did not arise until after 1800, and cannot explain Anglican business success before then.[28] Evangelicalism appears to have been largely a London-centred movement of the *non-business* well-to-do, mainly landed aristocrats and civil servants. There were, of course, many business families, especially in banking (like the Barings, Smiths and Martins) whose members became Evangelicals, but they were *already* wealthy and their business success cannot, certainly, be attributed to Evangelicalism; in any case, too little is known of Evangelicalism in the provinces to generalise about its effects there.[29] Moreover, the dissenting sects more affected by Evangelicalism and the revivals of enthusiasm, like the Methodists, produced the fewest wealth-holders, while those sects least affected, like the Quakers, produced the most. It is probably an implication of this that overt religious motivation was not a primary influence on the entrepreneurial performance of many Anglicans.

The statistics of the Church of Scotland are also significant and should be discussed. Their percentage among wealth-holders is fractionally higher than among the whole population by perhaps two per cent to three per cent. If the Weber Thesis is valid, Calvinism should have produced a Scotland notably wealthier and more prosperous than England. In fact it did not, and this was true of the whole population as well as of the handful of great fortunes. It is well-known that nineteenth-century Scotland was much poorer than England. While one English adult male in five had sufficient means to possess a vote in 1833, in Scotland the ratio was only one in eight.[30] The Income Tax returns by geographical area reveal that even in 1880, while Scotland's population amounted to about 16 per cent of England's, its income assessed under Schedule D (on business and professional incomes) totalled only about 11 per cent of the English figure.[31] For centuries, despite the Calvinist spirit pervading Scottish life, the brightest prospect that an enterprising Scot could see was indeed the high road to England, as the prominence of Scotsmen among English shipping magnates and merchants demonstrates. Scottish merchants overseas, straddling the trade routes to the West Indies, India, and Australia, existed in plenty.[32] Pervasive and established Calvinism did not affect Scottish society to the extent that it became either a paradise for capitalists or a land of affluence.

Finally, one might ask if the results indicated in Tables 5.1-5.2 were not skewed by the fact that so many wealth-holders inherited their fortunes from parents who were already wealthy. In other words, if 'self-made men' alone are counted in this study, would not the dissenting portion be much higher? The data in Table 5.3, which correlates the social class of the father of each non-landed wealth-holder with the wealth-holder's original religion does not endorse this suggestion.

In the first place, the number of 'self-made men' in the strict sense was – as we have seen – very small; secondly, the percentages by social origin are in no case seriously at variance with the overall percentages of each sect, except that there is some tendency for Anglicans to be overrepresented among those with upper-class fathers, and for adherents of the Church of Scotland and, to a lesser extent, Jews, to be drawn disproportionately from the lower ranks. As for dissenters, there are simply no discernible patterns at variance with a random sample at all.

It would be easy to conclude from these findings that there is essentially no correlation between religious affiliation and entre- preneurial achievement, even during the nineteenth century. Though, as a broad generalisation, this is probably more accurate than the Weber Thesis as it is normally stated, it is not yet refined enough to stand without amendment. The best way to approach the evidence given here, in my opinion, is not to take the view that certain religious groups are inherently more successful than others, but that *certain trades or occupations are inherently more profitable than others*, and offer far more room for the accumulation of vast fortunes than others. In modern Britain, as we have seen, there is abundant evidence that the most profitable trades, those productive of the largest incomes and fortunes, were in commerce and finance, while manufacturing industries were less lucrative. While there is no hard-and-fast rule, by and large Anglicans –

Table 5.3: Father's Social Class, by Original Religion of Wealth-holder

	Upper	Upper Middle	Lower Middle	Working	Unknowns
Millionaires:					
1. Anglicans	54=52%	14=38%	20=49%	2=25%	2=25%
2. Dissenters	18=17%	4=11%	4=10%	0	0
3. Church of Scotland	8= 8%	7=19%	10=24%	1=13%	2=25%
4. Roman Catholics	0	0	0	0	0
5. Jews	17=16%	6=16%	1= 2%	1=13%	3=38%
6. Lutheran	2= 2%	0	0	1=13%	0
7. Greek Orthodox	1= 1%	1= 3%	0	0	0
Total Known	100	32	35	5	7
Unknown	4	5	6	3	1
Half-millionaires:					
1. Anglicans	125=61%	65=40%	39=40%	4=10%	29=27%
2. Dissenters	31=15%	22=14%	11=13%	1= 5%	5= 5%
3. Church of Scotland	18= 9%	30=19%	18=21%	5=24%	3= 3%
4. Roman Catholics	2= 1%	2= 1%	0	1= 5%	2= 2%
5. Jews	14= 7%	11= 7%	3= 4%	2=10%	8= 7%
6. Lutherans	2= 1%	4= 3%	1= 1%	0	4= 4%
7. Greek Orthodox	1= .5%	3= 2%	0	0	1= 1%

Table 5.3: Continued

	Upper	Upper Middle	Lower Middle	Working	Unknowns
Half-millionaires:					
8. Others	0	0	0	0	1= 1%
Total Known	193	137	72	13	53
Unknown	13	24	12	10	55
Lesser Wealthy:					
1. Anglicans	65=77%	33=55%	4=36%	1=33%	32=20%
2. Dissenters	7= 8%	11=18%	1= 9%	0	7= 4%
3. Church of Scotland	0	6=10%	4=36%	0	10= 6%
4. Roman Catholics	1= 1%	0	0	0	0
5. Jews	2= 2%	2= 3%	0	0	3= 1%
6. Lutherans	0	1= 2%	0	0	1= 1%
7. Greek Orthodox	0	1= 2%	0	0	1= 1%
8. Others	0	0	0	0	0
Total Known	75	54	9	1	54
Unknown	7	6	2	2	112

Upper = top landowners, top businessmen, top professionals;
Upper Middle = intermediate levels of the three;
Lower Middle = farmers; small businessmen and professionals; clerical workers.

and immigrant groups like the Jews — were to be found primarily in commerce and finance, while English dissenters were disproportionately to be found in industry. If Jews and Anglicans had monopolised the cotton industry while dissenters had gone in heavily for merchant banking the figures would look quite different, and Weber might be confirmed. Yet, try as they might, with the rarest of exceptions manufacturers and industrialists, whatever their religion, could apparently not expand their businesses past a certain size. A recent historian of the Lancashire cotton industry, V.A.C. Gattrell, has noted that '(c)onstraints on growth — financial, "psycho-social", and in the areas of demand and technology alike, conditioned the expansive energies of industries as well as of industry as a whole. The result was a curious reticence about the advantages of expansion, witnessed in numerous contemporary recommendations of the advisability not of scale, but. to the contrary of moderation in enterprise'.[33] I would suggest that this was much more likely to occur in industrial firms — where dissenters were disproportionately to be found — rather than in commerce and finance, dominated by Anglicans, Jews and other migrants: this was governed by the nineteenth-century world economy, and probably varied from country to country. It is this fact which accounts for the great overrepresentation of Jews and other migrant groups so characteristic of the City of London, and it accounts as well for the curious phenomenon of the substantially greater number of Jews at the millionaire level than at lower stages on the wealth scale.

The question naturally arises from this, why did Anglicans, Jews and dissenters enter different fields in different numbers? No single easy answer can be given to this question; in certain cases it may have been simply a geographical accident, the presence in large numbers of particular religious or ethnic groups near the venues where particular businesses were carried on. With immigrants, the pattern was in many cases a carry-over from that of their old homelands in Europe where they were engaged in activities of this kind. A status factor may also have been at work: Anglicans, closer in their outlooks to the traditional status notions of landed society, may have avoided manufacturing industries where they dirtied their hands or were compelled to master a large-scale workforce, preferring to work in more genteel trades like banking and foreign trade. Most historians have assumed that this was an unfortunate choice in terms of economic advantage and growth. The evidence suggests that they are wrong. Finally, many religious and ethnic groups acted, in effect, as extended families or communities, serving as mutual benefit societies for their members, providing useful trading connections, venture capital, marriageable daughters with dowries and prospective business partners. This was especially true among the most successful minority groups like the Jews and Quakers, as well as among smaller groups like the Unitarians, Greeks and Huguenots. Among the Quakers for example, one finds the intermarried and closely related family trees of such families as the Barclays, Gurneys, Hanburys and Peases.[34]

However, though this is probably an important and valid factor in explaining the entrepreneurial success of some minority groups, it will not account for the success of the Anglicans. Surely the national and 'normal' Church of England did not act in this way. For upwardly-mobile and talented Anglicans, the way ahead led to the landed and professional elite, away from the business world. This argument, then, should not be pushed too far.[35]

Two major conclusions do nevertheless seem to follow from the interpretation offered here. One — and the acute reader may have seen it in other places in this work — is that entrepreneurial *effort* is not as important as *place in the total economy* in determining entrepreneurial rewards. A Calvinist cotton manufacturer may have in truth worked three times harder than an Anglican stockbroker in the City of London, but built up a fortune only a fraction as large: just as no shopkeeper, regardless of his religious beliefs or his tenacity of labour, would ever become as wealthy as a successful stockbroker unless he became something more than a shopkeeper. At best the drive provided by religion to the labours of the cotton spinner or shopkeeper would merely have made him into a very successful man of his trade.

Second, and following from this, it seems clear that entrepreneurial success has little or nothing to do with *religion*. The entrepreneurial spirit allegedly imbued into believers by Calvinism was surely, in nineteenth-century Europe, the common currency of acquisitive Western man, while the mechanism by which the Weber Thesis was supposed to operate — child rearing,[36] or family networks — belongs to other realms than religion or theology.

Politics

The political connections of wealthy men are ostensibly the best single clue to the relationship between wealth and power. For most of the period covered in this work, election to Parliament was considered to be an honour that many wealthy men wished to obtain, and for much

Table 5.4: Non-landed Millionaire MPs, by Type of Wealth and Party

	Industrial	Commercial	Miscellaneous	Total		Non-MPs
1809-58:						
Cons.	1			1 }	3	6
Whig/Lib.		2		2 }		
1858-79:						
Cons.	2	1	1	4 }	10	19
Lib.		6		6 }		
1880-99:						
Cons.	3	3	3	9 }		
Lib.	2	3	2	7 }	18	41
LU		2		2 }		
1900-19:						
Cons.	3	7	2	12 }		
Lib.	6	6	3	15 }	30	71
LU		2	1	3 }		
1920-39:						
Cons.	2	7	2	11 }		
Lib.	9	3	1	13 }	26	144
LU		2		2 }		

Cons. = Conservative
Lib. = Liberal
LU   = Liberal Unionist

of the period wealthy men were amply represented among both main parties. Below the national level there was an even greater participation by the rich in local politics, both as Justices of the Peace and after 1888 as members of the county councils, and in the towns as councillors and mayors.

As Tables 5.4-5.6 demonstrate, however, by no means all wealthy men went into Parliament. At the millionaire level, no more than about one-third of each cohort entered Parliament, and at the half-millionaire level the rate of participation was even lower, with about one-fifth of the first two cohorts serving in Parliament, a percentage which decreased to less than one-twelfth among the last cohort. The two groups of lesser wealthy show a rather higher degree of Parliamentary service than the worst-represented of the wealthiest cohorts, with about one-eleventh of the 1809-29 and one-sixth of the 1850-69 groups serving in Parliament. In absolute numbers there is a rather different picture, with the number

Table 5.5: Non-landed Half-millionaire MPs, by Type of Wealth and Party

	Industrial	Commercial	Miscellaneous	Total		Non-MPs
1809-58:						
Cons.	1	2	2	5		
Whig/Lib.	3	1		4	11	35
Unknown	1	1		2		
1858-79:						
Cons.	2	4		6		
Lib.	7	7		14	21	74
Unknown		1		1		
1880-99:						
Cons.	7	1	2	10	20	140
Lib.	6	2	2	10		
1900-19:						
Cons.	4	3	3	10		
Lib.	8	3	2	13	27	208
LU	2	1	1	4		
1920-39:						
Cons.	1	4	6	11		
Lib.	5	4	1	10	22	328
LU		1		1		

Table 5.6: Lesser Wealthy MPs, by Type of Wealth and Party

	Industrial	Commercial	Miscellaneous	Total		Non-MPs
1809-29:						
Cons.	3	2	2	7		
Whig	1	3	1	5		119
Unknown		2	1	3		
1850-69:						
Cons.	4	3		7		
Whig/Lib.	4	10	1	15		115
Unknown		1		1		

of MPs among both the millionaire and half-millionaire groups readily rising throughout the nineteenth century, reaching a peak among the 1900-19 cohort, and declining slightly with the 1920-39 group.

Although the Conservative party was largely the party of land while the Whig-Liberals held the support of most businessmen, until the great shifts in the occupational bases of party support that began in the 1860s and reached a climax in the 1880s, the Conservatives' representation among the non-landed wealthy was never negligible, generally producing only slightly fewer MPs in each cohort group than the Liberals.[37] Rather surprisingly, the Liberal lead was maintained to the very end, a generation after most wealthy Liberals had left their party for the Conservatives or Liberal Unionists. Among the lesser wealthy, the same pattern was evidenced among the 1850-69 group, but among the 1809-29 cohort there was a 2-1 Tory majority, probably evidence of the broad nature of the Pitt-Liverpool Tory party and the exclusive nature of the Whig opposition.

Among the millionaires, the early cohorts demonstrate a surprising majority for Conservatives engaged in commercial or financial fields as opposed to industrialists, although this was not the case until the 1880-99 cohort for half-millionaires. Among the Liberals, commercial millionaires were in a clear majority among the early groups although among the half-millionaires this picture is reversed. In the more recent periods the tendencies among both groups were less clear. Among the Conservative millionaires far more were in commercial than in industrial fields, and there were no industrial Liberal Unionists among the millionaires. Among Conservative and Liberal Unionist half-millionaires there is less of a clear pattern than among millionaires. At both levels the Liberals show a majority for industrialists.

The main conclusion of this is probably that there was a drift of the commercial and financial wealth, particularly among those in the City of London, away from Liberalism and into Conservatism or Liberal Unionism in the last decades of the nineteenth century, while the wealthy supporters of the Liberal party were increasingly drawn from among the industrialists. There are several plausible reasons why this is probably an accurate picture of what was in fact occurring among the upper-middle classes as a whole. First, as noted above, the social distance between the commercial wealthy and the traditional landed aristocracy was far less great than between the aristocracy and the industrialists, and hence the greatest bankers and merchants would have found an easier haven in Conservatism than previously. Second, the industrialists were disproportionately more dissenting in religion than those in commerce, and the Liberal party continued to be the party of dissent to the end. The drift of commercial wealth-holders — men like W.H. Smith, the millionaire merchant bankers Baron Ferdinand J. de

Rothschild (1839-98) and Sir Alexander H. Brown (1844-1922) – who were two of the original Liberal Unionist MPs – or Samuel Samuel (1855-1934), head of the merchant bank M. Samuel and brother of Lord Bearsted, founder of Shell Transport and Trading – from Liberalism to Conservatism represented a fundamental shift in the natural party of the Establishment, especially that part based on Anglicanism and London. The Liberal party, which in the 1850s might fairly have been described as the home of most businessmen, increasingly became the party of businessmen only of a few particular types: those with industrial works in factory towns or (with many exceptions as the above examples show) of dissenting or Jewish backgrounds. The 'bitter end' Liberal wealth-holders – those who remained loyal to Liberalism after the revolutions of 1886 and even of 1909 – were typified by such men as Sir John Brunner, 1st Bt. (1842-1919) and his son Sir John, 2nd Bt. (1865-1929), the chemical manufacturers of Swiss descent, the Jewish merchant banker Samuel Montagu, 1st Baron Swaythling (1832-1911), who possessed virtually the only safe Liberal seat in London (in Whitechapel) between 1885 and 1900, the Unitarian locomotive manufacturer James Kitson, 1st Baron Airedale (1835-1911), MP for Colne Valley between 1892 and 1906, or Sydney J. Stern, 1st Baron Wandsworth (1845-1912), another Jewish merchant banker who received a peerage after only four years service in Parliament and 'lavish contributions to party funds'.[38] The revolution in party affiliation that occurred in the late nineteenth century brought those wealthy groups with the least social distance from the traditional landed aristocracy – the London-based Anglican merchants and bankers and the provincial Anglican elites – into the Conservative party. It might also be noted that no wealth-holder served as a Labour MP, and only one appears to have been a Labour supporter, Sir Alexander Grant, 1st Bt. (1864-1937), a self-made biscuit millionaire who donated an automobile and 30,000 shares in his company to Ramsay MacDonald shortly before receiving a baronetcy in 1924: the cause of a considerable scandal.

At the same time that commercial wealth moved into the Conservative camp, there can be little doubt that the scale of wealth of all MPs was increasing. The Corn Law Parliament contained only seven men who left non-landed fortunes of £500,000 or more,[39] but the 1895 Parliament included among its members 56 Conservatives, 17 Liberal Unionists, and 20 Liberals – a total of 93 men, or nearly 15 per cent of the total membership of the House of Commons – who left fortunes of £500,000 or more. Even in 1906 there were 72 MPs (24 Conservatives, five Liberal

Unionists and 43 Liberals) with fortunes of £500,000 or more. After the First World War, however, both of the two old parties underwent a clear decline in their wealth levels: in the 1922 House of Commons, for example, only 30 Tories and six Liberals left fortunes of £500,000 or more.[40] The decline in the relative number of wealthy men *directly* represented in the British Parliament had its parallel in other countries, and probably should be seen as a common feature of democratic politics in this century.

The 1895 Parliament probably represented the peak of the overlap between wealth and formal power-holding. In 1895 there were probably 200 living millionaires in Britain, many of whom were members of the House of Lords, and 60 of whom sat in the House of Commons. It is likely that any state opening of Parliament at the time saw a greater concentration of Britain's economic wealth at one time in one place than ever in British history, and possibly among any legislature anywhere. One of the most notable aspects of the representation of the rich was the lifelong association with the constituencies they represented. Especially in small and middle-sized manufacturing boroughs it was common for a town to send its richest man — and largest employer of labour — to Westminster. One could easily cite 50 examples of this. Both Brunner and Mond were MPs for Cheshire constituencies near their alkali works; Spencer Charrington did not think it beneath him to represent Mile End, Stepney, where his great brewery stood; Mr Harland sat for Belfast North, and Mr Wolff, not to be outdone, for Belfast East. The position held by so many of these wealthy men in their towns was reminiscent of the landlord *vis-à-vis* his tenants, and it would be interesting to learn if the working-class supporters of these men retained any memory of their agricultural origins in a new context. With rare exceptions, class politics did not exist in any constituency: loyalties were largely derived from religious and political roots.[41] The 'abdication on the part of the governors' did not occur in these towns until the time of the real political revolution in modern Britain, in 1920-4.[42]*Most of these wealthy MPs, it should be noted, were the merest lobby fodder. The only non-landed millionaire MP to matter politically was W.H. Smith, who became First Lord of the Treasury before his death in 1891. Sir Robert Peel, 2nd Bt. (1788-1850), who left £400,000 (and much land), and who is included among the lesser wealthy, was the wealthiest non-landed Prime Minister.[43] One of the chief reasons for this, as James Cornford pointed out, was the late age of arrival of most MPs with business backgrounds in the period 1885-1914.[44]

Below the national level of representation, the wealthy were involved in politics to a greater extent than at the Parliamentary level. Clearly, only a minority even of the wealthiest men at one time will possess the time, interest or skills to enter politics at the Parliamentary level, but a far greater percentage would be willing to undertake the less arduous work of the JP or High Sheriff of a county. Involvement at the local level was a sign of the penetration of 'new men' in the very heartland of the traditional squirearchy. One should probably not, however, make too much of this. If one were rich enough, and not an obvious swindler or ex-Cockney, one could at practically all times and places in modern British history quickly achieve at least some measure of acceptability and status, particularly if one possessed dowered daughters. It is not surprising, therefore, that of the 250 non-landed millionaires who had no Parliamentary experience, no fewer than 122 held local office as Justice of the Peace, Deputy-Lieutenant, High Sheriff or Lord Lieutenant of a county, or mayor or councillor in a borough. This is a minimum number, since it is probable that for many other millionaires, holding similar rank, biographical details are lacking. Among the half-millionaires the percentage is probably somewhat lower, but still very high. Only among the lesser wealthy, and particularly among those deceased in the period 1809-29, does local office-holding appear to be slight. In this period local positions were largely still the monopoly of the landed gentry and Anglican clergy.[45]

Honours

The final seal of approval in the transformation of wealth into status was the acquisition of a title, preferably a hereditary one – a baronetcy or a peerage – in order to found a dynasty rather than a mere knighthood. As has been well-documented by Ralph Pumphrey, the peerage was to all practical purposes closed to businessmen until about 1885. Apart from the barristers who became Lord Chancellors or Masters of the Rolls, the only non-landed figures given peerages between about 1835 and 1885 were a handful of bankers or merchant bankers like the Barings (Barons Ashburton, Revelstoke, Northbrook, etc.), a few men with mercantile backgrounds like Macaulay or John Cam Hobhouse, 1st Baron Broughton (1786-1869, created 1856), the grandson of a Bristol merchant, and a solitary peer with an industrial origin, Edward Strutt, 1st Baron Belper (1801-80, created 1856). Thereafter, virtually overnight the peerage became open to a flood of businessmen of every sort and, it is interesting to note, between 1885 and 1905, to professionals and other public figures without aristocratic connections including several civil servants, the Poet Laureate Tennyson, the painter Leighton, the physicist Kelvin and the medical pioneer Joseph Lister, who was born a Quaker.[46] Few of these figures, it should be noted, were self-made men: most of the business peers had been wealthy for several generations. In the period between 1880 and 1905, it appears that only three or four newly-created peers started life poor.[47]

The reluctance among successive governments (and on the part of the Sovereign, who still had an important measure of control over the disposition of peerages) to reward all but the most minimal number of peerages to businessmen had several different roots. On one hand there was no doubt a strong element of resentment on the part of the land-owner against the new business order, a situation that was not relieved until landowners themselves acquired their share of City directorships.[48] It is also important to realise that a hereditary peerage was a permanent monument to the family rewarded, and for many years businessmen were in no position to claim permanence among their virtues. Even the wealthiest manufacturer might, after all, find himself bankrupted by a trade recession; even the most prosperous financier might turn into another 'Railway' Hudson. The acquisition of large amounts of land by a businessman might alleviate the anxiety over his impermanence but, as will be discussed later, few new businessmen became landowners on a great scale, and even this was no guarantee of peerage. The Arkwrights, who had always been Anglicans, had been awarded a knighthood in the eighteenth century, and owned 16,000 acres in 1883, never received a peerage. The Morrisons who, as has been noted above, owned 106,000 acres yielding £53,000 per annum had to wait until 1965 (!) to receive the very last hereditary peerage that was created.

Even in the best of times, only a minority of wealth-holders were given titles. Among the best-rewarded cohort, the non-landed millionaires deceased in the period 1920-39, only 53 out of 162 of these top wealth-holders were given a title of any kind — 21 peerages, 20 baronetcies, 12 knighthoods. Among most cohorts and at earlier times only a small percentage of these wealthy men received titles, even lowly ones. Among the non-landed half-millionaires deceased between 1809 and 1879, for instance, only eight titles were so bestowed — two peerages and six baronetcies. This niggardliness in the bestowal of titles throughout the nineteenth century must have had a considerable influence on the behaviour of many wealthy men. They were, in effect, in a 'no-win' situation: no amount of land purchase, no amount of charity, no degree of aristocracy-aping would gain them what they really wanted; in such a situation, there was little incentive to change one's life-style or habitual modes of thought. This was to change radically and quickly during the late nineteenth century.

There appears to have been little in the way of a definite correlation between the type of wealth (commercial, industrial or miscellaneous) earned by a wealthy businessman and the likelihood that he would receive a title, with each type of wealth represented in about equal proportions, although − as one might expect − it was probably the case that comparatively fewer industrialists were honoured in the earlier period. The trend in knighthoods (as opposed to baronetcies) is some-what curious: while one might have expected that new men would have received more such non-hereditary titles before the flood of baronetcies began, in fact the number of baronetcies exceeded the number of knighthoods bestowed upon top wealth-holders during the nineteenth century, while knighthoods began to flower only in this century. In all likelihood, it would seem, during the nineteenth century a baronetcy, when it was bestowed, was considered a substitute for a peerage rather than a promotion from a knighthood, and were hence granted to the types of men who would at a later time have been ennobled. Indeed, knighthoods appear to have been reserved for civil servants, military men and colonial administrators in a rather strict manner.

When peerages came in a flood they generally went to wealth-holders who had had some Parliamentary experience: among ennobled millionaires, 27 out of 37 had previously sat in the House of Commons, as had 15 of 24 ennobled half-millionaires. Oddly enough, however, at the very top, most of the peerages of superior rank were awarded to men without any Parliamentary experience. Apart from Wellington, no man in this study was granted a dukedom or a marquisate − a not unimportant commentary on the reluctance of the British elite to admit businessmen to equal consideration with landowners[49] − and only three were awarded earldoms: Lord Eldon during the period of Tory 'Old Corruption' and, in this century, the brewer Lord Iveagh and the foreign merchant and banker Lord Inchcape, neither of whom ever served as an MP. Six viscountcies were awarded to wealth-holders, three going to non-Parliamentarians: those bestowed upon Lords Northcliffe (newspapers); Bearsted (petroleum and finance); and Pirrie (shipbuilding). Finally, it remains to be noted that 13 of the 65 wealth-holders who ever received peerages received their original

ennoblement from Lloyd George, in addition to four other peers who
left £500,000 or more after 1939 — a high, but certainly not a startling
percentage of the total and, equally certainly, not a remarkable
percentage of the 91 peerages created in all by Lloyd George. Several
of these men, like Lords Leverhulme or Bearsted, might have received
their titles from any Prime Minister of the century, while several others,
like the distiller Lord Dewar or the brewer Lord Wavertree, were Tories.

Notes

1. Weber's *Die Protestantische Ethik und der Geist des Kapitalismus* first
appeared in *Archiv für Sozialwissenschaft und Sozialpolitik* vols. xx and xxi
(1904-5). The first English translation was published (London, 1930) as *The
Protestant Ethic and the Spirit of Capitalism*, translated by Talcott Parsons and
with an Introduction by R.H. Tawney. The most useful summaries of the
voluminous writings of historians and economists on the Weber Thesis are
Robert W. Green, (ed.), *Protestantism, Capitalism and Social Science. The Weber
Thesis Controversy* (2nd edn, Lexington, Mass., 1973) and S.N. Eisenstadt, *The
Protestant Ethic and Modernization. A Comparative View* (New York, 1968).
A well-known and vigorous general attack on the Weber Thesis is Kurt
Samuelsson, *Religion and Economic Action*, translated from the Swedish by
E. Geoffrey French and edited, with an Introduction, by D.C. Coleman
(New York, 1961).
2. Cited in E. Fischoff, 'The Protestant Ethic and the Spirit of Capitalism',
Social Research, 11 (1944), p. 62.
3. Ibid., p. 64.
4. Ibid.
5. Ibid.
6. Although Weber wrote of the Reformation, there are many references in
his work to the eighteenth and nineteenth century, for instance his celebrated
example of Benjamin Franklin as an 'ideal type' of rational Calvinist-derived
mind. The Weber Thesis was apparently first directly and causally applied by a
major economic historian to the British Industrial Revolution situation of the
eighteenth and nineteenth century by T.S. Ashton in his *The Industrial
Revolution, 1760-1830* (1948), though, of course, the folk notion of a
connection between dissent and entrepreneurship is far older.
Among historians who specifically and unequivocally reject the Weber Thesis
in its British post-1700 formulation are Samuelsson, *Religion and Economic
Action*, Charles M. Elliott, 'The Ideology of Economic Growth: A Case Study' in
E.L. Jones and G.E. Mingay (eds.), *Land, Labour and Population in the Industrial
Revolution* (London, 1967) and E.J. Hobsbawm, *Industry and Empire* (London,
1969), pp. 37-8.
7. See, e.g., Harold Perkin, *The Origins of Modern English Society, 1780-1880*
(London, 1969), pp. 71-2 (but note also Perkin's shrewd demurral, ibid., p. 72).
8. M.W. Flinn, 'Social Theory and the Industrial Revolution' in Tom Burns
and S.B. Saul (eds.), *Social Theory and Economic Change* (London, 1967), p. 25.
9. Everett E. Hagen, *On the Theory of Social Change* (Homewood, Illinois,
1962), pp. 294-309.
10. Ashton's book does not discuss innovations or entrepreneurial advances in
a number of fields like brewing; Hagen does not include entrepreneurs or

innovators in trade or finance, and has provided a detailed list of the men mentioned in Ashton's book whom he has excluded from his study (ibid., pp. 295, 303-4).

11. Hagen, *On the Theory of Social Change*, pp. 296-7. Flinn, 'Social Theory and the Industrial Revolution', p. 23) puts the figure even lower: at three per cent of the English and Welsh population in the 1770s, rising to five per cent in 1812. (This estimate excludes Methodists.)

12. Perkin, *The Origins of Modern English Society*, pp. 196-9; Table 4, p. 201.

13. A.D. Gilbert, *Religion and Society in Industrial England* (London, 1976), pp. 27-9.

14. Ibid., Table 2.1, p. 28.

15. Chris Cook and Brendan Keith, *British Historical Facts 1830-1900* (London, 1975), p. 219.

16. Ibid., pp. 221, 232-3.

17. This is no reflection, however, on the many merits of *On the Theory of Social Change* or on Hagen's pioneering efforts to test the Weber Thesis empirically.

18. Among the lesser points one might also mention: the religious affiliations of 21 of his 92 men are unknown, a large missing portion; the names used by him (following Ashton) can be questioned as to their relevance or completeness. For instance, he includes seven innovators in agriculture, hardly relevant to a discussion of business success. He includes some extremely obscure men, like 'Barlow' and 'Dobson' (*On the Theory of Social Change*, pp. 305-8) whose achievements or even forenames were untraceable in any source; conversely many important innovators are excluded (e.g., the Brunels). Finally, his evidence for religious affiliation is confused, sometimes taking religion in childhood and sometimes, irrelevantly, religion at death which would, of course, distort the real picture (see the sources, footnoted in Ibid., p.308n1-21).

19. It is doubtful whether the abilities required to be a successful inventor are much related to those of a successful entrepreneur. For example, an entrepreneur (and especially one in manufacturing or industry) must handle a labour force; inventors have, classically, worked alone or in small groups.

20. The four worth in excess of £500,000 were Richard Arkwright, Sir Robert Peel, Richard Crawshay and Josiah Wedgwood. The others worth over £100,000 include Matthew Boulton, Benjamin Gott, Josiah Spode, George Stephenson, Joseph Whitworth and (probably) some of his earlier businessmen like Ambrose Crowley and Abraham Darby. (See Hagen, *On the Theory of Social Change*, pp. 305-8.)

21. In the computer printouts from which Table 5.1-5.3 were derived, I included the categories 'Probable Anglican', and 'Probable dissenter' to cover those cases in which the conclusion is open to some doubt. The number of 'probables' amounts to about one-fifth of the total of cases where there is no doubt; there is about the same proportion of Anglicans as dissenters. It should also be noted that if 'final' rather than 'original' religion is taken, the proportion of Anglicans rises from about 55 per cent of the total to nearly 65 per cent.

22. The effect of this is probably to increase the percentage of dissenters among the total by two per cent to three per cent *vs.* actual religion. If entrepreneurial values are transmitted by subtle child-rearing methods, as some psychologically-oriented historians have suggested, formal conversions may not erase the disposition of parents to imbue their children with these values; disregarding recent conversions, as is done here, meets the possible objections of this school.

23. There was a rise in the percentage of dissenting wealth-holders deceased in the period 1920-39. For instance, about 26 per cent of millionaires deceased in

this period whose ancestral religion was known were dissenters.

24. See, e.g., R.S. Neale, 'The Bourgeoisie, Historically, Has Played a Most Revolutionary Part', in Eugene Kamenka and R.S. Neale, (eds.), *Feudalism, Capitalism and Beyond* (London, 1975) or the essays in J.T. Ward and P.G. Wilson, (eds.), *Land and Industry* (Newton Abbot, 1971).

25. Mention might also be made of the Catholic wealth-holders associated with the Howard family. Thomas J. Eyres (1780-1866) son of the Duke of Norfolk's Sheffield agent, went on to be a banker in Sheffield, eventually leaving over half a million. The father of Francis J. Sumner (1807-84), a Glossop cotton half-millionaire, married the daughter of the Duke's Glossop agent. The daughter of Joseph Tasker (1797-1861), a Catholic half-millionaire, became a countess of the Papal States and a notable philanthropist.

26. *The Times*, 3 February 1906; Roger Burdett Wilson, *Sir Daniel Gooch: Memoirs and Diary* (Newton Abbot, 1972), p. 55; Peter Ferriday, *Lord Grimthorpe, 1816-1905* (London, 1957).

27. He was Charles Middleton, Admiral Lord Barham (1726-1813), who left £150,000. None of the businessmen associated with Clapham was wealthy enough to appear in this study.

28. Rev. William Romaine was 'the only clergyman preaching in London inspired by the spirit of the (Evangelical) revival' until 'the very end of the eighteenth century' (Ian Bradley, *The Call to Seriousness* (London, 1976), p. 15).

29. Cf. John Foster, *Class Struggle and the Industrial Revolution* (London, 1974), p. 26. Foster uses 'Evangelical' far too loosely.

30. Cook and Keith, *British Historical Facts 1830-1900*, p. 116.

31. P.P. 1882, LII.

32. Among the more famous examples of Scottish mercantile enterprise abroad were Yule, Catto in India; Jardine, Matheson and the Burmah Oil Company (Founded by the Sime Cargill family) in the Orient; Robert Campbell and Co. in New South Wales; the Canadian financiers and railway magnates Donald Smith (Lord Strathcona) and George Stephen (Lord Mount Stephen); and Williamson, Balfour & Co. in the United States. See, e.g., W. Turrentine Jackson, *The Enterprising Scot. Investors in the American West After 1873* (Edinburgh. 1968).

33. V.A.C. Gattrell, 'Labour, Power, and the Size of Firms in Lancashire Cotton in the Second Quarter of the Nineteenth Century', *Econ. Hist. Rev.*, 2nd ser., XXX (1977), p. 107.

34. See, e.g., Paul H. Emden, *Quakers in Commerce. A Record of Business Achievement* (London, 1940).

35. There is, however, a recorded incident of this nexus at work among Anglican Evangelical families (see Bradley, *The Call to Seriousness*, pp. 158-9). It should also be noted that patterns of shop patronage were often divided along denominational lines. William Whiteley, the Yorkshire-born London department store millionaire, recalled that in every village trade was divided among Anglican retailers catering for Anglicans, dissenters catering for dissenters. (Richard S. Lambert, *The Universal Provider* (London, 1938), Chapter Two.)

36. See Flinn, 'Social Theory and the Industrial Revolution'.

37. On this subject see J.A. Thomas, *The House of Commons, 1832-1901: A Study of the Economic and Functional Character* (Cardiff, 1939). The term 'Conservative' was introduced about 1830, but the Tory party from Pitt onwards is here termed 'Conservative', while the Liberal party counted as a continuation of the Whig party.

38. *The Times*, 12 February 1912.

39. On the anti-Corn Law side (Division List, Third Reading of the Corn Law Bill, 13 May 1846): William Beckett, banker (Leeds); John Brocklehurst, silk

manufacturer (Macclesfield); Sir John Guest, ironmaster (Merthyr Tydfil); and George F. Muntz, metal manufacturer (Birmingham). On the Protectionist side: Sir Joseph Bailey, ironmaster (Worcestershire); Henry Kemble, tea merchant (East Surrey); William Thompson, ironmaster and banker (Westmorland).

40. See W.D. Rubinstein, 'Men of Property: Some Aspects of Occupation, Inheritance, and Power Among Top British Wealth-holders', in Philip Stanworth and Anthony Giddens (eds.), *Elites and Power in British Society* (Cambridge [1974]). Of course a large number of members of the 1846 Parliament were the sons of landowners who eventually succeeded to landed fortunes worth £500,000 or more. There were fewer in 1895 and succeeding Parliaments.

41. On this theme, see Patrick Joyce, 'The Factory Politics of Lancashire in the Later Nineteenth Century', *Historical Journal* xviii (1975).

42. See Maurice Cowling, *The Impact of Labour 1920-1924* (London, 1971).

43. Matthew White Ridley, 1st Viscount Ridley (1842-1905), Tory Home Secretary, banker and landowner, left £536,616. Disraeli left £84,020, an amazing sum for a man who spent much of his life a step ahead of the debt-collector; he actually left a larger personal fortune than Gladstone, whose estate totalled £58,569 plus land which yielded £18,173 per annum. Campbell-Bannerman left £54,909; Balfour £76,433; Asquith only £9,345; Lloyd George £139,855; Bonar Law £35,736; Baldwin £280,971; Ramsay MacDonald £21,502 − again, a goodly sum for a man who once came close to starvation − and Neville Chamberlain £84,013. Among the landed Prime Ministers, Wellington left a personal fortune of £500,000, Derby £250,000; Salisbury £301,000; and Rosebery a total fortune, real and personal, of £1,745,000.

44. James Cornford, 'The Parliamentary Foundations of the Hotel Cecil' in R. Robson (ed.), *Ideas and Institutions of the Victorians* (London, 1967).

45. However, according to Robert Shorthouse (Johns Hopkins University) in industrial Lancashire the majority of JPs as early as 1832 were non-landed.

46. See Ralph E. Pumphrey, 'The Introduction of Industrialists into the British Peerage: A Study of Adaptation of a Social Institution', *Amer. Hist. Rev.*, LXV (1959), pp. 1-16.

47. Among businessmen only George Stephen, 1st Baron Mount Stephen (1829-1921, created 1891), the Scottish-born son of a carpenter who left £109, and his cousin Donald A. Smith, 1st Baron Strathcona (1820-1914, created 1897), the son of a village tradesman, who jointly founded the Canadian Pacific Railway, appear to have been genuinely self-made.

48. See F.M.L. Thompson, *English Landed Society in the Nineteenth Century* (London, 1963), pp. 306-7.

49. Two wealth-holders became Privy Councillors, and one a member of the Order of Merit, without acquiring titles.

6   THE WEALTH-HOLDERS AS BUSINESSMEN

Thus far little has been said about what is presumably the central concern of non-landed wealth-holders in the course of their careers: their business connections and achievements. It was not even the case that every non-landed wealth-holder was a businessman: apart from those in the early period who built up their fortunes by government patronage and place, there have always been a number of professionals who left large estates mainly from their earnings in the professional sphere. Examples of this include the Liverpool solicitor John Shaw Leigh (1791-1871), the pioneering accountant William Quilter (1808-88) and the legal dynasty of Phillimore, including the judge Walter, 1st Baron Phillimore (1845-1929), all in the half-millionaire class. The numbers of such wealthy professionals, however, as was made clear in the discussion of occupational distribution, is very small compared with businessmen. And the probate data which has formed the basis of this investigation can provide only indirect information on this topic, which more properly forms the subject matter of business history, the history of the development of firms and their responses to entrepreneurial challenge.

Nevertheless, there are several aspects of this subject which are of great importance in understanding the role of businessmen, and of wealth, in modern Britain, about which the probate data may prove to be illuminating. In this chapter, three such questions will be examined: the motivating factors and ambitions of British businessmen and the self-perception of their role in British society; the typicality of wealth-holders among all leading British businessmen; and the place of the family firm in the portfolios of property held by wealthy businessmen.

What motivates men to accumulate great wealth? Several distinct views, all necessarily exaggerated, have been presented as the primary motivating factor in the pains taken by entrepreneurs. The first, which has been frequently associated with Protestant dissent,[1] and especially with sects like the Quakers, might be termed the Sense of Mission, the Christian duty of constant work and labour.[2] The second suggests that the primary motivating force behind much of the drive of British entrepreneurship has been the desire to achieve high status and gentility, if not for the businessman who founded the firm, then for his descendants.[3]

176

Third, there is the pursuit of money as an end in itself, rootless of permanent connection with any particular locale or indeed occupation: the financier, the company promoter, the gold magnate or the speculator. As psychologists have often pointed out, although affluence is a perfectly normal and natural desire, the wish to become as rich as Croesus is a mental affliction of a peculiarly unpleasant kind, a substitute for achieving affection, respectability or self-content.[4] ? ? ?

In England, it is not unlikely that the first of these motivating forces, the sense of mission, was indeed the primary driving force behind the activities of many entrepreneurs, especially during the nineteenth century, although the number of *wealthy* businessmen who were dissenters or who were — as we have seen — deeply religious, were fewer in number than might be supposed. Moreover, it is incontestable that the time-honoured tradition wherein business and professional wealth is transferred into status, title and land has been followed many times down the ages. However, a number of demurrals are in order: it would seem to be rather unlikely that many businessmen at the outset of their careers laboured with the end in view of a country house or a peerage — the latter of which would not have been obtainable before the 1880s in any case: such ends would have seemed the most fantastic of pipe-dreams. Furthermore, as will be shown in the next chapter, the majority of non-landed wealth-holders did not in fact buy landed estates of even 2,000 acres, and the notion that the transformation of non-landed into landed wealth was the rule during the nineteenth century stands in need of critical revision.

The last of the suggested forces, the rootless desire to make money in any field, occurs quite rarely in Britain, whatever the case might be in other countries like the United States. One of its more certain victims, however, was the richest of all British wealth-holders, Sir John Ellerman, 1st Bt. (1863-1933), who rose from obscurity to acquire a fortune of £36.7 million. According to Robert McAlmon, briefly married to Ellerman's daughter, the Ellerman mansion at South Audley Street was the epitome of vulgarity, its walls and halls lined with the most banal painting and statuary, conversation at mealtimes restrained in tone so that servants would not overhear; Ellerman was vindictive towards his business opponents, protective of his family and privacy beyond any reasonable bounds.[5] Similarly, the 'Randlords', like Werhner, Beit and Barnato, many originally foreigners and acquiring their fortunes in a frontier environment often by highly questionable means, were usually depicted as typifying the behaviour of *nouveaux-riches*. There is, for instance, Beatrice Webb's famous entry in her diary, written after attending a dinner party given by Sir Julius Werhner at Bath House, Piccadilly for his financier friends: 'There might just as well have been a Goddess of Gold erected for overt worship — the impression of worship, in thought, feeling, and action, could hardly have been stronger'.[6]

Where does the truth lie? Are such depictions typical or accurate? How, indeed, did most businessmen behave and what were their primary motivations and loyalties? It will be contended in this chapter that the key to understanding how British businessmen behaved lies primarily in the importance of the family firm, and secondarily in understanding the severe limitations and constraints on the amount of wealth to which British businessmen could aspire.

On the important place of the family firm — as opposed to large partnerships among different firms and to limited liability companies — there is little doubt. P.L. Payne, in a well-known work, has noted that 'there is little evidence of any significant divorce of control from ownership before the end of the nineteenth-century'.[7] The implications of this have not, I think, been clearly spelled out. Most businessmen, and especially the very wealthiest who, as we have seen, were 'self-made' only in a minority of cases, were simply carried along by their seemingly preordained roles as successors to their fathers and grandfathers, making the best of the situation in which they found themselves according to their personal abilities and outside circumstances. Conversely, most British businessmen, even the great wealth-holders, had no desire to rise above their family firms and become something greater.[8] There were few British businessmen, even among the wealthiest, who held directorships or chairmanships in businesses in widely different areas of the economy, and fewer still who accumulated numerous directorships. For the majority, the family firm was enough.

The number and variety of business interests may be measured fairly precisely from 1880 onwards, for it was in that year that the *Directory of Directors* first appeared, listing all of the directorships held by directors of public companies, and many held in private limited companies as well.[9] Although not a perfect measure of business participation — by definition, private companies and partnerships would be excluded — it is the best which is available, and the very large British businesses which were national in scope, particularly the railways, clearing banks, insurance companies and the largest industrial concerns, would certainly have been included from the first edition.[10]

For the period before 1880, the evidence for business participation is necessarily more inexact, and one must rely for information primarily upon available biographical accounts of a man's career. In comparing

Table 6.1: Business Interests of Non-landed Millionaires

	Multiple Interests	One Field	Idle	Non-Business
1809-58	1	7		1
1858-79	6	20	2	1
1880-99*	11	40	4	0
			Directorships:	
	7+	4-6	2-3	1	0
1880-99	3= 5.1%	5= 8.5%	12=20.3%	9=15.3%	30=50.8%
1900-19	9= 8.9	15=14.9	26=25.7	20=19.8	31=30.7
1920-39	18=11.6	27=17.4	45=29.0	30=19.4	35=22.6

* 1880-99 millionaires are given twice under each heading for comparative purposes.

Table 6.2: Business Interests of Non-landed Half-millionaires

	Multiple Interests	One Field	Idle	Non-Business	Unknown
1809-29	2	11	0	2	1
1850-69	6	40	1	0	1
			Directorships:		
	7+	4-6	2-3	1	0
1880-6	0	1= 2.8%	4=10.3%	8=20.5%	26=66.7%
1900-6	0	5= 6.4	20=25.6	10=12.8	43=55.1
1925-9	10=10.4%	19=19.8	13=13.5	21=21.9	33=34.4
1935-7	8=10.0	11=13.8	20=25.0	15=18.8	26=32.5

the pre- and post-1880 groups it is therefore necessary to adopt somewhat different criteria for assessing business participation. This has been done in Tables 6.1-6.3 in which the business connections of the non-landed wealth-holders are set out. Table 6.1 includes all those in the millionaire class, while Table 6.3 comprises both groups of lesser wealthy. However, because of the large numbers involved, only selected groups of half-millionaires have been included in Table 6.2, namely those deceased in 1809-29, 1850-69, 1880-6, 1900-6, 1925-9 and 1935-7.

For the pre-1880 groups, the wealth-holders have been ranked according to whether they held multiple business interests — that is,

Table 6.3: Business Interests of Non-landed Lesser Wealthy

	Multiple Interests	One Field	Idle	Non-Business	Unknown
1809-29	8=5.8%	96=69.6%	7= 5.1%	27=19.6%	26
1850-69	9=6.5	118=85.5	19=13.8	6= 4.3	14

significant interests in two or more different fields — or interests in one field only, were idle or earned their fortunes in a non-business field. The post-1880 wealth-holders have been ranked by the numbers of directorships held. It will be noticed that the criteria for the pre- and post-1880 groups are not strictly comparable, for all of the ten or more directorships held by an active member of the latter group may have been held in one type of business, while a wealth-holder described as holding multiple interests prior to 1880 might have held only two directorships in the post-1880 ranking. It should also be noted that even in cases in which a wealth-holder held multiple directorships, it was almost always possible to assign him to one occupation as his chief line of business; most multiple interests were clearly subsidiary to his main field.

Nevertheless, the picture which emerges both before and after 1880 is sufficiently similar that the change in categorisation probably does not signify a real change in the behaviour of British businessmen. The most important conclusion from this data is that for the most part the wealthiest British businessmen did not hold wide interests over a broad range of fields. The great majority of pre-1880 wealth-holders were concerned in only one field; the great majority of post-1880 wealth-holders held no more than three directorships, with only a small minority — about ten per cent among both millionaires and half-millionaires — holding as many as seven or more directorships.[11]

Most of the directorships held by wealth-holders, moreover, were in the wealth-holders' chief field of business. The numbers held in other areas of the economy, and particularly among the great national institutions like the railways, clearing banks and insurance companies, were smaller still, and the number of wealth-holders with wide-ranging interests of this type correspondingly smaller. This is detailed in Tables 6.4 and 6.5 which show the number of directorships held by millionaires and half-millionaires, deceased since the first edition of the *Directory of Directors* in 1880, in a major railway, clearing bank, insurance company or a very large industrial concern.[12]

The point to emerge most strongly here is that there is little conclusive evidence of the emergence of a large number of very wealthy

Table 6.4: Non-landed Millionaire Directors of Major Companies (Deceased 1880-1939)

	Number	Percentages of Total Non-landed
1880-99	9	16.4
1900-19	26	25.7
1920-39	40	27.6

Table 6.5: Non-landed Half-millionaire Directors of Major Companies (Deceased 1880-1937)

	Number	Percentages of Total Non-landed
1880-6	3	7.7
1900-6	9	11.5
1925-9	10	10.4
1935-7	13	16.3

businessmen who wielded influence and power over *multiple key areas* of the British economy. If there were such men in the period between 1880 and 1939, either they did not accumulate fortunes of £500,000 or more, or they exercised their power and influence in ways other than by sitting on company boards. There is manifestly no contemporary British entrepreneur who corresponds to J.P. Morgan or John D. Rockefeller in the United States; the fictional portrait of such a man in Trollope's *The Way We Live Now* — said to be based on the rise and fall of 'Baron' Grant (né Gottheimer), the financier[13] — is highly untypical of the careers of wealthy men in Britain. The 'Randlords', apart from being highly untypical as well, earned their money abroad or by speculation with their initial holdings in the City, and did not transform their wealth into influence among the important British industrial and commercial enterprises. It is also significant that socialist rhetoric of the period did not, so far as I am aware, ever identify any British businessman as playing an analogous role to Morgan or Rockefeller; the notion of 'finance capital' is simply inapplicable to late Victorian or Edwardian England.

British businessmen, even the richest, seldom rose above their lasts. They achieved wealth and success in one line of business and rarely if ever attempted to move on from there into dominance over a wide field, the 'commanding heights' of the economy. On the contrary, the temptations of idleness – the transformation into a country or Belgravia gentleman – were far more appealing a call than the drive for more power and influence. And if this call had no appeal to an active entrepreneur, it was certain to be irresistible to his sons and grandsons.

Central to coming to terms with the place of the wealth-holder among businessmen is the determination of how typical were such rich men among all businessmen. But just as no comprehensive listing of the very wealthy has hitherto ever been compiled, so until recently there has been no central index of leading company chairmen and other business leaders in Britain. Philip Stanworth and Anthony Giddens of the Department of Applied Economics at Cambridge University have rectified this to a considerable extent by compiling a list of 459 chairmen of the largest industrial concerns, banks, breweries, railways, iron and steel, shipping and oil companies serving between 1905 and 1972.[14] Though flawed in a number of important ways,[15] it is a pioneering venture, and allows us to make a reasonably accurate assessment of the place of the wealth-holder among major British businessmen, at least among those deceased in this century.

The results of this assessment are set forth in Table 6.6, detailing the valuations of those company chairmen in the Stanworth and Giddens study deceased before 1940, and ranked according to the occupational categories employed by the authors.[16] A total of 199 of Britain's leading businessmen included in the Stanworth and Giddens study were deceased prior to 1940 and of these, 52, or 26.1 per cent, left estates of £500,000 or more. It will readily be seen that these very wealthy businessmen were the exception rather than the rule, and that the majority of top British businessmen were considerably poorer, the plurality leaving estates between £100,000 and £300,000. Among the various occupational categories, the wealthiest were the merchant bankers,[17] followed by the shipowners, the food/tobacco magnates and those chairmen in engineering and oil. These are the only categories in which half (50.0 per cent), or more of the chairmen were wealthholders, while among the retailers, clearing bankers, railway chairmen and those in other industrial activities[18] (where there were no wealthholders), only 10.0 per cent or fewer left very large fortunes.

These differences in relative rewards among British businessmen point to a basic dichotomy among the various types of entrepreneurs. It is by now a commonplace that the growth of the corporation has meant a separation between the ownership of the shares in that concern

Table 6.6: Valuations of Leading Company Chairmen Deceased c. 1905-39

Lower Limit	'Miscellaneous Industrial'						Total Misc.	Iron & Steel	Oil	Shipping	Breweries	Banking			Railways	All Chairmen
	Engineering	Food/Tobacco	Chemicals	Textiles	Retail	Other						Clearing	Merchant banks	Bank of England		
£500,000+	4	8	5	5	1		23	6	1	2	8	3	3	3	3	52
£300,000	2	2	5	2		1	9	2			6	6		1	2	26
£100,000	2	1	2	8	3	5	22	6	1	1	7	7		3	11	57
£ 50,000	1			2	3	2	9	6			3	5		1	2	27
£ 25,000	2			3	2	2	9	2			2	4			4	21
£ 10,000			1				1	2			1				1	5
£ 5,000		1									1				1	2
£ 1,000				1			2				2				1	5
£ 100					1		1				2					2
0						1	1									1
Unlisted		1														1
Number	8	13	13	21	10	11	76	24	2	3	32	25	3	8	25	199
% above £500,000	50.0	61.5	38.5	23.8	10.0	0.0	29.6	25.0	50.0	66.7	25.0	8.3	100.0	37.5	8.3	26.1

and control of the running of its affairs, resulting in the creation of a new class of non-asset-owning corporate executives who own nothing beyond their salaries and pension rights.[19] This general theory needs to be modified considerably in the context of the British experience. Many large firms have remained in the control of the asset-owning family or families for many years after they became public companies. But it remains true that an increasing number of corporate executives, even at the level of chairman, are managers, unrelated to the family owning the company's assets and hired only for their talents. Virtually without exception, all wealth-holding businessmen, including those who died in the period 1905-39 without serving as major company chairmen, were asset-owners. At first glance this may appear a tautological or even a trivial statement, but it is not: in the first place, there are a number of wealth-holding businessmen who were not asset-owners in the businesses in which they served. Most of these were professionals – either solicitors or accountants – who were hired by a company for their expertise and managed to acquire a vast fortune, apparently by shrewd investment or from their professional fees. Examples of this include the half-millionaire accountants James Henry Stephens (1862-1937), who sat on the boards of 14 companies and served as chairman of Meux's Brewery and of Booth's Distillery, and his even more eminent colleague Sir William Barclay Peat (1852-1936), chairman of Samuel Allsopp, the brewers, director of National Provincial Bank and other companies, and also a President of the Institute of Chartered Accountants and the King's personal accountant; and the millionaire solicitors Sir George J. Fowler (1858-1937), director of Eagle Star Insurance and chairman of property companies, and Sir Joseph Hood, 1st Bt. (1863-1931), solicitor and deputy-chairman of Imperial Tobacco. Sir John Ellerman began as a trained accountant, moving on without any advantages of wealth or relationship, and in the post-1945 period virtually every millionaire property developer began with training in either accountancy or estate management.[20]

Nevertheless, the overwhelming majority of business wealth-holders, especially in the period of concern in this work, were the owners of the assets of their companies, either by founding them or succeeding to their ownership by inheritance. The major company chairmen who were not asset-owners were generally not immensely wealthy, and this points to the second conclusion to flow from the observation noted above. Among the 33 chairmen in Table 6.6 classified as 'miscellaneous industrialists', for example, who left under £500,000, at least 22 – and this is probably a minimum figure – were non-asset owners, rising to the chairmanship in the main by sheer ability at management.[21] These men could not from their salaries alone acquire a vast fortune, and in general left between £25,000 and £200,000, the equivalent of a middle-rank asset-owning manufacturer or merchant deceased at the same time, and far below the millions often left by the asset-owners, even by those with no real role in running their companies. Of the 23 wealth-holding 'miscellaneous industrial' chairmen in Table 6.6, only one appears to have been a non-asset owner, the millionaire Henry Greenwood Tetley (1851-1921), who served as chairman of Courtauld's Ltd., the great silk and rayon concern, just prior to his death. Tetley, a Bradford man without any connection with the Courtauld family, was first employed by the woollen manufacturers Lister & Co. for 22 years before joining Courtauld's in 1893 at a salary of £2,000 per annum.[22]

Tetley's is, however, a most exceptional case. Among those categories of businessmen in Table 6.6 of which only a small portion were wealth-holders, it is probable that most chairmen were managers or non-asset owners. This was particularly true among the retailers, where success on merit was early the rule, and among the railway chairmen, many of whom were either promoted chief engineers or, more commonly, elite figures – aristocrats and politicians – taken on for their names and connections. Among such groups as the brewers and textile manu-facturers, however, many asset owners left less than £500,000. Among the textile owners this was probably the case because of the peculiar corporate structure of the early limited companies in this field, where a very large number of small concerns retained their identities and considerable autonomy, producing absurdly large boards of directors – one possessed 84 members[23] – and the heads of these smaller concerns took their turns as chairman.

Although 52 non-landed wealth-holders deceased in the period 1905-39 were among the major company chairmen in the Cambridge study, over 500 were not. As has been shown, most of these retained at least a directorship in their family company, and others not included in Table 6.6 were heads of insurance companies or merchant banks excluded from this study. Nevertheless, the great majority of non-landed wealth-holders were not among the primary entrepreneurs of Britain during this period, just as they seldom held a very large number of multiple directorships. These less important wealth-holders may be divided into two groups, those holding only directorships or a sizable share of the assets of companies included in Table 6.6, and those whose fortunes came from heading companies smaller in size than those companies included in Table 6.6. Most of the less important wealth-holders belong to the second group, and their success is evidence that a man may become very wealthy by heading a medium-sized company as well as by heading one of the giants. Most of the textile manufacturers, merchants, colliery owners, shipowners and metal manufacturers who left over £500,000 in this century were heads of their own medium-sized companies, and unconnected with the giants in the field.

Of the 52 wealth-holders who were heads of major companies, 28 were millionaires[24] — 17 miscellaneous industrialists, one a shipowner, four brewers, five bankers, one a railway chairman. It is important to realise, however, that the 28 millionaires who were major company chairmen were far outnumbered by those who were not. No fewer than 235 non-landed millionaires deceased in the period 1905-39 were not major company chairmen. Of this number, 55 earned their fortunes in fields like newspaper-owning which were not a part of the Cambridge study, but the remaining 180 millionaires greatly outnumber those who were major company chairmen; this remains the case even if it is remembered that many early merchant bankers are unaccountably omitted from the Cambridge study. Divided according to their categories, in no field were more than 40 per cent of the millionaires deceased at this time major company chairmen. Among those in the various types of industrial activity, only in chemicals and among the Others were more than one-quarter of the total number of millionaires found among the major chairmen. In three categories — engineering, retailing and petroleum — not a single millionaire was a major company chairman.

Who, then, were the majority of millionaires who were not major company chairmen? Most, as we have seen, were directors of their family firms, both large and medium-sized. Some of these were the relatives of the chairmen, their brothers or cousins, and members of the same asset-owning family. This was especially the case among the many Willses of Imperial Tobacco and Coatses of J. & P. Coats Sewing Thread. Others were heads of smaller firms which merged into larger combines. But the great majority were the heads of medium-sized firms, not of giants. This is further evidence that the notion of an English plutocracy must be hedged with qualifications.

The third topic to be discussed in this chapter, and one which will provide further evidence for the limited nature of the ambitions of wealthy British businessmen, is obtainable from an examination of the inventories of their estates where this is possible. As explained in the first chapter, among persons leaving property in Scotland it is possible to consult the 'Inventory of Goods and Gear' drawn up by their executors or administrators, which details the specific holdings sworn for probate by the executors of the testator. It is thus possible to learn specifically what stocks and shares he owned, and from this to infer from another set of data the extent of his participation over wide areas of economic life.

The evidence to be had from the 44 inventories examined contains a definitive answer to the question of how the individual businessmen solved the challenges that were presented to him as an investor. These challenges were posed in a number of distinct ways. As the head of family or self-created business, both loyalty and the continuity of his dynasty demanded that a significant portion of his portfolio remain in shares in his own firm, regardless of their profitability or other strictly economic considerations. As a businessman and an investor, however, he had many other considerations to weigh. He wanted security – which meant investment in stocks of well-known companies and government bonds – and he wanted profitability and growth potential, which entailed investments of a more speculative nature. Finally, the ambitious businessman – the type we have been attempting to delineate in this chapter – might wish to acquire a controlling, or at least a major interest, in a number of nationally important firms. All of these possible considerations may be weighed in studying the inventories in detail.

A total of 44 such inventories were read in arriving at the information contained in Table 6.7. Those read included all non-landed Scottish millionaires deceased between 1858 and 1939 whose estates were resworn in London, and most Scottish half-millionaires deceased between 1876 and 1902, whose inventories were consulted in Edinburgh.[25] The occupations of these men cover a wide range of fields, including textiles, distilling, ironmastering, shipowning, chemical manufacture, etc., although there are probably fewer in finance than among the English wealth-holders.

Table 6.7 lists the percentage of these portfolios accounted for by the family business, which was almost invariably the most valuable portion of the wealth-holder's portfolio. Among millionaires, it will be seen that half or more of the total portfolio was accounted for by the value of the family firm, and that there is only a slight tendency for this trend to weaken in the final cohort group. Curiously, among the half-millionaires this tendency does not manifest itself, and the family firm accounts for a smaller portfion of the total portfolio than is the case among millionaires.

Several corollaries would seem to follow from the distribution in Table 6.7. First, it will be seen that there is less tendency toward multiple interest-holding among those who were sufficiently wealthy

Table 6.7: Percentage of Total Inventory in Family Firm

%	1858-79	1880-99	1900-19	1920-39
Millionaires:				
80+			2	1
60-79		2	5	5
40-59			1	7
20-39	1	1	1	2
0-19			1	1
Half-millionaires:				
80+	1	1		
60-79		1		
40-59	1	3		
20-39		3	2	
0-19		3		

to have become plutocrats in a meaningful sense than among those who were slightly less wealthy. This would tend to confirm the picture presented in the data for directorships and chairmanships — the wealthiest Scottish businessmen simply had no wish to expand beyond their own family firms in a major way. Among the four Scottish wealth-holders in this Table with estate of £2 million or more — the very richest of wealth-holders — the holdings of three in their family firms were in the 60 per cent to 79 per cent range, while the remaining one was in the 40 per cent to 59 per cent range.[26]

Second, it seems apparent that these wealthy businessmen grew wealthy primarily through the growth of their family firms rather than through shrewd investment in a wide range of offerings. Clearly, if one's family firm accounts for the major portion of the worth of one's portfolio, what happens to it is of greater importance to one's total prosperity than what happens to one's other holdings. Finally, the picture presented here suggests that wealthy businessmen were extremely reluctant, even at the end of their lives, to part with a major interest in their family firms.

Apart from their family holdings, the bulk of the wealth-holders' portfolios was characteristically composed of a very wide range of solid shares and bonds: in some cases shares in nearly 200 firms and institutions were held. It was rare for more than, say £10,000 to be invested in any one company apart from the family firm. As a rule, a millionaire held £10,000 or more in about 15-20 different firms; in his remaining companies he customarily held far less. The companies held were chiefly the best-known and most respectable of firms, including especially railway shares (with a very significant holding in American and Canadian railways); shipping companies; and industrial concerns like Armstrong, Whitworth, Burmah Oil, Shell, British Linen Thread; and the major clearing banks. None of the Scottish wealth-holders whose inventories were consulted could have held a controlling or, indeed, a major interest in many of these companies. Among those deceased from 1914 on, significant holdings appear in War Bonds and Loans, and among all wealth-holders there are invariably holdings in British government consols and in local bond issues in the wealth-holders' towns. These bond issues yielded between three per cent and five per cent in most cases. There appear to be remarkably few speculative or uncertain issues, apart from holdings in South American railways, Asian tea companies and the like. Similarly, few possessed bad debts or worthless shares, although such shares would have been included in the inventory. Finally, it should be pointed out that the great fraction of the wealth-holders' holdings were in stocks and bonds. Their chattels, including their country and town houses, art treasures, heirlooms, *et al.*, accounted for very little, on average for no more than three per cent of their total holdings. Apart from their shares, the largest portion of their portfolios was in cash at the bank or in personal loans to individuals or firms.

The picture presented here, taken in conjunction with the other evidence in this chapter, leads to the conclusion that British businessmen of wealth were modest in their ambitions and presumptions. Unlike their counterparts in America and possibly elsewhere, they did not bestride the world like colossi, seldom attempting to achieve economic power outside their own line of business. The remarks which were made in the previous chapter about *place* in the total economy being more important than *effort* ought surely to be recalled in this context. It seems likely that there were fairly rigid limits to the amount of wealth which it was possible to accumulate in any particular occupational sector of the British economy, with distinct differences in this regard among the occupational sectors: finance and commerce, by and large, were clearly more profitable than manufacturing. Conversely, it was also quite likely that, once having established his firm in at least a minimally successful way, an entrepreneur's course ran, as it were, in pre-arranged grooves, with less scope for anomalous patterns of success

190   *The Wealth-holders as Businessmen*

than one would have believed in advance. Two corollaries of this would
seem to be that beyond a probably fairly low level of entrepreneurial
skill, business acumen, ruthlessness and access to capital, no special, let
alone preternatural gifts of business ability were required for considerable
success within the constraints of the system,[27] and that genuine *tours
de force* of entrepreneurial achievement were accordingly extremely
rare, perhaps more so than in analogous industrial societies. The success
of an Ellerman, a Morrison or a Nuffield were thus all the more
remarkable.

The apparent limitations on the *potential* success of British entrepreneurs must be kept in mind in deciding whether the late Victorian
British economy 'failed': surely 'failure' cannot be impugned where
'success' was not possible. Britain's entrepreneurs were simply operating
within an entirely different milieu from businessmen in America and
Germany, and their responses, though no doubt conditioned to a large
extent by Britain's social institutions and traditions, can equally be
viewed as economically rational and efficient from the viewpoint of
their own immediate self-interests.

Notes

1. Low-church Anglicanism produced this mentality as well. The best
portrayal of this is in *Augustus Carp, esq. by Himself*, the humorous picture of
late Victorian hypocrisy published anonymously in 1924 by Sir Henry Howard
Bashford (1880-1961), a well-known physician. (See the Introduction, pp. xii-
xiv, by Anthony Burgess in the 1966 reissue of this work.)
2. See Arthur Raistrick, *Quakers in Science and Industry* (London, 1950)
and Roy Lewis & Rosemary Stewart, *The Boss* (London, 1958), Chapter VII.
3. Harold Perkin, *The Origins of Modern English Society, 1780-1880*
(London, 1969), pp. 63, 85.
4. See the useful summary of evidence in Thomas Wiseman, *The Money
Motive. A Study of an Obsession* (London, 1974), esp. Part One.
5. Robert McAlmon, *Being Geniuses Together* (London, 1974), pp. 1-5.
6. Beatrice Webb, *Our Partnership* (edited by Barbara Drake and Margaret I.
Cole) (London, 1948), p. 347.
7. P.L. Payne, *British Entrepreneurship in the Nineteenth Century* (London,
1974), pp. 20-1.
8. As has been suggested in a previous chapter, and from other research
(esp. James Cornford, 'The Parliamentary Foundations of the Hotel Cecil' in
R. Robson (ed.), *Ideas and Institutions of the Victorians* (London, 1967)), there
is little evidence of a direct overlap between business wealth or power and
political power, as judged by Parliamentary or Cabinet membership. This does
not, however, exclude the possibility that such men wield power by indirect
means or from extraparliamentary agitation, as in the case of the Repeal of the
Corn Laws.
9. A private limited company is one in which, although there are shares,

these are not publicly traded. The coverage of the *Directory of Directors* clearly becomes far more complete as the years pass, judging by the number of entries and the range of companies listed.

10. It is clear that the transformation of private into public companies in Britain was very uneven in chronology in different fields. As P.L. Payne makes clear in his article 'The Emergence of the Large-Scale Company in Great Britain 1870-1914' (*Econ. Hist. Rev.* 2nd Ser., Vol. XX, 1967), it was primarily in brewing and to a lesser extent in textiles that the change proceeded most quickly. In 1905, 17 of the 52 largest public industrial companies in Britain were breweries (Ibid., Table 1, pp. 530-40). Some of the firms on Payne's 1905 list are extremely implausible, among them, for example, Bovril, the meat extract manufacturers, and Maple's, the Tottenham Court Road furniture retailers. In contrast, the largest American companies at the time were nearly all in heavy industry or large-scale manufacturing (Ibid., pp. 540-1).

11. In ascertaining the number of directorships held after 1880, issues of the *Directory of Directors* at ten-year intervals were consulted, and the peak number of directorships held in any one year taken as the figure assigned to a man in these Tables. It is possible that a wealth-holder may have 'peaked' between the two years, but any directorship held for fewer than ten years was probably not a very significant interest. On the other hand, it should be noted that for most of a wealth-holder's career, he held far *fewer* directorships than the *peak* number.

12. The names of these companies is taken from the data compiled by Anthony Giddens and Philip Stanworth (now of York University) of the Department of Applied Economics at Cambridge University, forming the basis of their article in *Elites and Power in British Society*. The earliest list of industrial companies employed by them is Payne's of 1905. None has been compiled for the nineteenth century. I am grateful to Giddens and Stanworth for allowing me to use their 'raw data' for the SSRC Project on Elites and for my own research. Many of those holding directorships in a major company were of course chiefly concerned in this company and did not join later in their careers as additions to their corporate power.

13. W.T.C. King, *History of the London Discount Market* (London, 1936), p. 175.

14. Philip Stanworth and Anthony Giddens (eds.), *Elites and Power in British Society* (Cambridge, 1974). The occupational categories employed here are the authors', and in the case of the wealth-holders may differ from my own. Five company chairmen were the heads of major companies in two different fields, and are counted twice in their data.

15. Most importantly: only limited companies are included; many important occupational categories are excluded, particularly in finance (insurance companies and Lloyds brokers; the Stock Exchange), commerce (most wholesalers and foreign merchants), colliery owning, shipbuilding and newspaper proprietorship; the earliest list is Payne's of 1905, which, as has been noted, is not entirely representative of British industry; finally, the chairmanship of many companies is often held by a figurehead, while the real *locus* of power within a corporation is elsewhere.

16. Stanworth and Giddens, *Elites and Power in British Society*, p. 82. I might note in passing that I have some doubts about the methods of investigation employed by the authors in their article, especially concerning the social origins of these company chairmen. By relying exclusively or almost exclusively on attendance at elite public schools to categorise these chairmen as of middle class origin or above, they ignore the considerable differences in wealth and prosperity among the fathers and families of these chairmen, differences which could only be brought to light by much more rigorous research.

17. Only three merchant bankers in this study were deceased prior to 1939. The omission of most early merchant bankers is one of the most curious features of this study, slighting most of the great figures of the Golden Age of British merchant banking.

18. This category chiefly includes those in cement and tyre manufacturing.

19. Surprisingly, the best research on this point has been done by sociologists. See Ralf Dahrendorf, *Class and Class Conflict in Industrial Society* (London, 1959), esp. Chapters II and VII; Anthony Giddens, *The Class Structure of the Advanced Societies* (London, 1973), esp. Chapters 8-10.

20. *Dictionary of National Biography*, biography of Ellerman; Oliver Marriott, *The Property Boom* (London, 1967).

21. Other types of non-asset-owning chairmen include several elite figures — former Cabinet ministers, top civil servants or well-known landed aristocrats — chosen for their titles, connections or ability, but without any previous . business experiences; and professionals — accountants or solicitors — brought in temporarily during a period of crisis in the company's affairs.

22. *The Times*, 11 October 1921.

23. Payne, 'The Emergence of the Large-Scale Company', p. 528.

24. Actually, only 26 individual millionaires are included here, since two — Arthur Keen and Sir Thomas B. Royden — headed major enterprises in different fields. In addition, three chairmen were deceased prior to 1905: William, 1st Baron Armstrong (d. 1900), Spencer Charrington (d. 1904), the brewer and Sir John B. Maple (d. 1903), the furniture retailer. They are included in Stanworth and Giddens's list — it is uncertain why — but excluded from the data below.

25. I do not believe it is possible to see Scottish inventories prior to 1858 in London. Dr. W. Kennedy (London School of Economics) is at work on a thorough examination of a large number of wealthy Scottish inventories from 1870 to 1914, with the aim of studying investment decisions in a detailed manner.

26. There is no objective reason to suppose that wealthy Scottish businessmen behave any differently from their English counterparts. But if Scotsmen were 'cannier', more impressed by Calvinist-inspired economic doctrine and less 'sentimental' than the English, one would expect a *greater* willingness to move into new fields than among Englishmen. On the other hand, the City of London businessmen who might have been expected to possess very wide-ranging interests are not included in this breakdown.

27. It is for this reason that studies of the rich which focus on the bizarre, near-pathological behaviour of millionaires — as is so common in the United States (where, admittedly, there is good reason) — are not helpful to understanding their role or success.

7 LANDED WEALTH

With the exception of a brief discussion of the place of landowning in the occupational composition of the great fortunes, little attention has hitherto been paid to what is by far the single most important element in the British wealth structure, landed wealth. This topic raises its own set of special considerations, both because of the nature of the statistical sources and because of dimensions of British landed society itself, and surely deserves a separate chapter.

Incomes of Landed Wealth-holders

As has been explained before, the methods of evaluating real and personal property for the purpose of probate have been quite different. Realty was not included in the valuation figures before 1898, only unsettled realty between 1898 and 1925, and both settled and unsettled realty only from 1926. Although this is so, it is also true that the landed income − and hence the capital value of the land, which is commonly taken as a multiple of income − of all of the great landowners (except those owning urban land in London) is known in a definitive way for the early 1870s from the official compilation *The Return of Owners of Land* and from the figures which John Bateman derived from this *Return, The Great Landowners of Great Britain and Ireland* (4th edn, 1883).[1] Bateman revised and corrected the figures of acreage and rental in the *Return* and offered a county-by-county breakdown of the holdings of all landowners with 2,000 or more acres in the *Return*.[2]

For most of the nineteenth century, the probate sources provide the historian with a supplementary and, indeed, in some ways alternative source for studying the wealth of the great landowners, and it is the weaving together of the evidence of acreage and yearly income provided by Bateman with the data on personal wealth, which will provide the basis for much of the discussion here. It remains to be said that landed society has in many ways been better-served by its specialist historians than any other major division within eighteenth and nineteenth century British society.[3] There was a relative uniformity of social and economic behaviour (or at least of what was regarded as proper behaviour) among

Table 7.1: Gross Landed Incomes of £75,000 or More in 1883 — Revised Figures[a]

Name	Income (£'000)
£200,000 or more:	
1. Westminster, Duke of	c. 290-325
2. Buccleuch and Queensberry, Duke of	232
3. Bedford, Duke of	c. 225-250
£150,000-£200,000:	
4. Devonshire, Duke of	181
5. Northumberland, Duke of	176
6. Derby, Earl of	163
7. Bute, Marquess of	153
£100,000-£200,000:	
8. Sutherland, Duke of[b]	142
9. Hamilton and Brandon, Duke of	141
10. Fitzwilliam, Earl	139
11. Dudley, Earl of	123
12. Ancaster, Earl of	121
13. Anglesey, Marquess of	111
14. Londonderry, Marquess of	110
15. Portland, Duke of	108
16. Hertford, Marquess of,[c] Wallace, Sir Richard	104
17. Portman, Viscount	c. 100
£75,000-£100,000:	
18. Rutland, Duke of	98
19. Cleveland, Duke of	97
20. Downshire, Marquess of	97
21. Overstone, Baron (includes Sir L. Loyd-Lindsay and L. Loyd)[d]	93
22. Boyne, Viscount	88
23. Leconfield, Baron	88
24. Brownlow, Earl	86
25. Yarborough, Earl of	85
26. Richmond and Gordon, Duke of	80
27. Seafield, Earl of	78
28. Pembroke, Earl of	78
29. Norfolk, Duke of	76

a. The incomes of Westminster, Bedford and Portman include estimates, based on contemporary sources, of their London holdings – in the case of Westminster, £225,000, about £58,000 for Bedford and £55,000 for Portman. Several other prominent London landlords *might* have possessed landed incomes of £75,000 or more in the 1880s, especially Lords Howard de Walden and Cadogan. The Earl of Sefton, and the principal Weld-Blundell heir, owners of much Liverpool property, might similarly be placed on this list.
b. The 1st Duke of Sutherland (d. 1833), who inherited the canals of the Duke of Bridgwater, was unquestionably the wealthiest landowner of his day. After his death, however, his property was split between the succeeding Dukes of Sutherland and the Earl of Ellesmere.
c. Wallace was Hertford's illegitimate son and received his landed wealth from him.
d. These were Overstone's relatives who received virtually all of the land they are credited with owning in Bateman from Overstone.

the great landowners which has made possible a number of skilful group portraits drawn by later historians which could not be done so easily for the business world. Nor should it be overlooked that the family histories of nearly all of the great landowners are readily traceable in works like *Burke's Peerage* and *Burke's Landed Gentry*, whereas there are no consistent guides to the identities of the leading businessmen and professionals.

The point has already been made that the great landowners remained the richest group of men in Britain until the late nineteenth century. As Harold Perkin has observed, even in 1873 the number of purported individual business incomes of £50,000 or more assessed under Schedule D of the Income Tax were 77 in number, only just exceeding the 76 landed incomes of £50,000 or more reported by Bateman.[4] Although much has already been written on these super-rich landowners, it is perhaps worth naming them. In Table 7.1 are detailed the cream of even this group, the 29 richest landowners at the time of the appearance of the fourth edition of Bateman in 1883.[5] The figures given here differ from Bateman's in taking into account the probable incomes of a number of the greatest London landlords whose rentals were excluded from the *Return of Owners of Land*, in omitting four landlords whose stated income was in excess of £75,000, but whose actual income was probably much below this figure,[6] and in tidying up and bringing together a number of rentals distributed in Bateman's work among several members of a single family or what was to be a single heir, as in the case of the Earldom of Ancaster, created in 1892 following the succession by a single individual to the substantial property of the Aveland and Willoughby d'Eresby peerages. It also includes where relevant the mineral rents, hunting fees and the like of each of these landowners when they have been noted in the *Return.*

A number of very general points should be made about the families on this list and, indeed, about the financial circumstances of all of the wealthiest landowners down to those with, say £10,000 or more in rental income. In the first place, by and large they increased their incomes, together with the total capital value of their estates and of their non-landed property, in the course of the nineteenth century. In 1819, only four landowners (Northumberland, Grosvenor − later Westminster, Stafford − later Sutherland and Bridgwater − whose subsequent title-holder in 1883 does not appear on this list) were credited with total net incomes of £100,000 or more, estimates which are themselves probably exaggerated.[7] Second, in the course of the nineteenth century the gap between the very richest landowners and the minor aristocracy and gentry probably widened considerably; it was the super-rich, particularly those with lucrative non-landed sources of wealth, who could best weather the storms of the years following the start of the Agricultural Depression in 1879. Third, the capital value of the holdings of the richest landowners exceeded the total wealth of the richest businessmen down to the First World War or even later. The Duke of Buccleuch, for instance, would have been worth nearly £7m on the basis of his landed income alone in 1883, taking 33 years' rental in computing the capital worth of his property. This was a figure far in excess even of the £5m or so left by Nathan Rothschild or James Morrison. Conversely, it is difficult to imagine even a single British business figure of the 1870s or 1880s (with the possible exception of the Rothschilds, Lord Overstone and Charles Morrison) whose income from business sources came close to the £200,000-£300,000 per annum of the greatest landowners. Such a figure would not have been greatly exceeded by any British businessmen until the flourishing of the Ellermans, Leverhulmes and Nuffields just before or after the First World War. However, it must also be emphasised that many of even the greatest landowners were hounded by the constant necessity of debt repayments, especially during the earlier nineteenth century, so that the gross figures presented in Table 7.1 represent considerable over-statements of their *disposable* incomes. The final general point which should be made about the landed super-powers is that only one name among them belonged to a 'new' man, one whose fortune derived from post-Industrial Revolution wealth, that of Lord Overstone. All the others without exception are pre-industrial in origin, representing the end result of a process of familial acquisition which began, in some cases, with the Norman Conquest, and which was aided and abetted by all of the landmarks of British history through which the aristocracy consolidated its gains, from the spoils of the monasteries, to eighteenth-century 'Old Corruption', to the mineral income and urban rentals of the nineteenth century.

Perhaps the main omission from the picture of landed wealth provided by the statistics of landed income is the non-landed sources of income and wealth, often considerable, possessed by many of the great (and sometimes by the lesser) landowners. It has been remarked above that the probate figures of personal wealth provide a source of novel information on the wealthiest landowners. In using these statistics to supplement the figures of landed income, however, one should note that a degree of ambiguity enters into the probate calendar valuations from 1898 onward. Prior to 1898, the valuation figure consisted of personalty alone; thereafter, until 1926, both personalty and unsettled realty were included, but no distinction was drawn between the two in the calendar's single global valuation figure. From 1926, however, settled land has been proved and entered separately in the calendars (although it seems that the value of unsettled land has still been included in the global figure of the testator's estate which includes his personalty). Thus only until 1898 is there certainty that the real and personal property of the great landowners can be discussed as knowingly separate entities.

Nevertheless, throughout the nineteenth century, the probate calendars offer comprehensive information about a field of major importance which has seldom received any scholarly discussion.[8] Given the precariousness of what was seemingly an immutable form of wealth among all but the very greatest landowners, the peculiarly large expenses of their marriages and family settlements, reinvestment on their estates and the display and largesse normally entailed by the circumstances of their way of life, for many landowners their personal fortunes probably made the difference between leading the life which custom expected of them and, in some cases, disappearing from the land altogether.[9] This was never more true that during the periods of declining land values and rentals following the Napoleonic Wars and after the start of the Agricultural Depression in 1879.

Beyond the world of the rent-roll, which at one point in time at least lies fully exposed to the historian, there stands a separate shadow realm of the landowners' personal fortunes and non-landed incomes. Increasingly in the late nineteenth century this realm was becoming more crucial to most landowners. As F.M.L. Thompson has remarked of the period after 1879: 'The economic distinction was certainly

Table 7.2: Gross Annual Rentals of Wealth-holding Landowners

Rental (£)	1809-58	1858-79	1880-97	1898-1925	1926-39
Millionaires:					
100,000+	2	1	4	7	3
50,000-100,000	1	1	3	4	8
25,000- 50,000		1	1	7	4
10,000- 25,000		1		5	1
5,000- 10,000				1	1
Under 5,000				1	
Unlisted	1				
Half-millionaires:					
100,000+	1	4		2	1
50,000-100,000	3	5	1	8	6
25,000- 50,000	3	3	4	15	9
10,000- 25,000	3	2	4	9	5
5,000- 10,000	1		1	3	3
Under 5,000				1	1
Unlisted	1	1	1	4	

	1809-29	1850-69
Lesser Wealthy:		
100,000+	6	3
50,000-100,000	2	5
25,000- 50,000	8	9
10,000- 25,000	5	5
5,000- 10,000	4	5
Under 5,000	1	3
Unlisted	8	3

becoming more marked year by year between landowners who were purely agricultural and landowners who were guaranteed a share in the wealth generated by industry and commerce.'[10]

In Table 7.2 has been set out the gross annual rentals, according to Bateman, of those landowners leaving millionaire, half-millionaire and lesser wealthy estates recorded by the probate calendars. In this Table, as well as in some subsequent ones in this chapter, the periodisation adopted breaks in 1898 and 1926, when the changes in method of valuation took place, rather than in the years 1900 and 1920 as elsewhere.

It will be clear from this data that only a very small minority — even among the landowners with the very highest rentals — left personal fortunes or, in this century, fortunes with large components of personalty, of £500,000 or more. According to Bateman's figures, some 76 landowners were in receipt of gross annual rentals of £50,000 or more, a figure which does not include the great London (and possibly some other) urban property owners like Westminster and Portman, whose gross rental income certainly reached at least this figure. In the course of the period 1809-1939 probably on average five holders of each title or principal heirs of untitled landowners lived and died, suggesting that well over 300 landowners whose rental incomes exceeded £50,000 died and left estates to probate. Yet the total number of landowners leaving £500,000 or more according to the probate calendars was no more than 64 (many of whom were successive title-holders within the same family) and this figure counts as well those landowners deceased since 1898 whose valuation figure includes most or all of their personalty.[11] During the long period 1809-98, when the total number of landowners receiving £50,000 or more per annum certainly numbered more than 200 in all, no more than 26 landowners left personal estates of £500,000 or more.

In some cases the valuation of personalty was far less than what one might have expected from their recorded landed income or reputation as wealthy men. The celebrated Thomas Coke, 1st Earl of Leicester (1754-1842) left only £60,000 in personalty; the 1st Marquess of Westminster (1767-1845), whose London rent-rolls must even at the time of his death have been enormous, left £350,000; the 9th (1819-91) and 10th (1852-93) Dukes of Bedford left, respectively, £231,000 and £336,000; the 14th Earl of Derby (1799-1869), the Prime Minister, left £250,000. These examples are evidence of a puzzling randomness in this matter, for in each of these families the previous or succeeding title holder left far more. The 2nd Earl of Leicester (1822-1909) left £977,000; the 2nd Marquess of Westminster (1795-1869) left £800,000; the 8th Duke of Bedford (1809-72) left £600,000 and the 11th (1858-1940) left £4.7m, while the 15th Earl of Derby (1826-93) left £1,936,000. It seems clear that the personal wealth of the great landowners varied widely from generation to generation with little or no apparent pattern or reason. Even accepting the obvious facts that different landowners were by turn frugal or spendthrift, lucky or unlucky in their investments or lived in prosperous or depressed times, these differences still appear inexplicably wide, and require an explanation. It would seem that when inheritance of a title went from father to son, rather than to a more distant relative, the personalty of the heir to the title was likely to be greater than when a distant relative succeeded to it. For example, the 9th Duke of Bedford mentioned above was the son of General Hon. George William Russell (d. 1846), who left only £8,000 and succeeded his uncle, the 8th Duke, who died in 1872 leaving £600,000. The 9th Duke was followed by his brother, who held the title only for two years and also left, for a Duke of Bedford, comparatively little. Although instances of indirect succession were less common than succession from father to eldest son, they occurred within most of the great titled families at least once or twice during the nineteenth century.

This picture of fortuitous and wide variation in personal wealth-holding receives further support from a closer inspection of the names of the top leavers of personal wealth among the great landowners. It is apparent that not only were there far fewer top personalty wealth-holders than there were great landed income earners, but those leaving large personal fortunes were not always, or, indeed, commonly, the same individuals as those who received the greatest landed income.[12] Among millionaires, to be sure, high landed income and personal wealth did coincide fairly well, for there were few personalty wealth-holders with less than £25,000 per annum in landed income, but among the half-millionaires there were a great many, in fact the majority. Even among the millionaires there are cases, several extremely puzzling, of personalty wealth-holders with surprisingly little landed income. Hon. Henry Cavendish (1731-1810), the scientist who discovered phlogiston, was the son of the third son of the 2nd Duke of Devonshire and owned little if any land. A misogynist and virtually a hermit, he lived frugally, died a bachelor and allowed his large income to accumulate, leaving a fortune estimated by contemporaries at £1,175,000.[13] Another landed millionaire with little landed income was the virtually unknown Sir William Abdy, 7th Bt. (1779-1868) whose successor in 1883 owned only 3,121 acres yielding £9,710 per annum. Abdy owned real estate in Southwark (unlisted in Bateman) which may have been the source of his large fortune; but his father had left only £20,000.[14] During the twentieth century, when the valuation figures may include settled or unsettled land as well as personalty, there have been some landed millionaires whose fortunes were surprisingly large, even if the valuation figures be taken to include the capital value of their land. Such men as Alexander H. Thistlethwayte (1854-1915) (who left £1,490,000), a landowner in Hampshire credited with £9,929 per annum in 1883;[15] Rowland, 2nd Baron St Oswald (1857-1919) credited in 1883 with ownership of land worth £18,587 per annum, yet who left £1,782,000 and, perhaps most mysterious of all, Hubert, 2nd Marquess of Clanricarde (1832-1916) who left the truly enormous fortune of £2,500,000 are examples of this. At the time of Bateman's publication, Clanricarde owned only land in County Galway yielding £24,358 per annum which by 1915 had all been sold for only £228,000.[16] Clanricarde held no business directorships and was such an unfamiliar figure in London that he was once refused admittance to the House of Lords.[17] The remaining ostensibly landed millionaires with little agricultural land all certainly owned substantial urban property in London or elsewhere. Among them were Sir Richard V. Sutton, 6th Bt. (1891-1918), with important properties in Mayfair and Piccadilly, as well as land yielding £15,500 per annum; William B. Crigoe-Colmore (1860-1918), a Birmingham ground-rent landlord who left £1,367,000; John, 2nd Baron Llangattock (1870-1916), owner of properties in south London; Gerald, 6th Earl of Cadogan (1869-1953), John A. Berners (1869-1934) and James H. Benyon (1849-1935), all great London landlords.

That there was only a rough-and-ready correlation between landed income and personal wealth at the highest levels is further evidenced by the data in Table 7.3, which lists the names and gross annual rentals of all landowners leaving probate fortunes of £2m or more.

Except in the case of Lord Cadogan, who owned virtually no agricultural land at all, each of these men held extensive acreages and incomes in 1883. But it is also true that there were many other land-owners, such as the Dukes of Bedford or Westminster, with rental values just as large, but who fail to appear in this list. Two of these names call for special notice as they were highly anomalous. Andrew Montagu (1815-95), except for Sutherland the only nineteenth-century landowner to leave £2m or more, was a magnate in Yorkshire whose only entrance onto the stage of history occurred when, a keen Tory, he bought out Disraeli's sizable debts, charging him three per cent rather than the ten per cent he had been paying.[18] Born Andrew Fountayne Wilson, Montagu was a descendant in the female line of Charles Montagu, Earl of Halifax, Finance Minister to William III and a great placeman.[19] In 1883 with the Weld-Blundells of Liverpool (whose estates returned £60,000 per annum), he was the commoner with the largest rent-rolls among all of the landowners listed in Bateman. The other landowner whose listing here requires some comment is Wentworth B. Beaumont, created Baron Allendale in 1906 at the close of a 40-year career on the Liberal backbenches. He was certainly among the last truly great landowners to have been ennobled. His vast fortune,

Table 7.3: Landowners Leaving £2 million or More, 1809-1939

Name	Gross Annual Income (£), 1883	Estate (£'000)
1. George, 1st Duke of Sutherland[a] (1758-1833)	213,000[b]	'Above £1m.'
2. Andrew Montagu (1815-95)	53,000	2,005
3. William, 6th Earl Fitzwilliam (1815-1902)	139,000	2,882
4. W.B. Beaumont, 1st Baron Allendale (1829-1907)	35,000	3,189
5. Hubert, 2nd Marquess of Clanricarde (1832-1916)	24,000	2,500
6. Wentworth, 1st Viscount Allendale (1860-1923)	35,000	3,269
7. Alan, 8th Duke of Northumberland (1880-1930)	176,000	2,510
8. Gerald, 6th Earl of Cadogan (1869-1933)	(London land only)	2,000
9. William, 9th Earl of Dysart (1859-1935)	45,000	2,375

a. Sutherland's fortune was sworn 'Above £1 million': but certainly totalled above £2 million.
b. This represents the 1883 rentals of his two chief heirs, the Duke of Sutherland and the Earl of Ellesmere.

some £3,189,000, was heavily based on extensive lead and coal mines in Northumberland and Durham.[20]

The number of landowners among the half-millionaires with very low landed rentals far exceeded the number of low-rental millionaire landowners. No fewer than nine received rentals of less than £5,000 per annum, men like Stephen R. Delmé (1809-94) with £6,986 per annum in 1883, who left £543,000; the 5th Baron Kensington (1868-1900), who died in the Boer War at 32, with £5,379 per annum in landed rental and an estate of £855,000; John E.P. Spicer (1850-1928) of

Wiltshire and Surrey with £3,300 per annum and £672,000; and Owen L.J. Evans (1856-1928), of Broom Hall, Caernarvonshire, who similarly left £576,000 on a recorded landed income of £5,150 per annum. Several of these half-millionaire fortunes were clearly the products of ownership of London or other urban property which either did not appear in Bateman or which greatly appreciated in the intervening years to the deaths of their owners. Such men as Henry Browne Alexander (1799-1885), who inherited 60 choice acres of land in Kensington from his maternal grandmother and who developed them into prime residential properties;[21] Sir Robert Gunter, 1st Bt. (1831-1905) and his brother James Gunter (1833-1908), owners of large sections of the Earl's Court district as well as agricultural land yielding an income of £13,000; Thomas T. Townley-Parker (1822-1906), the ground-rent landlord in Burnley and Preston; William Hozier, 1st Baron Newlands (1825-1906) and Archibald Campbell, 1st Baron Blythswood (1833-1908), ground-rent landlords in Glasgow and James Griffith-Dearden, manorial landlord in Rochdale,[22] all left half-millionaire estates. In other such cases, the great size of the personal fortune can probably be ascribed to ancestral mercantile wealth which had never been entirely digested and transferred into the purchase of land, although the family in question had been removed from active trade for many generations. The Delmés, mentioned above, were descended from Sir Peter Delmé, Lord Mayor of London in 1723, the 'greatest merchant of his time'.[23] Sir Massey Lopes, 3rd Bt. (1818-1908), the well-known spokesman for the agricultural interest on the Tory backbenches, owner of land yielding £11,000 per annum, was the descendant of an eighteenth-century Jewish merchant in the City. Sir George Otto Trevelyan, 2nd Bt. (1838-1928), although his half-millionaire fortune was certainly in part the fruit of his landed holdings (which yielded £15,400 per annum in 1883), was probably substantially enriched by the royalties from the publications of his uncle, Lord Macaulay.

Among the other means of adding still further to a fortune were profitable marriage and lucky patronage, examples of which precede by many years the late-nineteenth-century marriages of American heiresses to British peers. Thomas Coutts (1735-1822), the renowned Charing Cross banker, who left £600,000, married his three daughters to the 3rd Earl of Guildford, the 1st Marquess of Bute and to Sir Francis Burdett, Bt., the last of whom of course fathered Baroness Burdett-Coutts, the celebrated philanthropist. Similarly Sir Henry Delves-Broughton, 9th Bt. (1810-99) although indeed the owner of lands producing £22,000 per annum, probably profited from his marriage in 1851 to the daughter of Louis Rosenzweig of the Paris Bourse.[24] Patronage as a source of fame and fortune is more universal still; the British ruling class of the eighteenth century has been described by one leading historian, for example, as an 'open aristocracy based on property and patronage'.[25] Probably the most dramatic nineteenth century instance of unexpected personal gain through patronage was the case of Sir John Edward Scott, 1st Bt. (1847-1912), whose father had been doctor to the 4th Marquess of Hertford and who was thereby introduced to Lord Hertford's illegitimate son, Sir Richard Wallace 1st Bt. (who left £1,226,000 in 1890). The younger Scott became Wallace's confidant and private secretary, gaining as well the confidence of Wallace's widow and eventually inheriting the bulk of her fortune. He was a prime mover in acquiring the Wallace Collection for the nation.[26]

Among the lesser wealth-holders, too, are many landowners with relatively low rentals in Bateman. This is not unexpected, for they were by definition poorer in personal wealth and the early dates of their death may have meant that there was little direct identity with their landed incomes and those given in Bateman.[27] However, a substantial number of these men — indeed fully half of those deceased in 1850-69 — were not minor landowners but among the very wealthiest in Britain, including nine landowners with rentals above £100,000 and seven others between £50,000 and £100,000. These are the earlier counterparts of the 8th and 9th Dukes of Bedford noted above, and included such men as William, 3rd Duke of Portland (1738-1809), who left £150,000; William, 5th Duke of Devonshire (1748-1811), who left £300,000; and Richard, 7th Viscount Fitzwilliam (1745-1816), who left £350,000 in the earlier period; Charles, 3rd Marquess of Londonderry (1778-1854), with £250,000; and Francis, 1st Earl of Ellesmere (1800-57), whose estate totalled £410,000 in the later period. Many of these lesser wealthy landowners possessed substantial but not princely estates, typical examples being men like James, 6th Earl of Cardigan (1725-1811) whose successor in 1883 was credited with an annual rental of £35,000 and George, 4th Duke of Marlborough (1739-1817), whose descendants received £37,000 per annum, according to Bateman.

As with their wealthier counterparts, there are here examples of men with very low landed incomes whose fortunes are inexplicably at variance with their stated incomes, such as Richard Thompson of Estrick, Yorkshire (d. 1820) who left £250,000 or Thomas Levett (d. 1820) of Packington in Staffordshire, whose personalty amounted to £180,000. The fortunes of others in this class can be assigned with some definiteness to 'Old Corruption', the world of government patronage and place. Notable examples of this were men like Charles, 1st Earl of Liverpool (1729-1808), Secretary at War and President of the Board of Trade during the late eighteenth century (and father of the long-serving Tory Prime Minister), who left £200,000; Charles Manners-Sutton (1755-1828), Archbishop of Canterbury from 1805 until his death, whose estate totalled £180,000; or Edmund Turnor (1754-1829), a landowner in Lincolnshire who was the great-grandson of one of the chief customs-farmers of his time and a relative of a Baron of the Exchequer.[28]

It is more than likely that personal fortune-holding among the great landowners was an important element in determining what role they, as individuals, would play in a society which automatically accepted their status as a sufficient, if not a necessary, precondition for wider political and social leadership; more attention ought surely to be paid to their total finances, of which their landed incomes were only a part. The three successive Earls of Stamford and Warrington of the period 1880-1939, for example, were owners of 31,000 acres in eight counties yielding £58,393 per annum, but left, respectively, £166,000, £3,800 (*sic*) and £95,000 in 1883, 1890 and 1910. They played no significant role in national affairs and only a limited one in local affairs. Although not every rich duke or earl was politically prominent, most of the poorer ones were not: witness the many dukes who did nothing during the nineteenth century, like St Albans, Leeds or Manchester. On the other hand, such important figures as the Marquess of Hartington, later the 8th Duke of Devonshire (1833-1908), who put his unsatisfactory family finances in order sufficiently to leave £1,165,000; Edward, 17th Earl of Derby (1865-1948), the 'King of Lancashire' who left £3,218,000; Henry, 5th Marquess of Lansdowne (1845-1927), the Foreign Secretary, whose estate totalled £1,278,000; or Lord Rosebery (1848-1929) the Prime Minister, worth £1,175,000 at his death, all possessed the ample personal means to match their place in society and to carry on even after the natural political leadership of the aristocracy was increasingly threatened.

It would, however, be too simple a generalisation that as the rentals and landed incomes of the aristocracy declined after 1879, so by degrees did the landowners' leadership of the political nation. At best this merely accelerated a process that was for many reasons inevitable. Nevertheless, the primary defining characteristic of those landowners who continued to play a leading part in national life after this period,

David Cannadine has recently suggested, was often the possession of great personal wealth, typically – after the late Victorian period – the product of selling off their agricultural or urban lands.[29] Dr Cannadine has studied in detail the Devonshires, a prime example of the staying-power of the very wealthiest landowners, whose financial accounts became much rosier during the unexpectedly competent stewardship of 'Harty Tarty', the famous 8th duke.[30] His successor was a Cabinet minister and Governor-General of Canada; *his* successor declined Churchill's offer of the Viceregency of India as late as 1943.[31] Cannadine notes that after 1939 'the battle for survival assume[d] new proportions', but does not discuss the much-publicised and equally unexpected renaissance of the Cavendish family during the years 1957-63, when the duke's son-in-law was Prime Minister and many of his relatives, including the 11th Duke of Devonshire himself, held Government office. The present Duke recently stated his belief that unless the present rates of Capital Transfer Tax were reduced, the remaining large estates would not survive more than two generations, and yet another renaissance is perhaps improbable – but who in 1880 would have guessed that they would survive this long?

The importance of the ownership of personal wealth should be kept in mind in any discussion of the vexed matter of aristocratic indebtedness during the nineteenth century. The debate in the literature between David Spring and F.M.L. Thompson, now 20 years old, was recently revived by Dr Cannadine.[32] Whereas David Spring contrasted the period of profligacy and excessive spending of the early nineteenth century with the more careful and sober mid-Victorian era, F.M.L. Thompson drew attention both to the ambiguous nature of indebtedness, which might indicate prosperity as well as adversity, and to the importance of relating the size of any repayments to the total disposable income of an aristocrat. Cannadine concludes 'it seems likely that the landed aristocracy as a class were in debt – but not ruinous debt – from the 1800s at least until the 1870s'.[33] Thereafter, it was the very richest landowners, above all those named in Table 7.1, who could best bear the strains of the Agricultural Depression and rising taxation, while the small and weak landowner increasingly went to the wall.[34]

Since the landowner's inventories of property left at death were not generally accessible to the historian and since, in fact, the probate sources provide very little direct evidence about indebtedness, especially before the 1880s,[35] the new information which these sources might provide on this question are limited, but still useful in their way. Table 7.4 compares the personal estates (before 1898) of two groups of landowners – all the successive title-holders among the very wealthiest aristocrats named in Table 7.1, and a sample of the successive title-holders of 29 substantial, but not astronomically wealthy, landowners. These are the first 29 (in alphabetical order) English or Welsh landed aristocrats (including baronets) with gross annual incomes of between £20,000 and £35,000 listed in Bateman.[36] For the period from 1898 to 1939, the numbers have been compiled of each succeeding title-holder who left £500,000 or more.

Table 7.4 indicates in a graphic manner the financial difficulties besetting the substantial, but not immensely wealthy, landowner in the course of the nineteenth and early twentieth centuries. The sample of substantial landowners taken here comprises such unquestionably major figures within the British aristocracy as the Earls Bathurst, Beaumont, Cardigan, Feversham and Grey, as well as baronets like Burdett and Graham of Netherby. It will be seen that although the personal wealth of the richest landowners increased in the course of the nineteenth century, the percentage of the group of substantial landowners leaving very large personal estates actually declined and, when the total capital value of their land becomes valued for probate in this century, only a single title-holder among this group left more than £500,000. This table, indeed, probably understates the economic distinctions between the two groups: many of the wealthiest title-holders left impressive sums just under £500,000 in this century; in other cases prior to 1926, the value of their settled land is clearly not included; while a number of major title-holders who died after 1939 left immense sums which they had held during the first 40 years of this century, like the 11th Duke of Bedford (£4.7m in 1940), or the 2nd Duke of Westminster (£10.7m in 1953). The decline in the personal wealth of the substantial landowners in the course of the nineteenth century quite possibly indicates that many were in grave financial straits long before the crunch actually came. They lacked a reserve of personal wealth which could be drawn upon in hard times; their relative lack of personal wealth points to a failure to save during good times. Disaster could occasionally strike anyone, as the celebrated example of the 2nd Duke of Buckingham and Chandos (whose debts in 1848 totalled £1.5m) demonstrates. Among the major sellers of assets in the course of the nineteenth century were at least two of the very wealthiest landowners, the Duke of Portland, who sold Bulstrode House and part of his Cumberland estate for about £350,000 and the Duke of Hamilton, whose family paintings, books and effects went for about £400,000.[37]

Table 7.4: Personal Estates (Before 1898) and Estates of £500,000 or More (From 1898) of the Very Wealthiest *vs* Substantial Landowners

1. Wealthiest Landowners (1809-97)

Size of Estate (£)	1809-58	Date of Death 1858-79	1880-97
1m+	2	1	3
500,000-£1m	3	5	1
300,000-500,000	3	1	1
200,000-300,000	3	4	3
100,000-200,000	8	7	3
Under 100,000	11	4	2
% Above £100,000	63	82	85

Size of Estates (1898-1939)

£	1898-1919	1920-1939
1m+	7	4
500,000-£1m	4	4
Under 500,000	9	4
% Above £500,000	55	67

2. Substantial Landowners (1820-97) (Incomes of £20,000-£35,000 in 1883)

Size of Estate (£)	1820-58	Date of Death 1858-79	1880-97
1m+	0	0	0
500,000-£1m	1	0	1
300,000-500,000	3	1	2
200,000-300,000	2	0	0
100,000-200,000	2	4	0
Under 100,000	21	15	19
% Above £100,000	28	25	14

Table 7.4: Continued

Size of Estates (1898-1939)

£	1898-1919	1920-1939
1m+	0	0
500,000-£1m	0	1
Under 500,000	14	11
% Above £500,000	0	8

The substantial but not immensely wealthy landowners surveyed here appear to have been vulnerable in another way: most were purely agriculturalists, possessing little in the way of mineral deposits or urban property. Of course the wealthiest landowners by and large were luckier in this respect too: the urban properties of the Westminsters or Bedfords, the mineral deposits of the Butes or Londonderrys, are too famous to require any special comment. With the passing of 'Old Corruption' during the Age of Reform these substantial men (and, *a fortiori*, lesser landowners and *nouveaux-riches* of all kinds) finally lost a lucrative source of income: hardly anything remained of the dutyless government perks or emoluments so frequent during the eighteenth century, either for themselves, their families or their favourites. Not long before it was quite different. The Earl Bathurst of the time of the 1832 edition of John Wade's *Extraordinary Black Book* was still in receipt of a useful £3,805 per annum as Teller of HM's Exchequer and Clerk of the Crown in Chancery; in addition at least five other members of his family were in receipt of Civil List pensions or government salaries, totalling nearly £7,000 annually.[38] Ironically, it was the Whig government headed by Earl Grey, one of the substantial but not immensely wealthy landowners in the sample used here, who probably did most to end these benefits forever.

It is clear from this evidence, as well as from what is more generally known about the nature of the nineteenth-century aristocracy, that personal wealth did not invariably correspond with title holding or rank in the peerage.[39] In Table 7.5, the millionaire, half-millionaire and lesser wealthy landowners have been grouped according to their rank in the aristocracy. (The category in this Table termed 'Sons of Peers' comprises those who were themselves the sons of aristocrats but did not inherit their fathers' titles.) As with the other correspondences

Table 7.5: Titles of Wealth-holding Landowners (By Date of Death Cohorts)

Title	1809-58	1858-79	1880-99	1900-19	1920-39
Millionaires:					
Duke	3	2	3	5	3
Marquess				2	2
Earl		1	2	5	11
Viscount					2
Baron				4	2
Sons of Peers	1				1
Baronets		1	2	1	
Commoners		2	4	2	
Half-millionaires:					
Duke	3	5	1		5
Marquess		3	1	1	4
Earl	4	3	3	5	11
Viscount				2	3
Baron	2	1	2	7	4
Sons of Peers		1	1		
Baronets	1		1	5	1
Commoners	3	2	5	9	7

	1809-29	1850-69
Lesser Wealthy:		
Duke	4	3
Marquess	1	3
Earl	8	8
Viscount	3	
Baron	2	3
Sons of Peers	4	1
Baronets	5	3
Commoners	11	10

noted in previous discussions, there appears to be a rough correlation between rank in the aristocracy and personal wealth, although as always with many exceptions. In particular, there were more millionaire earls than dukes (or any other category), while among the half-millionaires there were many earls and barons. Even at the highest wealth level there have always been a number of untitled landowners, like Andrew

Montagu or the Benyons, who left vast estates; there were many more such persons at the half-millionaire and lesser wealthy levels than among the millionaires. There were very wide extremes within each level of the peerage during the nineteenth century, with even dukedoms varying in acreage from St Albans, with just 9,000 acres, through Wellington with 19,000 to the Bedfords and Northumberlands and up to the Highland chiefs with their unimaginably vast, though largely barren, holdings. At the top of the table was the Duke of Sutherland with his 1,359,000 acres, of which 1,176,000 was in Sutherland. The earls, to take another category, ranged in acreage in the 1870s from Derby, Lonsdale (68,065 acres yielding £71,333), or Sefton down to the most recent political creations like the virtually landless Disraeli. Corresponding to this were the wide variations in the levels of personalty left within each rank of the peerage, with some earls or viscounts leaving vast fortunes and others never producing a single title-holder with more than a fraction of the minimum fortune required to appear in this study.

It is perhaps surprising that the wealthiest men within the lower ranks of the peerage − or those baronets or commoners without a peerage or title − should have failed to have advanced to the highest ranks of the aristocracy. In some cases, for example Derby, Lansdowne, or Salisbury title-holders declined the dukedoms which could undoubtedly have been theirs;[40] an eminent commoner like Coke of Holkham was said to have declined seven offers of a peerage, the earliest made in 1786, before accepting the first bestowed by Queen Victoria.[41] But in other cases, for instance with Andrew Montagu, Thistlethwayte or Benyon, it is difficult to see why they remained untitled. Ennoblements were until the late nineteenth century largely restricted (except for political, military and judicial creations) to landowners and their kinsmen, many of whom still received their title only because of their landed possessions. As late as 1880, in Disraeli's last batch of peerage creations − for instance, those bestowed on Alexander Wishart-Baillie, 1st Baron Lamington (12,708 acres yielding nearly £12,000 per annum) or upon Arthur Hill-Trevor, 1st Baron Trevor (23,694 acres returning £17,700) − one can see little obvious merit in the ennobled beyond long years on the Conservative backbenches and the possession of broad acres with rent-rolls to match. The Allendale peerage of 1906 appears to have been the last bestowed upon a really major landowner who was not a Cabinet minister.[42] It has often been pointed out that in the 1880s industrialists were given peerages in substantial numbers for the first time; it would be interesting to trace how and when they ceased to be given to land-owners. Only eight per cent of the peers created in the years 1920-39, it would appear, had agricultural backgrounds; this number includes several who were farmers. But even as late as 1935 Thomas Fermor-Hesketh (1881-1944) was created Baron Hesketh, his only political services up to that time consisting of one year in Parliament and a turn as High Sheriff of Northamptonshire. In 1883 Hesketh's father, a seventh baronet, realised £32,000 per annum from his land. By the time of his ennoblement, Hesketh was practically unique: among those ennobled within the same year were Lord Hirst, the German-born Jew who founded the General Electric Company; Lord Nuffield, the automobile manufacturer; Lord Portal, the paper-making millionaire; and John Buchan, Lord Tweedsmuir, author of *The Thirty-Nine Steps*.

A more curious phenomenon than the great landowners who lacked titles were the handful of peerage heirs and younger sons who left great personal fortunes. Among the millionaires, there are only two examples of this: Hon. Henry Cavendish, who died in 1810, and Edward, Lord Stanley, the heir of the 17th Earl of Derby, who died at the age of 44 in 1938, ten years before his father. Stanley's case would surely seem to be an example of intended estate duty avoidance which went amiss.[43] Many more such apparently anomalous cases occur, however, among the half-millionaires, like those of Lord Henry Bentinck (1804-70), fourth son of the 4th Duke of Portland, who left £600,000; Very Rev. Augustus Duncombe (1814-80), sixth son of the 1st Baron Feversham, who left £500,000; Hon. Algernon Tollemache (1805-92), brother of the 1st Baron Tollemache, whose estate totalled £816,000; and Thomas, Earl of Bective (1844-93), heir to the Marquess of Hertford, worth £776,000. Since the rates of duty on very large estates were minimal at the times these deaths occurred, presumably there was here little motive of death duty avoidance. Yet, equally clearly, some such cases run counter to the prevalent custom of primogeniture among the landowners, whereby the younger son could expect to inherit no more than an allowance and a small bequest, and where the oldest son would inherit only on the death of his father. Although these examples are few, they indicate that the notion of strict primogeniture ought to be considered critically. Indeed, it is implausible to imagine that the younger sons of the wealthiest landowners were simply left to their own devices, as might have been the case among the poorer gentry. But generosity toward younger sons much more often entailed the securing of lucrative or promising positions for them, whenever possible, in the Church, army and navy, or the diplomatic corps, rather than leaving them vast sums of money outright.[44]

Purchase of Land by Non-landed Wealth-holders

An equally important topic concerns us here; the movement of non-landed wealth-holders into the land, and it forms the subject of the remainder of the discussion in this chapter. Since the acreage and agricultural income of all significant owners of land are known from the *Return*, Bateman can also be used by the historian to trace the movement of new men of wealth into the land as this process stood in the 1870s and 1880s, and to identify the major business and professional wealth-holders who owned substantial amounts of land at this time.[45] In Table 7.6 below, the landed acreages of the business and professional (i.e. 'non-landed') wealth-holders deceased between 1840 and 1914 have been traced. Since the landed holdings detailed in Bateman are known only at a single point in time, it would become increasingly less accurate to use this source to trace the wealth-holders of periods very distant from 1883, and hence no wealth-holder deceased before 1840 or after 1914 has been listed.

It is a commonplace of British social history that down the ages, at least until just before 1914, wealthy businessmen and professionals quickly purchased land, transforming their wealth into status and permanence. In eighteenth-century Lincolnshire, for example, land purchases were made by City merchants and professionals, the newly-rich of towns as far afield as Hull, Sheffield and Nottingham, and local tradesmen and professionals.[46] The fact that such a movement undoubtedly took place throughout much of the British past, however, should not lead us to confuse two quite different contentions. It is one thing to assert that the purchase of land by the non-landed wealthy was common, another thing entirely to contend that it was universal or even the practice among the majority of wealthy businessmen and professionals. Even among a group of Jacobean London merchants, 44 of 140 did not own country estates;[47] by the nineteenth century, when the cost of land purchase was relatively much higher and the social distance between the aspirations of many businessmen and the traditional landed society had grown immense, the non-landed percentage was certain to rise. The fact that those peers, many with business backgrounds, ennobled after 1885 included for the first time a non-landed majority,[48] and that this break coincided with the decline of land values and the political influence of the landowning class, has led us to view

Table 7.6: Landed Acreage of Non-landed Wealth-holders (1840-1914)

Acreage	1840-58	1858-79	1880-99	1900-14
Millionaires:				
50,000+	1	1		
25,000-50,000		1	1	
10,000-25,000	2	5	7	2
5,000-10,000	1	1	5	1
2,500- 5,000		2	9	6
Unlisted	0	20	38	65
Percentage Unlisted	0.0	66.7	63.3	87.8
Half-millionaires:				
50,000+	2		2	
25,000-50,000		2		
10,000-25,000	2	6	9	4
5,000-10,000	1	8	6	3
2,000- 5,000	3	11	14	13
Unlisted	12	77	131	159
Total Number	20	104	162	179
Percentage Unlisted	56.0	74.0	80.1	88.8

Lesser Wealthy (1850-69):	Number
50,000+	
25,000-50,000	1
10,000-25,000	8
5,000-10,000	8
2,000- 5,000	9
Unlisted	129
Total Number	155
Percentage Unlisted	83.2

the decline in land purchase by the non-landed wealthy as much more sudden than in fact it was.[49]

As Table 7.6 makes clear, however, this commonplace view is quite wrong. There is no single cohort among the non-landed wealth-holders, with the exception of the millionaire group deceased in 1840-58 numbering four individuals, in which a majority owned land of sufficient acreage to be recorded in Bateman. Among both the millionaire and half-millionaire groups the non-landed portion was steadily rising, until by the First World War seven-eighths of the non-landed wealthy were landless. But even in the mid-nineteenth century landless wealth-holders were in a majority, and the increase in the landed portion may have been the result of the fact that the self-made men deceased in the years 1900-14 had owned no land when Bateman compiled his figures.[50]

Most of the minority of non-landed wealth-holders who did buy estates, moreover, did not purchase immense amounts of land. Fewer than half of those recorded in Bateman possessed estates of 10,000 acres or more; among the half-millionaires, the total was less than one-third. Some attention ought to be paid to these greatest purchasers of land. Only ten new men of wealth (among them one man in the lesser wealthy class) owned 25,000 acres or more. (The twelve individuals noted in Table 7.6 include two members of the same families as earlier wealth-holders.) In addition, a number of other descendants of wealth-holders dying prior to 1840, like Sir Robert Peel, 1st Bt. (d. 1830) and Lord Eldon (d. 1838) owned land sufficient to bring them into this table at this level: inclusion of these individuals brings the total number of post-Industrial Revolution great landowners to no more than 20 – at most – out of a total of over 200 great landowners recorded by Bateman as owning 25,000 or more acres.[51]

Probably the greatest of these new landowners were Lord Overstone (d. 1883), the banker; James Morrison (d. 1857), the warehouseman and merchant banker; Sir Josiah Guest, 1st Bt. (d. 1852), the ironmaster, whose son was created Lord Wimborne; Sir Alexander Matheson, 1st Bt. (d. 1886), the China merchant; the Baird family of Scottish ironmasters; and the Barings, the great merchant bankers. Lord Overstone spent £1,670,000 on the purchase of land,[52] and in the year of his death owned 30,849 acres yielding £58,098 per annum – a figure greater than the income of half of the dukes. Additionally, he transferred to his son-in-law Sir Robert Loyd-Lindsay, Bt. (later 1st Baron Wantage) much of the 20,528 acres yielding £26,492 per annum credited to him in Bateman, while Overstone's brother Lewis Loyd owned a further 3,237 acres yielding £8,795. Apart from his land, Overstone left a personal fortune of £2,119,000.

The Morrisons, less celebrated but even more remarkable in some respects, were credited in 1883 with the ownership of some 106,900 acres yielding £53,900 per annum. These estates, among them the entire Island of Islay in Argyllshire and the Fonthill estate in Wiltshire formerly owned by William Beckford, the great eighteenth-century merchant, were then in the possession of five brothers whose probated personal fortunes totalled nearly £15m. The great majority of this land, however, had been purchased by James Morrison before his death.[53] Although one son, Walter (1836-1921) became a prominent backbench MP, the family did not, as has already been mentioned, achieve a title of any sort until 1965 when John Granville Morrison, formerly Chairman of the Conservative Party's 1922 Committee, was created Lord Margadale.

In contrast, the Guest iron family of Dowlais in South Wales is among the most celebrated of early industrial families. They had been given a baronetcy in 1838, a peerage in 1880 and were elevated to a viscountcy in 1918. The first baronet, Sir Josiah Guest, a former Methodist who left £500,000 in 1852, had married as his second wife a daughter of the Earl of Lindsey; his son married a daughter of the Duke of Marlborough; his grandson a niece of the Duke of Westminster and served also as Lord-Lieutenant of Ireland. In 1883 the first Lord Wimborne – as the head of the family had become – was the owner of 83,500 acres in Glamorgan, Dorset and Ross-shire, worth £46,900 per annum, besides the sizable personal wealth still owned by the family.

The Bairds, the great Scottish ironmasters whose five Bateman-listed members held over 125,000 acres yielding about £59,000 per annum, were landowners throughout northern and central Scotland. The Barings, with the Rothschilds the most celebrated of merchant banking families, were credited in Bateman in 1883 with four members (Lord and Lady Ashburton, Lord Northbrook and W.H. Baring) owning a total of 89,000 acres yielding about £71,000 per annum, although no single member owned more than about 37,000 acres. The last of these greatest new landowners, perhaps not quite in the same class as the others, was Sir Alexander Matheson, 1st Bt., partner in the famous trading firm of the Far East, Jardine Matheson, and director of the Bank of England, who left £644,000 in 1886; although he owned no less than 220,663 acres in Ross and Inverness-shire, this yielded only £26,461 per annum.

Four other new families just below these were very nearly in the same class. These were the Scotts, the London bankers, with 59,923 acres but worth only £5,752 annually; the Baileys of Glanusk (later Lords Glanusk), ironmasters and relatives of the Crawshays, with 128,300 acres yielding £25,600 per annum; the Cunninghames of Craigends, ironmasters in Scotland, owners of 33,950 at £16,614 per annum, plus £2,500 per annum in mineral rents;[54] and Lord Ardilaun, at the time the head of the Guinness brewing family, with 31,300 acres worth £6,573 per annum in three Irish counties.

In the category of landowners below this level were about 35 new-wealthy families with holdings of between 10,000 and 25,000 acres, out of a total of well over 500 landowners throughout the United Kingdom in this class. Among the families at this acreage level were the Arkwrights, Goldsmids, Brasseys, Rothschilds, Meuxes, Whitbreads, Ridleys and Cunliffe-Listers. As a category it is quite probable that they exercised greater territorial influence than the very largest land-owning businessmen. The classic examples of this were the Whitbreads, for generations among the most important families in Bedfordshire, and the Rothschilds, for much of the nineteenth century nearly as important in Buckinghamshire as they were in the City. Further down still, the class of landowners with between 2,000 and 10,000 acres numbered among them many other important business families, for example the Gurneys, Watneys, Basses, Hardys and Armstrongs. Most of the business peers created between 1885 and 1914 who owned any land at all fell into this class.[55]

There was, it would seem, very little difference among the different occupational categories of non-landed wealth-holders in their eagerness to purchase land. Among the millionaires who purchased land recorded in Bateman, 18 can be classified in one or another of the commercial occupations, 19 as industrialists, and 11 among the miscellaneous (brewers, etc.) variety of production. At first glance this is somewhat surprising, as one might have expected the merchants and bankers, with their older and closer social ties to the landed aristocracy, to move more readily into full-fledged membership in it. Such men might, however, be readier to purchase very small but expensive estates in the Home Counties near London, while the growth of the West End and later of suburban London might have served as a kind of substitute for the country neighbourhood. Conversely, the very social distance between the industrialists and gentility as commonly understood may have required them, in their search for status, to imitate their social superiors in a much more obvious manner than their London counterparts. Or it may simply have been that the only pleasant places for a rich man to live in the north of England were in the countryside.

The fact remains, however, that the majority of wealthy business and professional men in nineteenth-century Britain were either landless or the owners of estates too small to be found in Bateman. In my opinion, this fact cannot be emphasised too strongly either when the structure of elites in nineteenth-century British society is discussed, or in any attempt to explain the decline of British business dynasties. Such families as the Crawshays of Cyfarthfa, the Coatses, Rylands,

Bulloughs, Cunliffes or Carr Glyns (Barons Wolverton) either owned no land in the 1870s and 1880s, or too little to be recorded in Bateman. By and large it is true that the very wealthiest of nineteenth-century businessmen, like Overstone, the Morrisons and the Rothschilds, purchased the most land, but certainly no hard-and-fast rule existed. Of the three wealthiest industrialists deceased up to the First World War, Thomas Brassey's sons owned about 12,000 acres, Sir Charles Tennant (d. 1906) owned 3,616 acres while John Rylands (d. 1887) apparently owned no land at all. Men like the financier Herman, Baron de Stern (1815-87), who left £3.5m, Hugh McCalmont (1809-87),[56] the stockbroker and foreign merchant who left £3.1m or John Gretton (1833-99), the brewer who left £2.9m, are not to be found in Bateman; nor are the heirs of Richard Thornton (1776-1865), the insurance broker whose estate was valued at £2.8m, while the son of Giles Loder (1786-1871), a Russian merchant who left £2.9m, owned a moderate estate of 10,241 acres spread among four counties. The failure of new men of wealth (which *a fortiori* was true of the thousands of successful business and professional men below the millionaire class) must also be seen in the context of the enormous and unprecedented growth of wealth and income in the wake of British industrialisation: not only did these new men purchase less land than any of their predecessors since the Middle Ages, but collectively they spent a much smaller fraction of their accumulated wealth on land purchases than ever before. Yet if one reads the obituaries or entries relating to these wealthy men and their families in works like Walford's *County Families* or *Who Was Who*, one is struck by the fact that most if not all *seemed* to own country estates, in some cases several such estates. The 13 members of the Crawshay ironmastering family noticed in the 1895 edition of Walford's *County Families*[57] are credited with 15 country houses, places with names like Cyfarthfa Castle, Glamorganshire; Haughton Castle, Simonburn, Hexham; Scole Lodge, Scole, Norfolk; and Brabourne Hall, Riverhead, Sevenoaks. Clearly in most such cases these country places were either rented, the wealth-holder not owning the freehold, or stood on very small estates without much surrounding agricultural land. It is important for the historian not to infer from such references the continuity of a landed aristocracy among the new rich. Nor should it be overlooked that even where great purchases of land by the newly-rich occurred, the bulk of their fortune almost invariably remained in the form of personalty like stocks and shares.

The reluctance of the post-Industrial Revolution rich to purchase land on a vast scale in the manner of their predecessors down the ages,

is evidence of several changes of the first importance in the structure
of the nineteenth-century British elites. Foremost is the fact that from
the beginnings of the Industrial Revolution down to the 1880s, the
British landed aristocracy was increasingly becoming a caste-like and
socially-isolated group, distancing itself from, and distanced from, the
newer business magnates, who found it nearly impossible in many
cases to gain full acceptance into the inner circle of high landed society.
Just as the landowner's now-frequent ventures into urban development
or mineral extraction did not indicate that he had become a *bona-fide*
businessman, so did the business magnate's occasional purchase of a
small, or even a larger agricultural estate, not point to a metamorphosis
into a fully-fledged landowner. As far as I am aware, there is no instance
of a major nineteenth-century landowner receiving more than half of
his income from non-landed sources like stocks or mineral royalties,[58]
just as there is no instance of a *major* nineteenth-century businessman
receiving more than half his income from the land. The passing of 'Old
Corruption' and the growth of agricultural rents and, indeed, supportive
non-landed sources of income, paradoxically removed the necessity
for the landed elite to form a close alliance with business or professional
men of wealth. Whereas a fair number of the major Tory figures even of
the late age of 'Old Corruption' had been the immediate descendants
of merchants or quasi-business placemen – for example Eldon, Goulburn
or Liverpool – thereafter for at least half a century an immediate
background in trade became despised almost in the same sense as among
the Spanish or Polish nobilities; the virtual absence of business peerages
until the 1880s – when the flood began – is well-documented.[59] Direct
participation in the new technology or the direction of industry in the
style of the Duke of Bridgwater (d. 1803) became an anachronism as a
new class of professional estate managers, colliery-owners and colliery-
viewers, large-scale builders like Cubitt, and the like, grew up: to the
great landowner, such things need no longer be visible.[60] The withdrawal
of aristocratic leadership from scientific societies, and the general
neglect by the aristocrat-dominated government of scientific and
technical education, is too well-known to require any extended mention.
Eighteenth- and early nineteenth-century Britain had had its share, and
indeed more than its share, of aristocratic scientists, like Hon. Henry
Cavendish or Sir George Cayley, 6th Bt. (1773-1857), inventor of the
glider. The list of Presidents of the Royal Society, which had been a
mixture of aristocrats and scientists until the term of Lord Wrottesley
(who served from 1854-8), thereafter was always headed by a
distinguished scientist, whose origins were irrelevant to his appointment.

Only in this century do there again appear scions of the nobility like Bertrand Russell, Hon. Charles S. Shelley-Rolls (1877-1910, co-founder of Rolls-Royce) or Sir Charles Parsons who again pick up the old tradition of aristocrat-scientist.

A similar pattern is to be discerned in the participation of Victorian landed aristocrats in business life. The railway-director peer is a well-known individual; the cotton-manufacturing peer — until cotton manufacturers became peers — is not. Elsewhere I have argued that there increasingly existed during the nineteenth century a closer political and social association between the landed and London-based commercial elite, especially after the 1870s, than between the landowners and industrial magnates;[61] 'the number of aristocrats, or even minor landed gentry, who were directly concerned with industry or manufacturing (apart from membership on boards of companies exploiting the minerals on their own land) was surely nil'.[62] It is in the late Victorian period that the landed aristocrat, particularly the younger son or relatively impecunious title-holder, became a common figure on the boards of City companies, occasionally companies of considerable dubiety. By the 1930s, as is true today, no one thought it strange to find a ninth Earl or a fifth Marquess on the board of a major business corporation;[63] many who were not there would prefer to be; many more were by then related by marriage to the business elite. But this change was a novelty.

The final point remaining to be made is that if the business wealthy did not become landowners, they nevertheless liked their residential comfort as much as anyone might expect. Virtually without exception[64] all wealth-holders by the end of their lives were resident either in a country house, a seaside resort town or in the West End of London or the wealthy section of a provincial town. The growth of the upper-class districts of London, expanding westwards from Bloomsbury to encompass vast regions in Mayfair, Belgravia, Kensington and Bayswater by the end of the century is a tribute as much to the attractions of London society for the wealthy as to any mere growth in their numbers;[65] it is as important to see the continuities as the changes in this process. Even in 1809-10, the first year of this study, many of the London-resident rich were already living in the familiar West End: addresses like Pall Mall, Portland Place, Curzon Street, Berners Street and Lower Grosvenor Street are already common among those leaving £100,000 or more in that year, and they already far outnumber those wealthy men and women still resident in the more easterly areas of central London, like John Puget of the Royal College of Physicians, who lived in Russell Square and left £175,000 or David Powell, a merchant who left £300,000 in 1810, whose addresses are given as St Helen's Place in the City and Hackney. Many other City merchants left London altogether for Bath or a country place, usually either in the Home Counties or the south-west. Although Lord Eldon (d. 1838), continued to live in Bedford Square, by 1874 Northumberland House, the Charing Cross seat of the Percy family, had become impossible to live in and was demolished. Except, indeed, for the virtually complete desertion of east and east-central London by the rich, the opening-up (made possible by the railways) of new suburban areas around London like Hampstead, the 'stockbroker belt' in Surrey and along the Metropolitan Line in Middlesex and Bucks., and the emergence of new south-coast watering places, above all Brighton and Bournemouth, to which these people retired, one can discern little difference between the 1809-10 London-resident rich and their counterparts dying in the late Victorian and Edwardian period. A duke or the Regency equivalent of a South African diamond millionaire might not then have dwelled in Park Lane, but he would certainly have lived nearby.

In the north of England, the shades of light and dark in this matter were sharper, the differences between the early and late nineteenth century more pronounced. The squalor and sheer physical dangers of central Manchester, Leeds or Birmingham led to their abandonment by the rich by the third quarter of the century, although they continued to dominate factory life, and the leadership of many of these towns as a whole, until the First or even the Second World War. Purpose-built urban enclaves like Toxteth Park in Liverpool, northern resorts and watering places like Harrogate, Scarborough and Chester, and country estates in Cheshire, north Wales, or the rural Ridings became the usual place of residence of these men (and their widows and daughters) in a distinctive way. Whether north or south, however, this must be seen as part of a regroupment of wealth in which urban neighbourhoods, rigidly defined by class boundaries, replaced both the former hetero-geneity of town life, and much of the snobbery of the country estate network. Landed aristocrats and new millionaires lived cheek-by-jowl in Berkeley Square or Park Lane, even while a *nouveau-riche* estate owner might wait decades for true acceptance into county society. The days when a Cobden lived over his place of business or when hundreds of middle-rank London merchants continued to live in the City, as was the case until the 1840s or 1850s, had passed by the 1880s or 1890s. As much as the passing of the traditional role and status of the landed aristocrat, this marked a fundamental shift in the way wealthy men perceived one another; perhaps unintentionally and spuriously, residential patterns lent a unity to men of wealth and property who had only that in common.

Notes

1. On the compilation of *The Return of Owners of Land*, see the Introduction to the 1971 reprint of Bateman's *The Great Landowners of Great Britain and Ireland*, edited by David Spring.
2. There are persistent rumours that a second return of landowners' acreage and income was compiled, at least in part, as a result of Lloyd George's land taxation ventures, in 1911. The surviving returns are said to be held by the Public Record Office. It goes without saying that access should be granted to historians to use these returns, if indeed they exist.
3. See especially, G.E. Mingay, *English Landed Society in the Eighteenth Century* (London, 1963), *The Gentry: The Rise and Fall of a Ruling Class* (London, 1976) and *Rural Life in Victorian England* (London, 1977); G.E. Mingay and J.D. Chambers, *The Agricultural Revolution: 1750-1880* (London, 1966); F.M.L. Thompson, *English Landed Society in the Nineteenth Century* (London, 1963); David Spring, *The English Landed Estate in the Nineteenth Century: Its Administration* (Baltimore, 1963); J.T. Ward and R.G. Wilson, (eds.), *Land and Industry* (Newton Abbot, 1971); and two recent articles by David Cannadine, 'Aristocratic Indebtedness in the Nineteenth Century: The Case Re-opened', *Econ. Hist. Rev.*, 2nd ser., XXX (1977) and 'The Landowner as Millionaire: The Finances of the Dukes of Devonshire; c. 1800-c. 1926', *Agricultural Hist. Rev.* 25 Pt II (1977). Many useful studies of individual landowners or landed families exist, e.g., Eric Richard, *The Leviathan of Wealth* (London, 1973), on the first Duke of Sutherland. On twentieth-century landowning there is far less, but see Roy Perrott, *The Aristocrats* (London, 1968) and Stephen Glover, 'The Old Rich: A Survey of the Landed Classes', *The Spectator*, 1 January 1977. The debate about the 'rise of the gentry' during the seventeenth century (Tawney, Stone, Hill, Hexter, *et al.*), and that on eighteenth-century landowning (e.g., Habbakkuk), must also be noted. See J.V. Beckett, 'English Landownership in the Later Seventeenth and Eighteenth Centuries: The Debate and Its Problems', *Econ. Hist. Rev.*, 2nd ser., XXX (1977).
4. Harold Perkin, *Origins of Modern British Society* (London, 1969), p. 431.
5. So far as I am aware, this is the first such *complete* list ever published.
6. These include, e.g., Lord Calthorpe, credited with an annual rental of £122,628. In this case, Bateman notes that Calthorpe is credited with *all* rentals in his extensive Birmingham holdings, despite the fact that he received only the ground rents. (Bateman, p. 22.) In the same category are Lord Haldon (credited with an annual income of £109,300), Sir John Ramsden (£181,300) and Sir John St Aubyn (£95,200).
7. Cannadine, 'The Landowner as Millionaire', p. 77, citing David Rush, *The Court of London from 1819 to 1825* (London, 1873), p. 9.
8. See however, Cannadine, 'The Landowner as Millionaire', and Thompson, *English Landed Society in the Nineteenth Century*, esp. Chapters 1, IX, X.
9. Bateman, *Great Landowners*, pp. xxxiv-xxv cites the imaginary but plausible case of 'John Steadyman', a squire of 'Wearywork Hall, Cidershire', whose gross income of £4,750 is reduced to little more than £1,000 through fixed expenses on his property or relatives. As Cannadine, 'The Landowner as Millionaire', rightly observes, it was just these lesser landowners who vanished

from the land most readily after the 1870s.

10. Thompson, *English Landed Society in the Nineteenth Century*, p. 268.

11. There is, of course, no necessary relationship between possessing a landed income of £50,000 per annum and a personal fortune of £500,000. These are merely convenient benchmarks situated at roughly equal points on the wealth pyramid. An income of £50,000 suggests an estate with a capital value in the range £1 million to £1.5 million, depending on the period.

12. It should be noted that although all individuals counted here as landowners were removed from trade or the professions for at least three generations, several ostensible 'landowners' probably still possessed great personal wealth earned during the family's rise. An example of this is the 3rd Earl of Eldon (1845-1926), great-grandson of the Lord Chancellor, who is counted as a landowner.

13. 'Hon. Henry Cavendish', *Dictionary of National Biography*.

14. Bateman, p. 1. Abdy is not noticed in the *Dictionary of National Biography*.

15. Thistlethwayte also owned 'a share' in 600 acres at Paddington held under lease from the Ecclesiastical Commissioners. (*The Times*, 5 July 1915.)

16. *The Times*, 14 April 1916.

17. *The Times*, ibid.; *Directory of Directors, 1880-1915, passim*. Clanricarde was a diplomat by profession; he had been known as the 'worst' Irish landlord.

18. W.F. Money and G.E. Buckle, *Life of Benjamin Disraeli* (London, 1929), vol. 5, p. 79.

19. Ibid.

20. *The Times*, 14 February 1907.

21. *Survey of London*, XXXVIII (London, 1975), pp. 8-11, 'Alexander Estate'.

22. Griffith-Dearden is unlisted in Bateman. His estate at Rochdale included the manorial rights over 32,000 acres and the privilege of Court Leet and Court Baron in the parish of Rochdale (*The Times*, 15 October 1912).

23. *Burke's Landed Gentry* (1937 edn), 'Delmé family'.

24. *Burke's Peerage*, 1937 edn; private information. The 8th baronet, father of the half-millionaire, had left only £4,000 in personalty in 1851.

25. Perkin, *Origins of Modern British Society*, p. 17.

26. *The Times*, 18 January 1912; 8 August 1913.

27. Eight lesser wealth-holders deceased in 1809-29 and three deceased in 1850-69, described in contemporary records as landowners, are unlisted in Bateman. In some cases their property was probably acquired by distant relatives whose succession I have been unable to trace.

28. 'Edmund Turnor', *Dictionary of National Biography*. (Liverpool died in 1808, but his estate was not proved until the following year.)

29. Cannadine, 'The Landowner as Millionaire'.

30. Ibid., esp. pp. 87-91.

31. Ibid., p. 91.

32. Cannadine, 'Aristocratic Indebtedness in the Nineteenth Century'.

33. Ibid., p. 645.

34. Ibid., pp. 645-50 and 'The Landowner as Millionaire'.

35. This might only be inferred from comparing the gross and net value of the personal estate, available only after 1880.

36. Because of the lack of early probate data, Scotsmen and Irishmen (or aristocrats who obtained the bulk of their landed income from Scotland or Ireland) have been excluded. Also excluded were all commoners, as succession to their property would have been too difficult to trace − while it could be argued that only title-holders would be truly a part of the aristocratic way of life − and

224   *Landed Wealth*

all post-Industrial Revolution fortunes, for instance that of Sir Joseph Bailey, the ironmaster, and his successors, who would otherwise qualify for inclusion. For similar reasons, Lord Overstone was excluded from the evidence concerning the very wealthiest landowners, as were the pre-Ancaster (Willoughby d'Eresby and Aveland) and the Hertford Wallace title-holders and a number of early title-holders deceased in Ireland or Scotland, for whom no probate valuation was available.

37. Cannadine, 'Aristocratic Indebtedness in the Nineteenth Century', p. 631. Cannadine unfortunately does not provide the dates of these sales. It would seem that the Portland sales occurred in the early nineteenth century, Hamilton's in the 1880s. (Ibid., p. 630.)

38. John Wade, *Extraordinary Black Book* (London, 1832), p. 510.

39. Nor did rank invariably correspond with landed wealth; but this cannot be discussed in depth here.

40. Disraeli, though nearly landless, was offered a dukedom (which he declined) upon his return from the Congress of Berlin in 1879. See Money and Buckle, *Life of Benjamin Disraeli*, vol. 6, p. 346.

41. *Complete Peerage*, 'Leicester of Holkham'.

42. Henry Chaplin, ennobled in 1916, owned 23,400 acres yielding £30,500 per annum and Walter Long, given a viscountcy in 1906, owned 15,400 acres worth £23,200 per annum. Both were of course leading politicians.

43. Yet Stanley (who left £2,210,000) actually left less than his father, who himself left £3.2 million in 1948.

44. On the practice among various agricultural classes in society during the early modern period, see Jack Goody, Joan Thirsk and E.P. Thompson, (eds.), *Family and Inheritance. Rural Society in Western Europe 1200-1800* (Cambridge, 1976) esp. J.P. Cooper, 'Patterns of Inheritance and Settlement by the Great Landowners from the Fifteenth to the Eighteenth Centuries'.

45. One qualification needs to be made in this statement: non-landed wealth-holders who purchased land sufficient to diminish their personal fortunes to a level below the half-millionaire mark would not be included in this study (although they might appear among the 'lesser wealthy' cohorts). To obtain information on these men, one would need to know the histories of all non-landed wealth-holders down to a level far below that which is traced here or, conversely, to make a special study of each and every substantial landowner in Bateman. Two local studies which have attempted just this are J.T. Ward, *East Yorkshire Landed Estates in the Nineteenth Century* (East Yorkshire Local History Society, York, 1967) and R.O. Knapp, 'Social Mobility in Lancashire Society With Special Reference to the "Modern Domesday Returns" of 1873-6' (unpublished doctoral dissertation, University of Lancaster, 1970).

46. B.A. Holderness, 'The English Land Market in the Eighteenth Century: The Case of Lincolnshire', *Econ. Hist. Rev.*, 2nd ser., XXVII (1974).

47. R.G. Lang, 'Social Origins and Social Aspirations of Jacobean Merchants', *Econ. Hist. Rev.*, 2nd ser., XXVIII (1974).

48. Thompson, *English Landed Society in the Nineteenth Century*, pp. 60-1, 294ff.

49. See, e.g., Ibid., pp. 36-42 and E.L. Jones, 'Industrial Capital and Landed Investment: the Arkwrights in Herefordshire, 1809-43' in E.L. Jones and G.E. Mingay (eds.), *Land, Labour and Population in the Industrial Revolution* (London, 1967).

50. Bateman revised the 1871-4 *Return* data for his final (1883) edition in so far as he could, but as I understand the matter he did not attempt to discover the new men unlisted in the Parliamentary Return who had purchased land after 1871-3. (See David Spring's Introduction to the recent (1971) reprint of

Bateman, pp. 7-22, esp. pp. 17-19.)

The total number of individuals in the 1850-69 lesser wealthy cohort is larger than in previous tables in this work which discuss this group. This is because all of those whose occupations or geography were unknown had not been included in the previous tables, but are included here unless they were known to have been (by our criteria) *bona-fide* landowners.

51. See Appendix I, Table 1 (p. 495) in Bateman.

52. D.P. O'Brien, *The Correspondence of Lord Overstone* (Cambridge, 1971) Vol. II, p. 862, no. 4 *et. seq.*

53. Information provided by Mr Richard Gatty JP of Pepper Arden, Northallerton, James Morrison's great-grandson. Morrison's unmarried daughter Ellen, who died in 1909, left another £2.4 million.

54. The Cunninghames were hardly strictly speaking new men and, perhaps, should be subtracted from the totals here. The Craigends estate had been in the Cunninghame family since 1479; the half-millionaire ironmaster, Alexander Cunninghame (1804-66) purchased this estate from his elder brother's son in 1858. (*Burke's Landed Gentry*, Cunninghame of Craigends.) Such anomalous types of social mobility were more common among Scotsmen than Englishmen.

55. Thompson, *English Landed Society in the Nineteenth Century*, p. 298.

56. In 1887 however, McCalmont purchased Bishops Wood on the Wye from the Partridge family (ibid., p. 319). This family is not recorded in Bateman.

57. Crawshays were millionaires prior to 1810 and would certainly have moved into the land well before the *Return* was compiled.

58. Cannadine, 'The Landowner as Millionaire'. Some rather minor noble landowners like the Earls of Leven and Melville were active businessmen; an exception to this general rule might be the Earls of Jersey, who were among the owners (through marriage) of Child's Bank, in addition to their rent-rolls of £34,600 per annum.

59. See Ralph E. Pumphrey, 'The Introduction of Industrialists into the British Peerage: A Study of Adaptation of a Social Institution', *Amer. Hist. Rev.*, LXV (1959).

60. See Spring *The English Landed Estate in the Nineteenth Century*; and Thompson, *English Landed Society in the Nineteenth Century*, esp. Chapters VI and IX.

61. W.D. Rubinstein, 'Wealth, Elites and the Class Structure of Modern Britain', *Past and Present*, 76 (1977), esp. pp. 112-15.

62. Ibid., p. 115.

63. See, e.g., Simon Haxey, *Tory M.P.* (London, 1938); Andrew Roth, *Lords on the Board* (London, 1971).

64. The only traceable wealth-holders who did not live in a wealthy neighbourhood were the solicitor and company director William F. Tibbitts (1842-1927), who lived in a slum district of Sheffield among the properties he owned, and the London water company owner Noel Whiting (1821-1903), who continued to dwell in Battersea long after it was deserted by the wealthy. (*Wandsworth Mercury*, 3 August 1903.)

However, out of interest, it might be noted that the post-1945 period has seen the death of several interesting wealthy eccentrics who made no effort to live their lives as wealthy men; their acquaintances were often unaware of their wealth. Harold Charles Burnet (1882-1961) lived the life of a recluse in a Worcester hotel. He was found dead in his room with a trunk containing £510,000 in share certificates, mainly in breweries. In the early 1970s *The Times* reported the probate of the estate of a Lancashire arc-welder who had left some £501,000, the source – or existence – of which was totally unknown to his family or friends! Football pools and taxation, working together, may some day move the centre of British wealth-holding from Mayfair to Coronation Street.

65. See Francis Sheppard, *London, 1800-70: The Infernal Wen* (London, 1971).

8 WEALTH IN THE POST-WAR WORLD

Prior to the Second World War, the basic patterns of wealth-holding are generally clear, if often surprising. With the post-war period, however, we enter perhaps the most confusing period of rapid change in the whole history of private wealth-holding in Britain. Has unprecedentedly high taxation, socialist measures of nationalisation, rapid inflation and Britain's secular decline as an economic power reduced the riches and power of its private wealth-holders to the vanishing point? Has the 'managerial revolution' now victorious throughout nearly every phase of industry made wealth-holding simply irrelevant to the wielding of economic power? Or have the rich, despite everything, managed to hold on and maintain their position in absolute and even relative terms? Folk wisdom, as usual, offers us various and contradictory answers to these questions, and it is safe to say that for every Englishman-in-the-street who believes that, as always, the rich rule, there is another man who thinks that, at least in the old sense, the rich have long since passed away and ceased to be.

It is difficult to know the truth of the matter, for just at the time when the patterns become more confused, the probate and other taxation sources unquestionably become less accurate. The major reason for this is, of course, the growth of estate duty avoidance (and other taxation avoidance schemes) coincident with the rising marginal rates of taxation and the growth of a sub-profession of lawyers and tax accountants who specialise in keeping their clients firmly attached to their fortunes. Since the amount of avoidance is probably unknowable even in a rough way and since, moreover, avoidance has presumably varied in its incidence between the Second World War and the present time, it is simply impossible — without making heroic assumptions — to compensate for in an accurate way, especially as this work has mainly focused on the wealth of specific *individuals*.

However, certain very general points about the effect of estate duty avoidance on the application of the probate data to the post-war world can be made with some confidence. First, if estate duties are now — as is often contended — a 'voluntary tax', then it is one that rich persons often volunteer to pay. Second, it is probable that, because of the nature of estate duties, wealth-holders in particular segments of the economy are taxed (and hence recorded) more frequently than in other

Table 8.1: Top Wealth-leavers, 1940-79 (Those Leaving £3 Million or More, 1940-69; £5 Million or More, 1970-9)

1940-9	£'000
1. Herbrand, 11th Duke of Bedford (1858-1940), landowner	4,651
2. William J. Yapp (1861-1946), tobacco manufacturer	4,501
3. Gerald, 7th Viscount Portman (1875-1948), London property owner	4,493
4. Walter M. Wills (1861-1941), tobacco manufacturer	4,433
5. Eleanor, Countess Dowager Peel (d. 1949), land; linoleum[a]	4,275
6. Hon. Arthur Ernest Guinness (1876-1949), brewer	3,322
7. Edward, 17th Earl of Derby (1865-1948), landowner	3,218
8. Philip E. Hill (1873-1944), investment banker	3,008
1950-9	
1. James A.E. de Rothschild (1878-1957), merchant banker	11,623
2. Hugh, 2nd Duke of Westminster (1879-1953), land and London property owner	10,703
3. Hastings, 12th Duke of Bedford (1888-1953), landowner	5,792
4. Sir Alfred E. Herbert (1866-1957), machine tool manufacturer	5,336
5. Gilbert Wills, 1st Baron Dulverton (1880-1956), tobacco manufacturer	4,268
6. Miss G.M. Yule (d. 1958), Indian Banking fortune[b]	4,100
7. William Weir, 1st Viscount Weir (1877-1959), engineer	3,304
8. John A. Dewar (1891-1954), distiller	3,272
9. Joseph A. Littman (1898-1953), property developer	3,213
1960-9	
1. Guy A. Vandervell (1899-1967), engine bearing manufacturer	10,950
2. Sir Alfred C. Beatty (1875-1968), mining engineer	7,181
3. Charles L. Arnold (1888-1968), electrical equipment manufacturer (MK Electric)	5,830
4. Gerald, 4th Duke of Westminster (1907-67), land and London property owner	5,489
5. Bernard Sunley (1910-64), property developer and civil engineer	5,205
6. William, 7th Earl of Radnor (1895-1968), landowner	4,552
7. Kenneth P. Allpress (1917-68), engineer	4,500
8. Howard Samuel (1914-61), property developer and publisher[c]	3,848
9. Hon. Dorothy Wyndham Paget (1905-60), American banking fortune[d]	3,803
10. Sir John R. Ritchie (1869-1963), engineer	3,500

Table 8.1: Continued

1960-9	£'000
11. William L. Stephenson (1880-1963), multiple retailer (chairman of Woolworths)	3,490
12. William Morris, 1st Viscount Nuffield (1877-1963), automobile manufacturer	3,253[e]

1970-9[f]	
1. Sir John R.Ellerman, 2nd Bt. (1909-73), shipowner	52,238[g]
2. Count Antoine Edward Seilern (d. 1978), of Salzburg, Austria – Estate in Britain	30,836
3. Felix D. Fenston (1915-70), property developer	12,671
4. Thomas, 10th Earl Fitzwilliam (1904-79), landowner	11,776
5. Thomas, 5th Earl of Leicester (1908-77), landowner	11,314
6. Archibald, 6th Earl of Rosebery (1882-1975), landowner[h]	9,942
7. Joseph Rank, 1st Baron Rank (1888-1972), cinema; foodstuffs	5,993
8. Sir Richard J. Boughey, 10th Bt. (1925-78), landowner	5,956
9. Joseph Sunlight (1889-1978), architect and property developer	5,714
10. William, 7th Earl of Sefton (1898-1970), land and Liverpool property owner	5,243

a. She was the daughter of Lord Ashton (d. 1930), the linoleum multi-millionaire. This was the largest woman's estate ever left in Britain.
b. Daughter, Sir David Yule (d. 1928), Anglo-Indian banker said to be worth £20 million in India.
c. Despite his wealth, Samuel was a socialist who served as a director of the *New Statesman* and the *Tribune*.
d. Grand-daughter, William C. Whitney, American banking millionaire. She was the daughter of the 1st Lord Queenborough, Conservative politician.
e. Nuffield gave away an estimated £30 million in charitable and educational bequests in his lifetime.
f. Includes estates probated to mid-1979 only.
g. This was much the largest estate ever left in Britain.
h. Rosebery was the son of Hannah Rothschild, (d. 1890), who left £765,000 in her own right.

areas: in particular, it is likely that landowners are actually recorded in the contemporary probate data more disproportionately than business-men. This is because agricultural and forested land is taxed at a considerably lower rate than other forms of property, and hence it is in the interests of a rich man to own agricultural land *as opposed* to other forms of property (though avoiding taxes altogether is, of course, better still). Third, even if the contemporary probate statistics are not a complete sample, it is likely that in most respects — and apart from the distinction which we have just drawn — they are a random sample reflecting most of the changes which have plainly come over the British wealth structure in the past 40 years, and hence — at least to a certain extent — valid as material for research.

These points would probably be illustrated more clearly with individual examples. Perhaps the best examples are the very richest individuals, and Table 8.1 records the largest estates left since 1940 — all those leaving £3 million or more between 1940 and 1969, and those leaving £5 million or more in the period 1970-9.

Some conclusions about the quality of the contemporary probate data will be evident from even a superficial glance at this list. Although it certainly contains some names not well-known to the general public or even to the business historian, it will be clear as well that, whatever else this list may or may not be, it is not an index of little old ladies who leave their fortunes to the home for stray cats. Certainly no one would claim that it contains the names of *all* of Britain's richest men and women of the time. No one would pretend that Agatha Christie (d. 1976) was worth only £106,683, Lord Sieff (d. 1972) of Marks and Spencer only £165,000 or Lord Beaverbrook (d. 1964) — whose lawyers managed to persuade the Inland Revenue that he was a Canadian, and hence dutiable in Britain only to a limited extent — only £380,000. But this list does include Ellerman, Nuffield, Rank, Dulverton, Weir and many great landowners. Many other great businessmen and land-owners left large fortunes, but below the £3 or £5 million noted here. All of these are mysterious if death duties are indeed a 'voluntary tax'. Lord Rosebery, for example, a former Cabinet minister, who died at the age of 93 after holding the title for 46 years (and whose mother was a Rothschild): why did he volunteer to pay duty on an estate of some £9,942,000? Why did successive Dukes of Bedford leave £4.7 million and £5.8 million? These matters are as inexplicable as they are fortuitous for the researcher. One must surely conclude that whether for economic, legal or psychological reasons, avoiding death duties is simply not as easy as it seems. And it is simply not true that death duties are paid on very substantial estates only by the unlucky or the unsophisticated.

The best that one can say about the probate statistics in the post-war period is that they are good in parts — though which parts remains unknown. Research making use of them is probably valid, therefore, for some purposes, largely invalid for others. As a statistical *sample* of the 'real' rich (though bearing in mind what we have said about the disproportionate place of land in these figures) it is probably valid enough, although even here some qualifications will probably be needed.

It is also valid, though to a more limited extent still, as an indicator of the names of the great individual wealth-holders and the size of their fortunes. On the other hand, the use of these statistics to infer conclusions about the distribution of wealth throughout society is probably much more hazardous, because so much slips through the net — and not only by the very rich. Similar doubts may be expressed about other measurements of affluence which are available, like the Income Tax. These are all probably better at showing trends over time than a precise anatomy of wealth at any one time; it is unlikely that the student of this subject would wish to be much more precise.

The aim of this chapter is to trace each of those dimensions of wealth-holding we examined throughout the book in the post-1939 period, keeping squarely in mind the comparative limitations of the data. Since the data alone are insufficient for a full appreciation of the changing nature of wealth in contemporary Britain, more weight will be placed on non-quantitative and impressionistic indicators of wealth than has been usual.

It seems evident that the rich have fared very differently at different times since 1940. It seems fair to divide this period into the following main chronological periods.[1]

(1) The period of the Second World War seemed to be marked by top wealth-holding and income-earning closely resembling the pattern of the last pre-war years, despite the very high levels of wartime taxation and the very limited opportunities for profitable investment. Whether this was truly the case, or merely reflects greater patriotic honesty on the part of the very rich, is difficult to ascertain.

(2) The post-war era of austerity was marked by an apparently genuine diminution of (especially) high incomes and top fortunes. But statistically, the diminution in wealth-holding probably began in earnest sometime after the war, and reached its nadir only in the 1950s, i.e., well after the end of the 1945-51 Labour government, and after the date (1948-9) usually taken to mark the high tide of wealth equalisation in Britain.

(3) A period of easier times and greater affluence lasting from the late 1950s until the early 1970s, marked by patchiness in growth among the various occupational elements in the wealth structure, with the birth or increase of very large fortunes in such fields as property development, agricultural landowning and consumer products and services at the expense of older (but not newer) manufacturing industries and (perhaps) of old-style commerce and finance.

(4) The economic vicissitudes of the mid and late 1970s appear to have passed the very rich by, except momentarily, and there is evidence of another inflation-fanned rise in the number of top income- and wealth-holders in the late 1970s. But equally, this may have been due to the introduction of the Capital Transfer Tax, making *inter vivos* gifts more difficult and pointless.

Some statistical evidence for this periodisation can be found in Table 8.2, which presents the average annual number of gross *probate calendar* estates of £500,000 or more left between 1940 and 1979, and the number of pre-tax incomes of £50,000 or more each by five-year periods. Several points should be borne in mind here, however. Firstly, the Inland Revenue Statistics of (net) worth for probate are different and higher, although they vary according to the same general trend.[2] Secondly, income statistics are apparently unavailable for the wartime period, while they are much more difficult to come by during the 1970s. Thirdly, it goes without saying that these statistics must be read against the background of rapid and increasing inflation, general affluence, and much higher rates of taxation than during the pre-war years.

In considering these figures, it should be remembered that in the last pre-war five-year period (when the pound was worth more than twice its post-war value and taxes were substantially lower) an average of 8.6 probate calendar millionaire and 20.2 half-millionaire estates were left each year while there were 92 incomes of £100,000 or more, with 288 between £50,000 and £100,000. The decline in wealth-leaving and high income earned, which reached their nadirs in the early and middle 1950s, was thus much more severe than any similar effect which the Depression (except at its very bottom) may have had upon the wealthy. Was this decline genuine? Even allowing for a greatly increased incidence of tax avoidance in the wake of higher taxes and the coming to power of a Labour government, it seems right to conclude that this was largely so. Certainly the way of life of the very rich in Britain changed more substantially in the decade between 1939-49 than at any time in history since the seventeenth century: the virtual end of servant-keeping and of aristocratic display in the old grand manner. To be sure, some of these changes were exogenous, the results of the war, of the loss of Empire, of the freer style of living of young people, of domestic convenience appliances. But not all were, and in assessing the role of the post-war Labour government, one should surely keep these in mind as a balance to the now fashionable view of the Attlee

Table 8.2: Top Wealth-holders and Income Earners, 1940-79

	£2 million +	£1-£2 million	£500,000-£1 million
Average Annual Number of Estates, £500,000 or More:			
1940-4	1.4	5.6	15.2
1945-9	2.8	7.6	22.4
1950-4	1.6	5.2	10.8
1955-9	1.2	4.0	14.8
1960-4	2.0	2.6	24.6
1965-9	3.0	6.6	26.4
1970-4	3.6	9.4	51.0
1975-9	7.2	18.6	_a
		£50,000-£100,000	£100,000 +
Average Annual Number of Pre-tax Incomes of £50,000 or More:			
1940/1-1944/5		223.0	67.8
1945/6-1949/50		213.0	50.6
1950/1-1954/5		180.6	39.6
1955/6-1959/60		224.0	56.4
1960/1-1964/5		408.6	102.2
1965/6-1968/9 (four years)		434.6	119.8

a. N.A. — 73 estates were recorded at between £800,000 and £1 million, or 14.6 annually at this level.

government as essentially a conservative one.

The 1950s and 1960s — and beyond — are another story, however, and a large part of the ambiguous and chameleon-like image of wealth-holding in contemporary Britain has been caused by the fact that while the changes in the life-styles of the rich since 1939 are apparently permanent and irrevocable, the size of fortunes and numbers of very wealthy individuals began to grow and reach — in current values at any rate — levels unprecedented in British history. Many of these fortunes were in the fields of property development and newer consumer products while others were in long-established areas of wealth-holding like land and shipping. Much of this growth, especially in the size of the top fortunes, has not been recorded by the probate statistics, and it is

perhaps in the *size* of top fortunes, rather than their *number*, that the
probate statistics have become most deficient. Certainly there were
and are men in modern Britain worth far in excess of the figures indicated
in Table 8.1, and the total wealth held by men like, say, the Duke of
Westminster or Lord Rank (and many others leaving substantial fortunes
but not large enough to figure in this table) was much greater than that
recorded in the probate calendars.

Some evidence as to the range of wealth and identities of the richest
men of contemporary Britain was provided by the *Daily Express* of
31 March 1969, which published a putative list of Britain's richest
individuals and families. Five fortunes were said to be worth £100
million or more at the time — those of Garfield Weston, the Toronto-
born food (Associated British Foods) and retailing (ABC teashops)
magnate, worth over £200 million; the Pilkington glass family,
collectively worth £200 million; Lord Cowdray of the petroleum and
engineering family, now much diversified and said to be worth £150
million; Sir John Ellerman, also said to be worth £150 million; and the
Moores family (football pools and retailing), at £125 million. As we
have seen, Ellerman (who died in 1973) left £52 million, while Lord
Cowdray's personal fortune was reliably detailed at £100 million in
1969.[3] The *Daily Express* also named ten other individuals or families
as worth between £25 million and £100 million at the time: Sir Godfrey
Mitchell of Wimpey Construction (£63 million); Lord Thomson, the
Canadian newspaper magnate (£60 million); property developer Harry
Hyams (£50 million); the grocery retailing Sainsbury family (£50
million); Roland 'Tiny' Rowland, the mining magnate (£26 million);
the Cayzer shipping clan, headed by Lord Rotherwick (£34 million);
Sir Charles Clore (£25 million); the Schroders of Schroder Wagg, the
City merchant bank (£30 million); the Sobells of General Electric
(£25 million); and the Sangsters of Vernon's Pools (£25 million).

Obviously such lists must be taken with a considerable pinch of salt.
Yet they point to the fact that the very wealthiest men and women in
contemporary Britain are now possessed of fortunes whose size, in
absolute and even relative terms, far exceed anything in the past. Other
estimates of the scale of wealth now held by Britain's richest multi-
millionaires are higher still: Ellerman was often said to be worth anything
up to £500 million; Harry Hyams and another great property developer,
Lord Samuel of Wych Cross (claimed to be worth only £17 million by
the *Daily Express*) were regularly credited, at the height of the property
boom of the early 1970s, with fortunes of between £500 million and
£1,000 million; while the total fortunes of a great hereditary London

landowner like the Duke of Westminster — which of course exists in the form of family trusts — has recently been estimated at £4,000 million, possibly not an inaccurate sum for the owner of most of Oxford Street, Mayfair and Belgravia.

Though there is less hard evidence here, it is also clear that the scale of very high incomes has increased as well, though possibly not at so marked a pace. British top professional and managerial incomes still lag behind most of the other European countries, although perhaps not so far behind as previously. The bulk of the great unearned incomes are probably carefully camouflaged for fear of incurring the extraordinarily high rates of taxation they continue to attract. However, the combination of professional opportunities, working women and ever-present inflation have raised the thresholds of wealth enormously: there must be many thousands of younger married couples, still on the bright side of 35, whose family incomes total £10,000, £15,000, £20,000 or even more, sums associated only a generation ago with the poorer dukes. Yet most of these couples, one suspects, do not feel particularly affluent and probably struggle along with the quiet desperation characteristic of the middle class in this century. Inflation in housing, which has increased the cost of middle-class housing in south-eastern England by perhaps 3,000 per cent in 40 years (and by 1,000 per cent in 15 years) is probably the main reason why the lower limit of the wealth held by the top one per cent of wealth-holders as measured by the probate statistics, climbed to over £100,000 in 1976, more than four times the sum held by this class in 1961.[4] Such a statistic would indicate that more than 300,000 persons in Britain own net assets of £100,000 or more.

What sort of people have left very large estates during the past 40 years? Much the same as always, generally speaking. As Table 8.3 indicates the overall occupational figures are similar to those in the past. (No occupational breakdown for those deceased during the 1970s is available.)

These figures, however, conceal a number of trends of some importance. The number of very wealthy old-style City of London merchant bankers, bankers and other financial figures has quite definitely declined in recent years, if the probate statistics are to be believed. The £11.6 million fortune of James de Rothschild (d. 1957) was virtually the only fortune, and certainly the very largest, left by a Rothschild or any member of a classical City financial dynasty. This is, frankly, exceedingly difficult to credit, although, as we have seen, the inter-war period did mark a period of decline for such families. It is far more likely, however, that this seeming decline is in fact the product of

Table 8.3: Occupations of Non-landed Wealth-holders, Deceased 1920-39

	1940-59	1960-9
Millionaires:		
I Manufacturing	23=23.5%	19=28.8%
Food-Drink-Tobacco	29=29.6%	11=16.7%
II Commerce	41=41.8%	30=45.5%
III Professionals, etc.	4= 4.1%	4= 6.0%
IV Others	1= 1.0%	2= 3.0%
Unknown	0	0
Total	98	66
Half-millionaires:		
I Manufacturing	74=32.6%	48=35.8%
Food-Drink-Tobacco	35=15.4%	11= 8.1%
II Commerce	89=39.2%	51=37.8%
III Professionals, etc.	19= 8.3%	15=11.1%
IV Others	3= 1.3%	2= 1.5%
Unknown	7= 3.1%	8= 5.9%
Total	227	135

disproportionate and careful estate planning and trust establishment by these older dynasties (situated so close to the sources of legal and financial advice in these matters) and, to the extent that this is true, it distorts the value of the probate statistics as a source of meaning and insights about contemporary Britain.

The continuing high percentage of fortunes in the commercial sector is accounted for by a number of countervailing factors. First, there has been an increase in the number of financiers from independent or small company backgrounds, particularly in insurance and stock broking, men like the millionaire Lloyds underwriters Arthur D'Ambrumenil (1873-1958), and Henry E. Lyons, 1st Baron Ennisdale (1878-1963); stockbroking millionaires like Leslie H. Wilson (1884-1968) and John, 2nd Baron Glendyne (1878-1967); and independent financiers like Richard J. Pinto (1892-1969) and Harley Drayton (1901-66). It is possible that in such cases the lack of a family company of ancient lineage has made the avoidance of death duties by family trusts or *inter vivos* giving somewhat less imperative. Second, among the recent wealth-holders there are a fair number of multiple retailers of the type who have profited so mightily since the 1930s — men like Hugh Fraser, 1st Baron Fraser of Allander (1903-66), of the House of Fraser; Michael Kaye (1902-66) of the Pricerite supermarket chain; Horace Moore (1894-1959) of British Home Stores; Simon Marks, 1st Baron Marks of Broughton (1888-1964), of Marks and Spencer; and Sir Montague Burton (1885-1952) of Burton's, all but the last of whom left millionaire estates (Burton left £687,000). Third, and perhaps most importantly, there have appeared an ever-growing number of wealthy property developers — who are, of course, properly classified as financiers rather than in some other occupational category. Felix D. Fenston's £12.7 million estate was the largest of these, and one of the very largest left since the war, but virtually every year brings its rich harvest — the fortunes of Philip E. Rose (£4.3 million); Reginald M. Phillips (£2.8 million); Joseph Sunlight (£5.7 million); and Christopher H.R. Reeves (£3.6 million) are representative of the many property development fortunes left in the 1976-9 period alone.

Like old-style banking and merchant banking fortunes, old-style manufacturing and heavy industry have also declined as a source of great fortunes — though, unlike the old City dynasties, the decline here is probably not illusory. Nevertheless, some continue to be left, even as the products of fields where private wealth-holding is no longer legally possible, as the millionaire estates of pre-nationalisation colliery owners like Christopher W. Batt (1929-73)[5] and Col. Claude Lancaster (d. 1977) who left £3.2 million, demonstrate. But many of the recent fortunes in manufacturing and industry are the products of newer, consumer-oriented industries developed or greatly expanded during the twentieth century. The fortunes of Lord Nuffield, of William Rootes first Baron Rootes (1894-1964; £1.8 million) or Sir Reginald Rootes (d. 1977; £1.3 million) in autos, Ernest Barlow (1874-1966; £1.3 million) in metal box packaging; of Charles L. Arnold (1888-1968; £5.8 million) in electrical equipment or of John Jobson (1887-1971; £1.5 million) of the Qualcast lawnmower company, are indicative of the wide range of trades which produced their top wealth-holders. There is, indeed, much evidence of a considerable spread in the range of fields which in the post-war period were productive of fortunes. The estates of Dame Barbara Hepworth, who left £2,970,000 in 1975, and of Benjamin Britten (created Baron Britten of Aldeburgh shortly before his death), who left £1,665,000 in 1976, were easily the largest ever earned by creative artists through their own works in modern British history, and show that the affluent society may have broken the nexus between creativity and poverty which has existed for much of modern history, especially among experimental artists. This same apparent expansion in the areas in which the ingenious may earn truly large fortunes is evident in many other areas as well — for instance in the £1.7 million estate of Elkan M. Jackson (1891-1971) of the London Rubber Company, by Herbert Showering (d. 1975, £995,000) of Babycham champagne, or by Jacob Green (d. 1970), whose £1.3 million represented the proceeds of the Evans outsize shops, of which he was chairman.

Despite the apparent (and probably illusory) diminution in the wealth of the great City of London dynasties, there is little evidence that London has decreased in importance as the national centre of wealth-making: if anything, its importance has increased. This has come about in large part because the old locally-based provincial firms, especially manufacturing firms in the northern cities, have disappeared or been absorbed in giant, largely London-based corporations, their old entrepreneurial dynasties severing their local ties and becoming an indistinguishable part of the national upper or upper-middle class. With this has come a continuing loss of local patriotism and spirit, and a secular trend throughout the British economy and population away from the manufacturing north and to the commercial and service-oriented south, with profound political and demographic effects. The net result of this has been an increase in the London-based wealth-holders, and a steady decrease in those based in the northern conurbations. An exception seems to be Birmingham, where engineering and metal industry wealth-holders have become considerably more numerous, especially at the half-millionaire level. Conversely, the decline of Clydeside and Merseyside (in particular) has been very marked. This is illustrated in Table 8.4, which details the venues of the wealth-holders' main business interests in the recent past. The cohort deceased 1920-39 has been included for the purpose of comparison. Unfortunately, the data on the 1970-9 period has not been analysed in sufficient detail to be included here, but on a superficial examination, it would be surprising to find that the relative importance of London *vis-à-vis* the northern conurbations has not continued to increase further.

The central position of London to the world of wealth-holding in contemporary Britain is enhanced further if two other factors, not evident from the tables here, are taken into account. One is London's magnetic role as the urban centre of the old landed aristocracy; the other is its attractiveness for foreigners as compared with any place in provincial Britain. Numerous foreigners have left very large estates in Britain in recent years — despite the high levels of death duties,

Table 8.4: Venues of Non-landed Wealth-holders' Business Interests, by Main Conurbations, 1920-69

	1920-39	1940-59	1960-9
Millionaires:			
1 City of London	32=20.9%	15=15.3%	14=21.2%
2 Other London	15= 9.8%	11=11.2%	14=21.2%
Total London	47=30.7%	26=26.5%	28=42.4%
3 Greater Manchester	6= 3.9%	4= 4.1%	2= 3.0%
4 Merseyside	12= 7.8%	2= 2.0%	2= 3.0%
5 West Yorkshire	11= 7.2%	7= 7.1%	4= 6.1%
6 Greater Birmingham	5= 3.3%	3= 3.1%	3= 4.5%
7 Clydeside	12= 7.8%	5= 5.1%	3= 4.5%
Total all Non-landed Wealth-holders	153	98	66
Half-millionaires:			
1 City of London	72=20.6%	41=18.1%	25=18.5%
2 Other London	33= 9.5%	38=16.7%	22=16.3%
Total London	105=30.1%	79=34.8%	47=34.8%
3 Greater Manchester	26= 7.4%	4= 1.8%	7= 5.2%
4 Merseyside	25= 7.2%	15= 6.6%	8= 5.9%
5 West Yorkshire	22= 6.3%	6= 2.6%	7= 5.2%
6 Greater Birmingham	11= 3.2%	12= 5.3%	13= 9.6%
7 Clydeside	24= 6.9%	14= 6.2%	6= 4.4%
Totals all Non-landed Wealth-holders	349	227	135

among them Europeans like Count Antoine Seilern of Salzburg (d. 1978) whose £30.8 million estate was the second largest left since the war; Americans like Frederick M. Mayer of New York (who left £2.4 million in Britain in 1975); and — a sign of the times — Middle Easterners like General Mohammed Khatami, brother-in-law of the Shah (£1.2 million in 1977), and Sheik Sabah Al Salem Al Sabah, the Emir of Kuwait (£1.5 million in 1978). Most of these lived in London or, occasionally, in country estates in the Home Counties.

The twentieth century has indeed seen its full share of locally-based, often self-made entrepreneurs, owing as little to London as their nineteenth century counterparts: men like Nuffield of Oxford, Rootes or Austin in the West Midlands or Bristol's aeroplane builders. Yet such men often leave incompetent heirs, and control of the family firm generally passes into other hands. Moreover the continuing drift of large-scale capital, talent and international trading links to the south-east is a self-reinforcing process, almost impossible to counteract, as the history of Britain's major automobile firms is testimony. Lord Leverhulme, a preeminent figure in the life of Merseyside, was succeeded as chairman of Unilever on his death in 1925 by Francis D'Arcy Cooper, a London accountant, one of the earliest examples of the continuing trend.

Although wealth has probably become more centralised in London during the post-war period, this has not meant, curiously enough, that there is less scope for the self-made man than in the past. On the contrary, there have possibly been more genuine self-made fortunes since 1945 than in any period of British history, including the Industrial Revolution. The seeds of these fortunes were often to be found in the unpromising atmosphere of the immediate post-war years; many a property tycoon or electronics millionaire got his start with his demobilisation money. Angus Maude's remark regarding the post-war Labour government, that 'since the war ended it has been easier to make higher profits without being really efficient than probably at any period in my lifetime',[6] was not simply partisan banter.

The available statistics of wealth-holding bear this out to a certain extent although, as with geography and occupation, they probably do not reveal the true extent of the change.[7] Among non-landed millionaires, the percentage whose fathers were of lower-middle-class occupation or status increased from 18.3 per cent in 1920-39 to 21.2 per cent in 1960-9, while lower-class fathers increased from 5.9 per cent to 13.6 per cent in the same period. Upper-class fathers declined from 59.5 to 50.0. Half-millionaires continued to be drawn from almost precisely the same backgrounds as before, indicating — as was perhaps the case with some religious groups — that to the very richest entrepreneurs, a relatively meagre background was no barrier to advancement. Even taking the probate statistics at face value, the most recent cohorts have seen some very notable examples of dramatic social mobility to the very highest levels of wealth. Lord Nuffield's origins as the son of a commercial clerk who left £74 are well-known, but such men as Henry Lyons, 1st Baron Ennisdale (1878-1963), an insurance millionaire,[8] son of a Wandsworth musician who left £300; Bernard Sunley, the property developer who left £5.2 million — the son of a Catford gardener who left no estate at all; Harley Drayton (d. 1966) another financier multi-millionaire who was the son of a domestic gardener; or Fred Pickup (1879-1968), the son of a Lancashire farmer who left nothing and who made his £1.1 million by inventing and successfully marketing 'Tizer', the soft drink, are evidence of a seeming openness to those with sufficient entrepreneurial skills. But even these examples (most of which had their origins in the pre-1939 period) probably do not reveal the extent to which Britain's wealth structure is dominated by self-made men and families. Among those noticed in the *Daily Express* list of multi-millionaires, at least one-third, and possibly one-half, are self-made men. Garfield Weston, described as Britain's richest man in 1969, was the son of a Toronto baker; the Moores, 'Tiny' Rowland and many a millionaire property developer, retailer and financier mentioned in the newspaper accounts, were all self-made men.

If the question of the social origins of contemporary Britain's top wealth-holders is a difficult one to pinpoint, their religions and ethnic origins seem impossible (and moreover increasingly irrelevant) and little can be said with confidence about this matter. In keeping with the decline of the self-conscious, confident and disproportionately dissenting old-style north of England entrepreneurs, it would seem fair to conclude that committed Protestant dissent has declined as a significant element in the British wealth structure — though, plainly, in the context of the decline of all committed dissent and, indeed, of all organised religion. Still, dissenting religious activity and philanthropy continue as with, for instance, the gift of nearly £500,000 to the Friends' Service Council by the will of Peter Selwood of Southampton, who left £978,000 in 1976. Nevertheless, most of the old dissenting business dynasties are now certainly at least nominal Anglicans, and any specifically *dissenting* element among them has long been lost, a casualty of three generations of attendance at the public schools and the consequent homogenisation of the English upper classes.

One religious group whose status can be checked with somewhat greater accuracy, however, is the Jews, because of their distinctive names.[9] We have seen that the inter-war period was one of decline for Britain's Jews, especially for the old City of London families of the 'Cousinhood'. There can be little doubt that the post-war period has seen a considerable revival of the wealth of Britain's Jewish community, and it now seems probable that perhaps 15 per cent to 20 per cent of Britain's wealthiest men and women are Jews, a figure unapproached since the Edwardian period. This figure is, if anything, an underestimate, for the (disproportionately Jewish) wealth-leavers of the City of London are probably underrepresented in the probate data, while as a group the (heavily Jewish) property developers of the post-war period are probably still too young to figure in these statistics in their rightful percentage. As before, Jews are mainly to be found in commercial and financial trades, with a significant representation in newer types of manufacturing, in entertainment and in the professions. Many of these successful Jews were refugees from Hitler, often arriving penniless and literally one step ahead of the Gestapo: for instance Erich Markus (d. 1978), who founded the Office and Electronics Machine Company in the late 1930s and left £4.1 million. There can be little doubt that other, more recent migrant groups like the Kenyan Asians are in the process of taking this same road to prosperity.

Another significant matter is the direct interrelation of wealth-holding and politics. Figures are hard to come by,[10] but it seems as if the pattern here has been a two-step one: a continued decrease in the scale of wealth held by Members of Parliament during the 1940-70 period, and a general rise in their wealth since then, especially since the mid-1970s. The decline of Parliamentary wealth in the earlier of these stages was the joint result of two factors: the general poverty of Labour members, and the continuing reluctance of very wealthy men, particularly the great business tycoons, to seek election to Parliament. In their place, the full-time politicians, often men of professional or managerial background but occasionally genuinely self-made men (like Edward Heath), have dominated the Tory benches since 1945. In the recent past there seems to be a resurgence of the *direct* participation of wealthy men in Parliamentary life — certainly the present (elected 1979) Conservative Cabinet stands in this respect with any of its predecessors in the distant past — but more importantly, there has been a considerable upward rise in the salaries, earnings and savings of all parliamentarians, occasioned by the general rise in incomes and secondary earnings possible through journalism and other sources. Certainly most prominent Labour politicians of the present day, whatever their social origins, are now well-to-do or even wealthy. The half-million pound advance which Sir Harold Wilson is said to have received for the first instalment of his memoirs was probably not as anomalous as it may have seemed. While the American situation, where multi-millionaire Kennedys and Rockefellers often participate in national politics at the highest levels (generally as left-liberals) has not reached Britain, certainly the affluence of most politicians, especially Labour ones, is far more general and widespread than even 20 years ago. No one would wish to infer too much about political or ideological attitudes from this, but one cannot readily imagine such men making a profound revolution.

The prominence of the self-made portion of the contemporary

wealth structure has often been masked by several factors. One of the most important of these is the continuing significance of landowning and hence of the old landed aristocracy. The same irresistible pressure of a spreading population on a land area which remains constant, plus the inflationary psychology which continues to view land as an utterly safe investment, have rescued the fortunes of a class generally seen as doomed to extinction earlier in the century. In addition, the tax advantages of owning land have ensured that, in all likelihood, there is less duty avoidance and more accurate assessment of the true wealth of the great landowners than with many other groups. Looking again at the names of the very richest wealth-leavers of the past 40 years, one will see clearly the effects of the inflation of land prices. The 11th Duke of Bedford who died in 1940 left £4.7 million; his son, deceased only 13 years later, left £5.8 million — *after* subtracting, presumably, the substantial losses to the Russell estate occasioned by the payment of death duties on the previous duke's estate. By the 1970s very substantial landowners like Lords Leicester, Rosebery and Sefton were once again among Britain's wealthiest men, as they had been a century before. So rapid has the increase in land values been that a relatively minor Staffordshire baronet, Sir Richard Boughey, could leave the eighth largest estate probated in Britain in the 1970s. In 1883, Boughey's ancestor owned only 10,975 acres yielding £16,715 per annum, and no member of this family has ever left an estate remotely large enough to figure in this study.

This great revival in the fortunes of the hereditary landowners has occurred despite the very considerable decrease in the size of their landed holdings. Stephen Glover, writing in the *Spectator* of 1 January 1977, has provided a list of the 1976 acreage of the largest landowners listed in the 1876 edition of Bateman's *Great Landowners* (which excluded Scotland and Ireland).[11] Every landowner without exception had lost some land; nearly all had lost most. To take the first three names on his list, the estate of Lord Ailesbury had shrunk from 53,362 to 5,500 acres, that of Lord Ancaster from 67,638 to 22,690 acres, that of Lord Bath from 41,690 to 10,000. But despite this, nearly all of these landowners were richer than ever before, purely because the capital value of the land had increased so markedly — from £53 per acre on the average in 1876 (Glover's figure, and possibly an exaggeration) to only £56 in 1950, but then to £200 in 1970 and £600 in 1974. Thus the three much-diminished estates just mentioned were worth not less than (respectively) £3.3 million, £13.6 million and £6 million in 1974. The four old landed magnates still retaining 50,000 or more acres in

1976 — Beaufort (52,000), Devonshire (56,000), Lonsdale (72,000) and Northumberland (105,000) were thus each worth in the hundreds of millions; and such figures take no account of the stocks, art treasures or other personalty owned by these families or of the urban land particularly in London, still owned by aristocratic families like the Westminsters, Cadogans and Portlands and worth possibly thousands of millions. Glover also noted that three new men, whose families owned no agricultural land whatever in 1876, were now among England's largest landowners — Lords Leverhulme (90,000 acres), Iveagh (24,000) and Cowdray (20,000). It is because of this that many landed families, having lived through the long period of agricultural depression which lasted for three-quarters of a century after 1879, believe that the golden age of the British landowner is now, despite the constant threat of extinction by taxation hanging over them and the fact that the income from agricultural land is a lower proportion of its capital value than is the case with practically any type of investment. This same spectacular rise in land prices has also meant that, for the first time in British history, owner-occupying *farmers*, often former tenants, appear among leavers of the wealthiest estates. All that was required to make a farmer a paper millionaire in the mid-1970s was ownership of at least 1,800 acres, and on this reckoning the number of millionaire farmers must run into the hundreds.

There is, finally, the matter of business control and entrepreneurship. As with so many areas we have discussed in this chapter, the overall picture is paradoxical and contradictory. On one hand, the replacement of the old-style tycoon by the corporation has proceeded apace, while on the other, the wealth of individual managers who rose through corporate channels of promotion has risen as well, again in keeping with the overall rise of all top salaries and rewards. Millionaire and half-millionaire estates, once virtually unknown among major corporation chairmen who rose by the managerial route, are now much more common, for instance the £1.2 million left in 1978 by Sir Harold Peake, formerly chairman of the Steel Company of Wales. Most corporate managers, even those of genuinely self-made backgrounds, are affluent by any standard. Alexander Fleck, 1st Baron Fleck (1889-1968), who rose from a lab. boy at 14 to chairman of ICI, left £278,000, while Leonard Lord, 1st Baron Lambury (1896-1967), chairman of Austin and British Motors and the son of a licensed victualler who left £564, himself left £171,000. Such examples are very typical. The dichotomy between ownership and control is thus not a clear one, since the controllers are invariably owners, although not of the companies they control. And there has certainly been no dearth of new-style tycoons, building up their own personally run and managed endeavours even if these are seldom at the heart of the modern economy. If a dichotomy may be truthfully said to exist, it is simply one between these latter-day tycoons (some of whom are corporate managers) and the impersonal corporations which are indeed not owned by their controllers, but by institutional and corporate investors, often insurance companies and pension funds, including those operated by trade unions. To such companies, the laws of economic or human nature may not apply. To the extent to which they dominate the contemporary economy — and the extent to which non-capitalist sources of power like the government effectively control it — the whole venture of this book, with its focus on individual and family wealth, is irrelevant. But it would be equally wrong to exaggerate the extent to which the individual entrepreneur or wealth-holder is obsolete; so long as Britain's economy continues to be essentially capitalistic, he will be a central figure in it.

The overall picture, then, is one of paradox: of an increase in the size of fortunes and probably of the opportunity for making them, in the context of a society and economy which have changed in the most profound ways. Above all, there has probably been a reduction in the *authority* of the wealth-holders, now subject to the impudent challenge of the government, the trade unions and the nature of the economy. This has both been caused by, and in turn affected, their lifestyles: when Edward Sieff, chairman of Marks and Spencer, and certainly a very rich man, was shot and wounded in his London home by an Arab terrorist in 1973, newspapers recorded that his household consisted of exactly one servant, a Filipino houseboy. Lord Lucan's household comprised two servants when he disappeared in 1974. The larger-than-life millionaire of the nineteenth and early twentieth century, controlling the lives and destinies of thousands of working people, has now disappeared, and a more modern, smaller, less exalted millionaire has succeeded, though he is probably just as rich as his precursor. Tocqueville pointed out that revolutions were made when elites were seen to wear no clothes, but he was certainly wrong, for in an affluent society nearly everyone has a vested interest in maintaining private property, even if multi-millionaires are the result. But the overall product is mystification, for responsibility without power, no less than its converse, puzzles nearly everybody.

Notes

1. An essentially similar periodisation was made by Richard Titmuss in his famous work *Income Distribution and Social Change*, (London, 1962), esp. Chapter 3. Titmuss dates the trend away from greater equality from the late 1940s, earlier than I do.

2. The average annual number of net *Inland Revenue* estates over £500,000 recorded in 1955/9-1965/9 was:

	£1 million +	£500,000-£1 million
1955-9	8.6	21.4
1960-4	10.0	42.2
1965-9	14.8	41.0

3. *New York Times*, 24 April 1969.

4. *Social Trends, No. 9*, (1979 Edition), (London, Government Statistical Service, 1978), Table 6.37, p. 119.

5. Batt was the great-grandson of Robert Millington Knowles (1843-1924), a half-millionaire Nottinghamshire colliery owner. Batt's father was still living at the time of his son's death at the age of 43.

6. Cited in Paul Foot, *The Politics of Harold Wilson* (Harmondsworth, 1968), p. 58.

7. Professor Colin Harbury, who undertook very detailed studies of the social origins of wealth-holders deceased in 1956-7 and 1973, comparing the wealth of the father of all wealth-leavers (worth £50,000 or more) with the wealth of the sons, has found a 'significant decline' in real terms in the valuations of the estates of the father of wealth-holders between 1956-7 and 1973. C. Harbury and D.M.W.N. Hitchens, 'The Inheritances of Top Wealth Leavers: Some Further Evidence', *Economic Journal* 86 (1976), p. 321.

8. He was a prominent member of the Liberal National Party within the National Coalition of the 1930s, and received his peerage for that reason in 1939.

9. Though, without further research, Jews who anglicise their names cannot, of course, be identified.

10. See W.D. Rubinstein, 'Men of Property' in Philip Stanworth and Anthony Giddens (eds.), *Elites and Power in British Society* (Cambridge, 1974), where the wealth left by members of the 1950 and 1951 Parliaments who were deceased to mid-1973 was traced. I have not had the opportunity to carry this research any further.

11. Glover notes that 'the accuracy of the information below, which comes from various sources, cannot be guaranteed'.

9 SOME CONCLUSIONS

Although we have examined the very rich in Britain from a variety of perspectives, there are certain common patterns implicit in all of these discussions, and which might serve to summarise the kind of wealthy class we have discovered. Perhaps the most striking features of the individual wealth-holders we have discussed are three in number: their conservatism compared with the innovative dynamism of the British economy in this period, the limitations which the nature of the British economy imposed upon their ambitions and their power, and their variegated and diverse nature.

The British wealth elite during the eighteenth, nineteenth and twentieth centuries has been one where land and commerce predominated, and where industrialism in the strict sense comprised a surprisingly small fraction of the total number of wealth-holders. The *direct* impact of the Industrial Revolution upon the British wealth structure was thus rather limited and tentative, whatever its direct impact upon the population as a whole. Nathan Rothschild and Lord Overstone were both more 'typical' and wealthier examplars of nineteenth-century British capitalism than Arkwright and Peel; the City of London much more 'typical' than Manchester, however greater the impact of Manchester upon the consciousness of the economic and social historian may have been. And neither Rothschild nor Arkwright was as typical or wealthy a figure within the British wealth structure as the Duke of Devonshire or the Earl of Derby. These peculiarities of the British wealth structure must, clearly, have had the most profound implications for the development of British society, and for the relationship between the British elite structure and the rest of society. I have elsewhere previously suggested how these may have affected the evolution of modern British history,[1] and I hope to discuss this evolution in the detailed manner it must be discussed in a future study.

Closely related to the British wealth structure's conservative nature are the limitations which the nature of the British economy imposed upon even its most active and successful entrepreneurs. There were no British Morgans or Rockefellers, perhaps no British Krupps or Beits. The wealthiest American multi-millionaires of the late nineteenth and early twentieth centuries were approximately *twenty times* wealthier than the richest British business millionaires of the period[2] —

Rockefeller's $1 billion (£200 million) *vs.* Charles Morrison's £11 million are the approximate orders of magnitude – and Britain's millionaires were therefore compelled to function in a network of constraints and restraints upon their goals, methods and behaviour which American multi-millionaires were wealthy enough to avoid. Although the topic is not fully explored in this work, these constraints clearly extended to a slavish imitation of the landed aristocracy and its mores in the countryside or the West End of London, and most certainly in the life-styles expected of their sons and grandsons. The peculiarly disaggregated nature of the British economy and its development during the nineteenth century also meant that one cannot speak of a British 'finance capital' in any real sense until the inter-war period at the earliest, whatever the case might be in Germany, France or elsewhere.

The third striking feature of the British wealth structure, although at first glance it may seem paradoxical in view of what we have just said, is the variegated and diverse nature of the individuals and categories of businessmen who became wealth-holders. This emerged most clearly in our detailed discussion of several major occupational groups, but is also implicit in much of the other discussion. There was no clear-cut royal road to wealth in nineteenth-century Britain and, on occasion, men of every type and of high and low degree could amass a fortune. We have noted, however, two important qualifications to this picture which must certainly be drawn: place appears to be more important than entrepreneurial effort, above all place at the centre of wealth-making, the City of London, and the opportunities for truly dramatic upward intergenerational social mobility were exceedingly rare as, indeed, they were in other societies, including the nineteenth-century United States.

The picture which emerges here, though in many respects anomalous and *sui generis*, is probably situated recognisably on the continuum of wealth structures among advanced capitalist countries. Britain's wealth structure was in some respects more comparable to those in other analogous European countries, especially France and even Germany, than to the United States or the smaller or more primitive Western societies of the time like Australia or Italy.[3] It is toward the international typology of wealth structures that the historian of this subject must hope to turn, providing that any such typology or cross-national comparisons are made with a sophisticated and painstaking use of the available quantitative data, and with the understanding of the fact that every national history is different.

Notes

1. W.D. Rubinstein, 'Wealth, Elites and the Class Structure of Modern Britain', *Past and Present*, 76 (1977).
2. See W.D. Rubinstein, 'Introduction' in W.D. Rubinstein, (ed.), *Wealth and the Wealthy in the Modern World* (London, 1980).
3. See the essays in Ibid.

APPENDIX: WOMEN WEALTH-HOLDERS

Women in Britain were not often very wealthy in their own right. In the entire period between 1809 and 1939, only 16 women millionaires and 46 women half-millionaires were deceased.[1] By the periodisation adopted in this work, the number of women wealth-holders was:

	1809-58	1858-79	1880-99	1900-19	1920-39
Millionairesses	0	0	0	6	10
Half-millionairesses	5	0	11	10	20

As will be readily seen, the number of women wealth-holders was increasing at the end of the span. (After the Second World War the number increased even more rapidly.) During the nineteenth century, however, no millionairesses were deceased and no half-millionairesses died between 1849 and 1887. It was, of course, considered most unusual for a woman to inherit property of such value absolutely, and in most of the pre-twentieth century cases, one suspects, she was a substitute for a non-existent male heir.

In virtually every case where information on the woman wealth-holder is available, her fortune is readily traceable to a related previous male wealth-holder or to a wealthy family. The exceptions to this — apart from those for whom information is lacking — are a number of women whose chief sources of inheritance were from men (husbands or fathers) who did not themselves leave very large fortunes. In some of these cases, the money may have been passed on in order to avoid death duties, although if the heritor was the wife — of the same generation as the husband — the payment of duties would not have been long deferred. In other cases, several smaller legacies may have been substantially increased, through shrewd investment and cautious spending, by the heiress or her advisers.

A third possibility is that the woman earned it herself. There have been examples of self-made women in the early part of this century, most notably the black American 'Madame' Walker, the former laundress who invented the hair straightening process, and the cosmetics manufacturers Elizabeth Arden and Helena Rubinstein, but none of these was British. The only woman on the list below who was active in trade was Miss Annie L. Watson (1862-1936), a permanent director of Sutton

& Co., the carriers. But she, too, was the daughter of a wealth-holder, in this case of Thomas Watson (d. 1910), a London carrier who left £596,000. The barriers to women in business at high levels in Britain were and are extremely severe: women were admitted to the London Stock Exchange, for example, only in 1974. Of the 450 major company chairmen in the study of Stanworth and Giddens, discussed in Chapter 6, the only woman was Margaret, Viscountess Pirrie (1857-1935), President of the shipbuilders Harland & Wolff following the death of her husband in 1924. (Many readers will be surprised that there was even one.)

One of the most striking features of the list below is the paucity of those who inherited industrial fortunes. Of the 47 women wealth-holders whose source of wealth is known, 19 were earned in commerce, 11 in land, seven in miscellaneous trades or the professions and only 10 in industry or manufacturing. It would seem that both commerce and landed society were more likely to grant women large fortunes absolutely than were the beneficiaries of the Industrial Revolution. A final point of interest is that three of James Morrison's women relatives left vast fortunes in their own right.

Data on women wealth-holders are, generally speaking, much more difficult to obtain than equivalent information on men. The findings outlined in the list below have been compiled mainly from obituaries and wills in *The Times* and from standard reference works, in addition to birth and marriage certificates. Women's dates of birth are not usually given in works like Burke's *Peerage*. In certain cases membership in a wealthy family is known but not the precise relationship to other wealth-holders.

Women Wealth-holders

Name, Date of Death, Valuation ('000)	Probable Source of Wealth
Millionairesses:	
1. Mrs Alexandra Ralli (1841-1903) £1,012	Daughter, J. Ralli, foreign merchant; widow, Peter P. Ralli (d. 1868), left £500,000
2. Mrs Ada Lewis-Hill (1846-1906) £1,168	Widow, Samuel Lewis (d. 1901), millionaire money-lender
3. Mrs Enriquetta Rylands (d. 1908) £3,602	Widow, John Rylands (d. 1887), cotton manufacturer and millionaire

4. Miss Ellen Morrison (1834-1909) £2,351 — Daughter, James Morrison (d. 1857), warehouseman and millionaire

5. Emily M. Easton (1818-1914) £1,101 — Sister (?) John Easton (d. 1880), colliery, half-millionaire

6. Miss Emily Talbot (1879-1918) £2,000 — Daughter, C.R.M. Talbot (d. 1890), landowner and millionaire

7. Miss Alice de Rothschild (d. 1922) £3,062 — Daughter, Baron Anselm de Rothschild

8. Mrs Millicent Salting (1848-1924) £1,869 — Widow, W.S. Salting (d. 1905), Australian half-millionaire

9. Mrs M. Hamilton-Fellowes (1874-1928) £1,900 — Daughter, Sir Frederick Wills, tobacco millionaire

10. Mrs Edith Douglas-Hamilton (1871-1928) £1,756 — Sister of preceding

11. Mrs Emma Marryat (d. 1927) £1,200 — Daughter, Sir James Caird (d. 1916), jute half-millionaire

12. Mrs Helen Hornby-Lewis (1851-1930) £1,648 — Daughter, J.R. Stewart (d. 1896), half-millionaire ironmaster

13. Lady Emma de Rothschild (1844-1935) £1,151 — Widow, Lord Rothschild

14. Dame Fanny Houston (1857-1936) £1,528 — Widow, 9th Lord Byron, landowner, and Sir Robert Houston, shipowner[2]

15. Mrs Mary W. Wharrie (1847-1936) £1,486 — Daughter, Sir Henry Harben (d. 1911), President of Prudential Insurance (he left £394,000)

16. Miss Annie L. Watson (1862-1936) £1,006 — Daughter, Thomas Watson (d. 1910), half-millionaire carrier

Half-millionairesses:

1. Elizabeth Whittingstall (d. 1825) — Widow, George Whittingstall, (d. 1822) half-millionaire

2. Dame Harriet Holland (d. 1825) — Unknown (landed?)[3]

3. Harriet, Duchess of St Albans (d. 1837) Widow, Thomas Coutts and 9th Duke of St Albans
4. Susannah Houblon Newton (d. 1837) Huguenot merchant family
5. Jane Innes (d. 1839) Daughter, George Innes (d. 1780), Scottish banker and placeman
6. Charlotte, Countess of Bridgwater (d. 1849) Widow, 8th Earl of Bridgwater (d. 1823), landowner
7. Anna Maria Heywood (d. 1887) Daughter, John P. Heywood (d. 1877), millionaire banker
8. Mary Ann Morrison (d. 1887) Widow, James Morrison (d. 1857)
9. Hon. Dame Charlotte Scarlett (d. 1888) Daughter, John Hargreaves (d. 1874), half-millionaire
10. Louise Ann Ryland (d. 1889) Ground-rent landlord family in Birmingham
11. Hannah, Countess of Rosebery (d. 1890) Merchant banking family (Rothschilds); Wife, Lord Rosebery
12. Elizabeth Rawson (d. 1890) Relative, Viscount Mountgarret, landowner
13. Jane Smith Allan (d. 1892) Widow, Alexander Allan (d. 1892), shipowning half-millionaire
14. Mary Ann, Baroness Forester (d. 1893) Widow, George, 3rd Baron Forester (d. 1886), landowner
15. Yolande Lyne-Stephens (d. 1894) Widow, Stephen Lyne-Stephens (d. 1860), half-millionaire foreign merchant
16. Dame Amelie Wallace (d. 1897) Widow, Sir Richard Wallace (d. 1890), millionaire landowner
17. Fanny Gretton (d. 1897) Brewing family, wealth-holders
18. Mrs M.J. Ralli (d. 1900) Foreign merchant family, wealth-holders
19. Miss Emily Montefiore (d. 1902) Stockbrokerage family, wealth-holders
20. Mrs Anne Turner (d. 1902) Widow, Charles Turner, Liverpool merchant and half-millionaire
21. Hon. Emily Meynall-Ingram (d. 1904) Landowner — owned in her own right 25,205 acres at £45,491

22. Miss Lucy Cohen (d. 1906)	per annum in Bateman Stockbrokerage family, wealth-holders; sister-in-law, Rothschilds
23. Mrs Martha MacEwan (d. 1909)	Widow, Dr. Patrick Fraser (d. 1896), physician who left £419,421
24. Mrs Marion P. Smart (d. 1913)	Widow, Thomas Jones-Gibb (d. 1884), China merchant half-millionaire
25. Miss Sarah Anne Adams (d. 1914)	Unknown
26. Dame Emily F. Smyth (d. 1915)	Widow, Sir J. Henry Greville Smyth, Bt., landowner
27. Mrs Mary L. Burns (d. 1919)	Sister, J.P. Morgan, financier
28. Harriet, Baroness Wantage (d. 1921)	Daughter, Lord Overstone (d. 1883), millionaire banker
29. Mrs Anne E. Croft (d. 1922)	Widow, Henry Croft, (d. 1893), millionaire maltster
30. Dame Lelia B. Herbert (d. 1924)	Daughter of Mr Gammell, Rhode Island, USA, manufacturer; her son Sir Sidney Herbert (d. 1939), left £572,000. Her husband's father was Lord Herbert of Lea
31. Elizabeth, 3rd Baroness Masham (d. 1924)	Widow, 3rd Baron Masham (d. 1924), silk plush manu-facturer, left £1,558,000
32. Mrs Sarah Grove-Grady (d. 1926)	Daughter, John Beaumont (d. 1889), woollen manufacturer half-millionaire
33. Mrs Agnes Wood (d. 1927)	Widow, James Marke Wood (d. 1908), shipowning millionaire
34. Mrs Virginia Schillizzi (d. 1929)	Widow, John S. Schillizzi (d. 1908), foreign merchant millionaire
35. Mrs Kate Boyd (d. 1929)	Daughter, Thomas Coats (d. 1883), millionaire sewing thread manufacturer
36. Dame Edith J. Durning-Lawrence (d. 1929)	Daughter of John B. Smith, MP, manufacturer, and widow, Sir William Lawrence, MP, a London merchant

37. Mrs Jeanette Coats Barclay (d. 1931)	Sewing thread (Coatses) family, wealth-holders
38. Mrs Jane E.C. Caulfeild (*sic*) (d. 1932)	Relative, Lord Charlemont, landowner
39. Annie, Viscountess Cowdray (d. 1932)	Widow, first Viscount Cowdray (d. 1927), petroleum millionaire
40. Laura, Baroness Aberconway (d. 1933)	Predeceased her husband, Charles McLaren, first Baron Aberconway (d. 1934), Liberal MP, barrister and company chairman (Palmers of Jarrow; John Brown & Co.), who left only £15,000. Almost certainly an instance of estate duty avoidance gone amiss
41. Mrs Ellen Boswell (d. 1934)	Described as 'life insurance widow' in *Daily Mail Yearbook, 1935*: exact details not traced
42. Mrs Mary Ann Hudson (d. 1935)	Widow, William Hudson, 'partner in an exporting business', (*The Times*, 6 May 1935), but he was not a wealth-holder
43. Dorothy, Viscountess St Cyres (d. 1936)	Daughter, Alfred Morrison (d. 1898), half-millionaire, a son of James Morrison (St Cyres is the courtesy title of the Earldom of Iddlesleigh)
44. Mrs Marie de Rothschild (d. 1937)	Merchant banking family, wealth-holders
45. Miss Winifred de la Chere (d. 1938)	Unknown
46. Miss Katharine A. MacKinnon (d. 1938)	Relative, shipping family, wealth-holders
47. Cara, Baroness Fairhaven (d. 1939)	Widow, Urban Broughton (d. 1929), US mineral and utility owner who settled in Britain and was given peerage but died before it was gazetted. She was given the rank and style of a baron's widow and her son created Baron Fairhaven. Her husband left

£105,000 in Britain; her son
(d. 1966) left £2,485,000

Notes

1. Only two 'lesser wealthy' women were deceased, both in the period
1850-69. They were Margaret Wilson (d. 1854) and Anna Maria Booth (d. 1856).
Little could be traced of their biographies.

2. Her husband, (Sir Robert Houston) was reputed to be worth £7 million,
but took up domicile in the Channel Islands to escape death duties. She later
paid the Treasury £1,500,000 'as an act of grace pending settlement of the legal
position' regarding her husband's domicile. (*The Times*, 30 December 1936.)
There is no trace of her husband's estate in the English probate calendars. On her
controversial career, see Alan Jenkins, *The Rich Rich* (London, 1977), pp. 139ff.

3. Curiously enough, I have been unable to trace any person, or indeed,
titled family of the time with this surname. This may well be an error in
transcription, either in the manuscript probate calendars of the period, or on my
part. An executor was Earl Cardigan, her uncle.

INDEX

Aberconway, Lady 255
Allendale, Lord 44, 201-2, 211
American wealthy: in Britain 94-5,
   239; scale of wealth 46, 247-8;
   social origins 131-3
Anglicans: as wealth-holders 145-63,
   167, 241; brewers 89-90; chemical
   manufacturers 80-1; colliery
   owners 77; cotton manufacturers
   80-1; in northern towns 107;
   merchant bankers 92
Arkwright family 20, 37, 83-5, 136,
   157, 170, 217, 247
Armstrong, Sir William (Lord) 20,
   157, 189, 217
Ashton, Lord 44
Asquith family 79, 81, 175n43
Assessed taxes 17
Atkinson, J.R.S. 19
'Austerity' period 231-2
avoidance, estate duty: extent 15-16;
   post-1945, 227-31

Baird family 27, 78, 216
Baldwin, Stanley, 175n43
bankers 61, 70, 91-7, 236; and
   politics 163-9
Baptists 84, 90, 145-63
Barclay family 136, 154-5, 163
Baring family 93-4, 106, 136, 169,
   216
baronetcies 170-3
Bass, Michael (Lord Burton) 88
Bateman, John 15, 18, 59-60, 193-
   207, 243-4
Bearsted, Lord (M. Samuel) 46, 167,
   171-2
Beaverbrook, Lord 230
Bedford, Dukes of 44, 50, 193, 199,
   200, 204, 207, 209, 211, 228-9,
   243
Beecham family 79-80
'beerage', the 88
Beit, Alfred 41, 44, 77, 247
Belfast 168
Birmingham 108, 221, 238
Blackburn 82-4, 85-6, 107
Bonar Law, Andrew 175n43

Borthwick Institute (York) 10
Bradford 131, 185
Brassey, Thomas 20, 37, 44, 131,
   157, 217-18
brewing 86-91
Bridgwater, Duke of 196, 219
Bright, John 121
Bristol 88, 108, 239
Brown (merchant bankers) family 92,
   94, 167
Brunner family 80-1, 167-8
Buccleuch, Dukes of 193
Buckingham, Duke of 207
Burton-on-Trent 69, 88
business interests of wealth-holders
   178-82
businessmen, wealth-holders as
   176-90
Buxton family 90

Cadbury family 69, 154-5
Cannadine, David 206
Canterbury Prerogative Court 12-13,
   28, 34-7
Capital Transfer Tax 206, 232
Catholic Apostolics 155
chairmen, wealth-holder 182-6, 245-6
Chamberlain, Joseph 121
Chamberlain, Neville 175n43
Chapman, Stanley 37
Charrington family 69, 87, 90, 107,
   136, 168
chemical manufacturers 68, 82-6
Christie, Agatha 230
Church of Scotland 85, 92, 100,
   145-63
City of London 69, 91-7, 102-10,
   162-3, 170, 221, 235-6, 247
Clanricarde, Lord 201
Clark (cotton) family 84-6, 108
class, social barriers 119, 130
Clore, Sir Charles 234
Clydeside see Glasgow
Coats family 84-6, 108, 186, 217,
   254-5
Coleman, D.C. 137
colliery owners 76-8
Combe family 69, 87

257